Hands-on ESP32 with Arduino IDE

Unleash the power of IoT with ESP32 and build exciting
projects with this practical guide

Asim Zulfiqar

BIRMINGHAM—MUMBAI

Hands-on ESP32 with Arduino IDE

Group Product Manager: Preet Ahuja

Publishing Product Manager: Suwarna Rajput

Senior Editor: Sayali Pingale

Technical Editor: Yash Bhanushali

Copy Editor: Safis Editing

Project Coordinator: Uma Devi

Proofreader: Safis Editing

Indexer: Hemangini Bari

Production Designer: Alishon Mendonca

Marketing Coordinator: Rohan Dobhal

First published: January 2024

Production reference: 1141223

Published by Packt Publishing Ltd.

Grosvenor House

11 St Paul's Square

Birmingham

B3 1RB, UK

ISBN 978-1-83763-803-1

www.packtpub.com

Dedicated to my parents, Zulfiqar Ahmed and Aneela Zulfiqar, as well as my wife, Alfiya Shaikh, for their continuous support and encouragement.

Contributors

About the author

Asim Zulfiqar is a blogger and tech content creator who has been writing tutorials on embedded systems and the IoT on his blog and YouTube channel, *High Voltages*. Currently, he is working as a scientific programmer for IoT research projects.

He completed his bachelor's degree in electronic engineering at Sir Syed University of Engineering and Technology, Pakistan. After that, he completed his Erasmus Mundus joint master's degree program in photonics integrated circuits, sensors, and networks at Scuola Superiore Sant'Anna (Italy), Aston University (UK), and Osaka University (Japan).

I express my sincere gratitude to my parents and family for their continuous support and encouragement during this project.

I would also like to extend my thanks to Uma Devi, Suwarna Patil, Sayali Pingale, Aryaa Joshi, Shagun Saini, and the entire Packt team for their invaluable guidance throughout this project, as well as Kalbe Abbas and Vishwavardhan for their technical insights.

About the reviewers

Vishwavardhan Yeseskar has worked in the design and development of embedded systems for more than 12 years, especially focused on IoT. He has work experience with some of the best German companies in this domain, and he has been a part of teams that have rolled out multiple embedded devices with IoT integration.

He has a bachelor's degree in electronics and communication from Visvesvaraya Technological University and a postgraduate diploma in artificial intelligence and machine learning from Amity University. He is currently employed as a product architect at a leading German firm.

I would like to thank my wife, who encouraged me to contribute to the learning community by active participation, and also for her patience during the period of review of this book.

Kalb e Abbas, Jafferi is an embedded systems engineer with more than five years of experience working in the embedded systems domain. His main interest is creating networks of devices using wireless technologies such as BLE, Wi-Fi, and LPWAN, and monitoring these devices remotely.

He has collaborated with many web and application developers that required integration of data collection and monitoring using embedded devices.

I am indebted and thankful to my parents, friends and colleagues, and all the employers who saw potential in me and always made me feel special.

I am very much thankful to the author of the book and my friend, Asim Zulfiqar. His knowledge, experience, and humbleness have inspired me in many ways.

Table of Contents

Part 1 – Introduction: Getting Familiar with ESP32

1

2

3

Interfacing Cameras and Displays with ESP32   51

Part 2 – IoT Protocols and ESP32

4

Implementing Network-Based Protocols with ESP32   73

5

Choosing the Right Data-Based Protocols for Your ESP32 Projects   105

Part 3 – Practical Implementation

6

Project 1 – Smart Plant Monitoring System Using ESP32, Messaging Services, and the Twitter API   143

7

Project 2 – Rent Out Your Parking Space   175

8

Project 3 – Logging, Monitoring, and Controlling using ESP32   203

9

From Arduino IDE to Advanced IoT Development – Taking the Next Steps   241

Preface

The ESP32 is a great microcontroller for learning and creating **Internet of Things (IoT)** applications. It's especially good for beginners in the IoT world. Setting up and connecting sensors to the ESP32 can be complicated, but the Arduino IDE makes it easier to write code, upload it to the ESP32, and use its features. This book is designed to help you understand the basics of using sensors, connecting to networks, processing data, and creating applications with the ESP32, giving you a solid foundation for IoT development.

Starting with the basics of the ESP32 and the Arduino IDE 2.0, you'll learn how to connect sensors to the ESP32 through practical examples. Then, the book shows you how to use the ESP32 camera and display modules with examples. It also explains IoT networks and data protocols, providing you with different options for various IoT applications. Toward the end of the book, you'll use your knowledge to work on exciting projects, from smart connected devices to data loggers and automation, experiencing real-world applications.

By the end of the book, you'll be able to confidently work on ESP32 projects, choose the right IoT protocol for your application, and successfully create and deploy your own IoT projects.

Who this book is for

This book is for people who like electronics and IoT, whether you're just a fan, enjoy it as a hobby, or work in the field. It's written to help you really understand ESP32 and IoT protocols by giving you practical examples. You should know a bit about electronics and have some experience with programming, but it's designed to be easy for beginners. So, if you're interested in learning about ESP32 and IoT, this book is a good choice for you.

What this book covers

Chapter 1, IoT with ESP32 using Arduino IDE, begins with an introduction to IoT, outlining its characteristics and various applications. Following that, the ESP32 is introduced, and its capabilities are explored in detail. The chapter concludes by explaining and utilizing the Arduino IDE for a "Hello World" example.

Chapter 2, Connecting Sensors and Actuators with ESP32, provides an overview of the ESP32's **General Purpose Input/Output (GPIO)** and peripherals. The chapter also explores communication protocols used to connect different sensors, including examples of UART, I2C, and SPI.

Chapter 3, Interfacing Cameras and Displays with ESP32, offers both theoretical insights and practical guidance on utilizing the ESP32-CAM board, along with various display modules in conjunction with the ESP32.

Chapter 4, Implementing Network-Based Protocols with ESP32, provides an overview of network-based protocols such as Wi-Fi, **Bluetooth Low Energy (BLE)**, Cellular (5G and NB-IoT), and LoRaWAN. The chapter also explores the distinctions between these protocols, offering insights to help you select the most suitable network protocol for your upcoming projects.

Chapter 5, Choosing the Right Data-Based Protocols for Your ESP32 Project, explores various data-based protocols such as HTTP, MQTT, and webhooks. The chapter outlines the differences between these protocols, aiding you in selecting the most appropriate data-based protocol for your ESP32 projects.

Chapter 6, Project 1 – Smart Plant Monitoring System Using ESP32, Messaging Services, and the Twitter API, offers a step-by-step guide to reading environmental parameters such as temperature, humidity, and soil moisture using ESP32. Additionally, the chapter covers how to share these status updates on Twitter, Email, WhatsApp, and Telegram using ESP32.

Chapter 7, Project 2 – Rent Out Your Parking Space, provides a step-by-step guide to creating a prototype system. This system enables you to accept payments via PayPal to rent out your parking space.

Chapter 8, Project 3 – Logging, Monitoring, and Controlling Using ESP32, outlines a step-by-step approach to reading data from various sensors in different locations within a house, such as the kitchen and bedroom, using ESP32. Moreover, the chapter covers how to log this data in a database, visualize and monitor it, and control components using your smartphone.

Chapter 9, From Arduino IDE to Advanced IoT Development – Taking the Next Steps, offers a roadmap to advance your IoT development skills and suggests the next steps you can take to build on the knowledge gained from this book.

To get the most out of this book

This book is designed for beginners, so you only need a little knowledge about electronics and programming. To work on the projects in the book, you'll also need some devices listed in the following table. For the software part, you'll need the Arduino IDE, which works on all major operating systems. Additionally, the book mentions some free third-party services in different chapters, such as the OpenWeatherMap API, Twitter API, CallMeBot API, InfluxDB, Grafana, and PayPal API.

Software/hardware covered in the book	Operating system requirements
An ESP32 development board	Windows, macOS, or Linux
An ESP32-CAM board	
Display modules	
Sensors and actuators	
Free API services (OpenWeatherMap, Twitter, CallMeBot, and PayPal APIs)	
InfluxDB Cloud and Grafana Cloud	

If you are using the digital version of this book, we advise you to type the code yourself or access the code from the book's GitHub repository (a link is available in the next section). Doing so will help you avoid any potential errors related to the copying and pasting of code.

The specific uses of both software and hardware are thoroughly explained in their respective chapters with detailed instructions.

Download the example code files

You can download the example code files for this book from GitHub at `https://github.com/PacktPublishing/Programming-ESP32-with-Arduino-IDE`. If there's an update to the code, it will be updated in the GitHub repository.

We also have other code bundles from our rich catalog of books and videos available at `https://github.com/PacktPublishing/`. Check them out!

Conventions used

There are a number of text conventions used throughout this book.

`Code in text`: Indicates code words in text, database table names, folder names, filenames, file extensions, pathnames, dummy URLs, user input, and Twitter handles. Here is an example: "The `WiFi.softAP()` function is used to set up the ESP32 as an access point."

A block of code is set as follows:

```
#include <WiFi.h>
const char* ssid = "MyESP32AP";
const char* password = "password123";

void setup() {
  Serial.begin(115200);
  WiFi.softAP(ssid, password);
  IPAddress apIP(192, 168, 4, 1);
  IPAddress subnet(255, 255, 255, 0);
  WiFi.softAPConfig(apIP, apIP, subnet);
  Serial.print("Access Point IP Address: ");
  Serial.println(WiFi.softAPIP());
}
void loop() {
  // Your code goes here
}
```

Bold: Indicates a new term, an important word, or words that you see on screen. For instance, words in menus or dialog boxes appear in **bold**. Here is an example: "Now, you can upload the code using Arduino IDE and open **Serial Monitor**."

Tips or important notes
Appear like this.

Get in touch

Feedback from our readers is always welcome.

General feedback: If you have questions about any aspect of this book, email us at customercare@packtpub.com and mention the book title in the subject of your message.

Errata: Although we have taken every care to ensure the accuracy of our content, mistakes do happen. If you have found a mistake in this book, we would be grateful if you would report this to us. Please visit www.packtpub.com/support/errata and fill in the form.

Piracy: If you come across any illegal copies of our works in any form on the internet, we would be grateful if you would provide us with the location address or website name. Please contact us at copyright@packt.com with a link to the material.

If you are interested in becoming an author: If there is a topic that you have expertise in and you are interested in either writing or contributing to a book, please visit authors.packtpub.com.

Share Your Thoughts

Once you've read *Hands-on ESP32 with Arduino IDE*, we'd love to hear your thoughts! Scan the QR code below to go straight to the Amazon review page for this book and share your feedback.

https://packt.link/r/1837638039

Your review is important to us and the tech community and will help us make sure we're delivering excellent quality content.

Download a free PDF copy of this book

Thanks for purchasing this book!

Do you like to read on the go but are unable to carry your print books everywhere?

Is your eBook purchase not compatible with the device of your choice?

Don't worry, now with every Packt book you get a DRM-free PDF version of that book at no cost.

Read anywhere, any place, on any device. Search, copy, and paste code from your favorite technical books directly into your application.

The perks don't stop there, you can get exclusive access to discounts, newsletters, and great free content in your inbox daily

Follow these simple steps to get the benefits:

- Scan the QR code or visit the link below

https://packt.link/free-ebook/9781837638031

- Submit your proof of purchase
- That's it! We'll send your free PDF and other benefits to your email directly

Part 1 – Introduction: Getting Familiar with ESP32

In this section, you'll familiarize yourself with the fundamental elements of this book, including ESP32, the **Internet of Things (IoT)**, and the Arduino IDE 2.0. Additionally, you'll learn the utilization and integration of sensors, actuators, cameras, and displays with ESP32 and the Arduino IDE. By the end of this part, you'll have acquired the necessary hardware-interfacing knowledge, enabling you to move on to exciting IoT projects.

This part has the following chapters:

- *Chapter 1, IoT with ESP32 using Arduino IDE*
- *Chapter 2, Connecting Sensors and Actuators with ESP32*
- *Chapter 3, Interfacing Cameras and Displays with ESP32*

1

IoT with ESP32 using Arduino IDE

The **Internet of Things (IoT)** has revolutionized the way we interact with everyday objects, making them smarter, more efficient, and more connected. One of the key components of IoT is the microcontroller, which is required for the collection and processing of data from sensors and other devices. The **ESP32 microcontroller**, a product of Espressif, is one of the most popular choices for IoT projects due to its low cost, high performance, and built-in Wi-Fi and Bluetooth connectivity.

Through this chapter, we will take a deep dive into ESP32 and compare it with other **microcontroller units (MCUs)** available on the market. We will also explore the power of ESP32 and discuss why it is the ideal choice for IoT projects.

Furthermore, we will introduce you to the world of IoT and its application in various domains, including healthcare, agriculture, and smart homes. This section will help you understand how IoT is revolutionizing the world and how you can contribute to it.

Lastly, we will introduce you to the **Arduino Integrated Development Environment** (IDE) 2.0, one of the most popular programming platforms for IoT projects and a beginner-friendly environment. We will discuss various other available options for programming ESP32.

In this chapter, we'll cover the following topics:

- A brief introduction to IoT
- Understanding the capabilities of ESP32 for IoT
- Deep dive into the Arduino IDE 2.0 to program ESP32

By the end of this chapter, you will have achieved the following:

- Gained knowledge about IoT and its applications in various domains

- Understood the features and advantages of ESP32 over other microcontrollers

- Become familiar with the Arduino IDE 2.0

- Learned how to program ESP32 using the Arduino IDE

- Written a Hello World program using ESP32 and the Arduino IDE

We hope this chapter will be informative and will inspire you to explore the endless possibilities of IoT with ESP32. Let's get started!

A brief introduction to IoT

Before diving into the main subject of this book, which is using ESP32 with the Arduino IDE 2.0 for IoT projects, it's important to first learn about IoT. Understanding the basics of IoT will help us see why it is important to pick the right microcontroller and the best communication method for our project. By knowing the basics of IoT, we can better use its potential in our ESP32 projects with the Arduino IDE 2.0. Additionally, knowledge of IoT and its applications will provide a sense of motivation and direction for getting started.

To keep this introduction brief, in this section, we are going to describe what IoT is, its main characteristics, and the basic architecture of IoT technology, which includes all the core parts and key components of IoT. Then, we will discuss the applications of IoT in different sectors and domains.

IoT and its main characteristics

IoT refers to a network of physical objects, devices, and systems that are connected to the internet and are equipped with sensors, software, and network connectivity, enabling them to collect and exchange data. To simplify it, a *thing* can be a smartwatch you wear that tracks your activity and health data and sends that information to your phone or your doctor using the internet or a network. Overall, IoT is about making things more connected, efficient, and convenient for people in their everyday lives.

After explaining what IoT is, it's important to understand the main characteristics of IoT to explain the idea of IoT in more detail; this will help you distinguish it from other technologies and develop effective IoT solutions that can deliver real value and impact. The main characteristics of IoT are connectivity, sensing and perception, data collection and perception, interoperability, security and privacy, scalability, and user experience. These characteristics enable IoT to be used in a wide range of applications, and it has use cases in various domains, from healthcare to agriculture and smart homes.

To give you a better understanding of these characteristics, each of these is described as follows, with a real-world example in the field of smart farming or agriculture:

- **Connectivity**: As we discussed, IoT is a network of physical objects; connectivity is a fundamental trait of IoT. IoT devices are connected to each other, to the internet, and to other networks, which allows them to exchange data and communicate in real time through automation. In the context of smart agriculture, wireless sensor networks for real-time monitoring, remote access, and control of irrigation systems using mobile or web-based interfaces are examples of connectivity.

- **Sensing and perception**: Another important trait of IoT is that it enables devices to collect data and analyze it to gain insights, make decisions, and automate processes. Sensing involves the collection of data from the physical environment using sensors, while perception involves processing and analyzing data to derive insights and take action. One example of sensing and perception in IoT can be seen in smart agriculture, where sensors are used to monitor soil moisture, temperature, and humidity, and a perception algorithm analyzes this data to determine the optimal time for watering and adjusting the temperature of a greenhouse.

- **Data collection and analysis**: Data collection and analysis is a characteristic that enables devices and systems to collect large amounts of data from various sources and analyze it to generate insights and support decision-making. Data collection and analysis in smart agriculture can involve processing the data collected by sensors and using it to make decisions about crop management. For example, by analyzing data on soil moisture and weather patterns, farmers can determine when to plant, irrigate, or fertilize crops. This is where **machine learning** (**ML**) algorithms can be applied for enhanced decision-making.

- **Interoperability**: Interoperability is the ability of different devices and systems to communicate with each other seamlessly, enabling them to work together to achieve common goals and improve overall efficiency. For example, in smart farming, farmers can collect and analyze data from multiple sources that are interconnected and work together to make informed decisions about crop management, such as soil moisture, temperature, and weather conditions.

- **Security and privacy**: Security and privacy are important characteristics of IoT as they ensure that the data collected and transmitted by IoT devices is secure and private. In smart agriculture, security and privacy can include encryption and authentication protocols to prevent unauthorized access to data, as this data could be exploited by malicious attacks for financial gains or to cause harm to farmers.

- **Scalability**: Scalability in IoT refers to the ability to handle a growing number of devices and data traffic in a network without a significant decrease in performance. Scalability in the case of smart agriculture can include the addition of more sensors to cover larger areas of the farm and the integration of new technologies as they become available.

- **User experience**: User experience in IoT refers to the ease of use and convenience of the technology for the end user. In the context of smart agriculture, it includes providing a simple and intuitive interface for farmers to access and interpret the data collected by sensors; for example, designing a user-friendly mobile application, providing real-time alerts and notifications in case of issues, or creating a customizable dashboard to view and analyze data. This characteristic plays a vital role in the adoption or success of IoT applications.

All these characteristics are crucial for the successful implementation and operations of IoT applications. Without all the aforementioned characteristics, IoT systems cannot function effectively. Their characteristics ensure that IoT devices and systems are reliable, efficient, and secure, ultimately leading to better user experiences and outcomes.

The basic architecture of IoT

The architecture of IoT can be defined as the components of IoT interconnected with each other and how they interact to provide a complete solution. The components that make up the IoT architecture include devices, sensors, connectivity, applications, storage, and so on. The IoT architecture can be divided into four layers at a high level:

- **Sensing or perception layer**: The perception layer is responsible for sensing the environment. Sensors and actuators are the core components of this layer, and this stage of the layers is responsible for data gathering.

- **Network layer**: The network layer is responsible for data transmission by providing connectivity between devices. It includes internet gateways, network gateways, and network technologies such as Bluetooth, Wi-Fi, Zigbee, and cellular networks, which we are going to discuss in upcoming chapters in detail.

- **Data processing layer**: The data processing layer is responsible for processing data, managing storage, and making decisions. The task of this layer is to process information and make required decisions.

- **Application layer**: The application layer is the bottommost layer, and it makes a bridge between the end user and the IoT system. The application layer also includes various software applications that run on devices and servers, such as mobile applications, web applications, dashboards, and analytics tools.

Figure 1.1 shows the basic architecture of IoT. The arrow on the left of the diagram shows the data flow or control flow:

Basic IoT Architecture

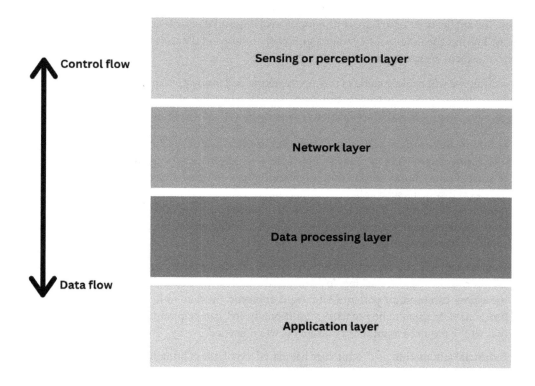

Figure 1.1 – Basic architecture of IoT

The data flows from top to bottom, where the sensor collects data, the network layer transmits the data, the data processing layer analyzes and stores the data, and the application layer is responsible for showing that data to the end user, whereas the control flow is from bottom to top; take an example of a thermostat.

In the case of controlling a thermostat using a mobile application, the process involves several layers of interaction. At the application layer, the user interacts with the mobile application to adjust the thermostat's temperature setting. The user's command is then analyzed and translated into a specific action at the data processing layer. This action includes determining which thermostat device to control based on the user's input. Subsequently, at the network layer, the command is sent over a network connection to the designated thermostat device. The thermostat device receives the command and adjusts its temperature settings accordingly, effectively regulating the temperature in response to the user's input. This layered approach ensures seamless control of the thermostat through the mobile application.

Applications of IoT

IoT has changed the way we live, work, and interact with the world around us. From smart homes and wearables to smart cities and industrial automation, IoT is making its way into every aspect of our lives. The applications of IoT are continuously evolving and diverse, with new use cases emerging every day. IoT has the potential to gather significant amounts of data, and data being the new gold can help transform everything around us.

In this section, we will explore some of the most exciting and innovative applications of IoT and how they are transforming the way we live and work. Since the number of IoT applications is enormous, we are going to discuss selective applications categorized in the form of the following industries:

- **Smart homes:** Smart homes are a popular application of IoT, which involves the use of interconnected devices to manage, optimize, and automate various things in your daily life. In smart homes, home automation is one example of IoT that allows users to control various devices and systems such as lights, heating, and entertainment systems through mobile or other interfaces. Security, surveillance, and energy management are other examples that make our home smarter, more secure, and energy-efficient, which results in reduced energy bills and a smaller carbon footprint.

- **Healthcare:** IoT has revolutionized the healthcare industry by introducing remote health monitoring and patient tracking. IoT-enabled devices or, more specifically, wearable IoT devices these days can monitor patients' vital signs and send the data to healthcare providers in real time, enabling them to be proactive. Additionally, IoT can help improve asset management so that all the required equipment is available when needed.

- **Industrial automation:** IoT technology has played a vital role in bringing significant advancements in predictive maintenance, which has ensured the continuity of production. Also, IoT helps in supply chain management and quality control. All these applications of IoT in industries have reduced downtime and increased productivity and cost savings.

- **Transportation and logistics:** IoT has helped the transportation and logistics sector as well by offering efficient ways of managing fleets, tracking assets, and improving parking management systems. With the help of IoT devices and sensors such as GPS trackers, fleet managers can track the location, speed, and condition of their vehicles in real time, which makes it easier for them to plan routes and manage fuel. Asset tracking enables logistics managers to track and monitor shipments and ensure they are in good condition.

- **Agriculture:** IoT has a lot of potential to increase productivity in the agriculture sector, with applications such as precision farming, livestock monitoring, and crop management. Farmers can use IoT sensors and data analytics to monitor the growth and health of crops, irrigation and fertilization processes can be optimized, and it also aids in the detection of diseases and pests.

The aforementioned applications are the most popular ones, but IoT has helped other businesses and industries as well. In the last part of this book, we will make our own projects that will use the potential of IoT to help us with different daily tasks.

In this section, we learned what IoT is and what its main characteristics are, and we discussed the basic architecture of IoT, from the sensing layer to the application layer. Toward the end of the section, we familiarized ourselves with IoT applications and discussed how these applications can contribute to our daily lives and make them easier. In the next section, we will discuss the capabilities of ESP32 and will learn why it is one of the best candidates for IoT-enabled applications.

Understanding the capabilities of ESP32 for IoT

In the previous section, we discussed a lot about IoT. ESP32 is equipped with built-in Bluetooth (supporting **Low Energy**, or **LE**), and Wi-Fi makes it the perfect candidate for IoT use cases. It can help in various layers of the IoT architecture. For example, it can serve as a sensor node in the sensing layer, which can help us collect and transmit data from various sensors; it can also work as a gateway or a hub in the network layer, collecting data from multiple nodes and forwarding it to the cloud or other devices; it can be used for data analysis and processing, and can also be used in the application layer in the form of wearable devices or robotics.

The versatility of ESP32 makes it an ideal candidate for IoT applications, and in this section, we will be discussing more details about ESP32, its different variants, and a brief comparison of ESP32 with other development boards available for IoT development.

A brief overview of the ESP32 board and its variants

As discussed in the introduction, ESP32 helps a lot in IoT development, but there are several variants of ESP32 microcontrollers on the market. Some popular ones include ESP32-WROOM, ESP32-WROVER, ESP32-DevKitC, and ESP32-SOLO. The difference between all these variants is in their features, such as the amount of memory and number of pins, but the features that make it perfect for IoT development are common in almost all these variants. All variants of ESP32 are based on the same chip (that is, the ESP32 **System on chip (SoC)**, which has a dual-core processor), and all variants have built-in Wi-Fi and **Bluetooth LE (BLE)** support and various input/output interfaces such as **Universal Asynchronous Receiver-Transmitter (UART)**, **Serial Peripheral Interface (SPI)**, **Inter-Integrated Circuit (I2C)**, **analog-to-digital converters (ADCs)**, **digital-to-analog converters (DACs)**, and **pulse-width modulation (PWM)**. You can read more about this at https://www.espressif.com/sites/default/files/documentation/esp32_datasheet_en.pdf.

ESP32 versus other development boards

When we say ESP32 is a perfect candidate for IoT development, it is not the only one. There are other options for IoT use cases. The following table will conclude why ESP32 is the best beginner-friendly option for getting started with IoT:

Development Board	Processor	Connectivity	Power Consumption	Price
ESP32	Dual-core Xtensa LX6, up to 240 MHz	Wi-Fi, Bluetooth, BLE	Low power consumption modes	$4-$10
Arduino UNo	ATmega328P	None (can be added with shields)	Low	$20
Arduino MKR 1000	SAMD21 Cortex-M0+	Wi-Fi	Low	$35
ESP8266	Tensilica L106, up to 160 MHz	Wi-Fi	Low	$2-$5
Raspberry Pi Zero	Broadcom BCM2835, up to 1 GHz	Wi-Fi, Bluetooth (with add-ons)	Moderate	$5-$10
Raspberry Pi Pico	RP2040, up to 133 MHz	None (can be added with add-ons)	Low	$4-$10

Figure 1.2 – Comparison of ESP32 with other IoT-enabled development boards

From the comparison table shown in *Figure 1.2*, we can see that ESP32 outperforms the other available development boards for IoT development in terms of price, power consumption, and connectivity options. However, other boards have other features that make them suitable for other applications; for example, Raspberry Pi Zero has a microprocessor and can run on the Linux OS, making it suitable for applications that require more computation power, and can be used to perform more complicated tasks.

To conclude, ESP32 provides Wi-Fi, Bluetooth, and BLE connectivity and provides interfaces for connectivity such as I2C, SPI, and UART, which can be used to connect other connectivity options such as a 5G shield, **NarrowBand-IoT (NB-IoT)** shield, or **Long Range (LoRa)** transmitter and receiver. Another advantage of using ESP32 is it provides low power consumption modes, such as deep sleep, and so on, which is one of the required features for IoT development.

In this section, we learned that built-in Wi-Fi and BLE capabilities enable ESP32 to be used in IoT-based applications, and the low power consumption and low prices make it one of the best development boards for IoT-based projects. Furthermore, we compared ESP32 with other development boards on the market. In the next section, we will learn about the capabilities of the Arduino IDE and program ESP32 using it.

Deep dive into the Arduino IDE 2.0 to program ESP32

In this section, we will discuss the ESP32 board and its programming using the Arduino IDE 2.0. As discussed in the previous section, ESP32 is a powerful microcontroller and can be programmed in several ways. We will discuss some common ways in which we can program ESP32 and discuss why the Arduino IDE is a beginner-friendly IDE to get started with ESP32. We will have a brief introduction to the Arduino IDE, install the Arduino IDE, and will get ourselves familiarized with the Arduino IDE user interface. Then, we will move on to setting up the IDE for programming ESP32, and finally, we will walk through a simple "Hello World" example using an LED to demonstrate the basics of ESP32 programming with the Arduino IDE.

How can ESP32 be programmed?

ESP32 can be programmed in several ways, including the Arduino IDE, the Python programming language, the **Expressif-IoT Development Framework** (**ESP-IDF**, the official development framework by Espressif), and many more. Some of the most common and widely used methods are described as follows:

- **Arduino IDE**: A beginner-friendly IDE that can help you write, compile, and upload code to ESP32 using the Arduino programming language.

- **MicroPython**: A Python-based interpreter that runs on ESP32, allowing developers to write Python code and execute it directly on the device.

- **ESP-IDF**: The official development framework for ESP32 offers several APIs for low-level hardware access and allows for more flexibility in programming and debugging.

- **Other programming options**: Other ways can be used to program ESP32, such as Visual Studio Code with PlatformIO, JavaScript and Node.js, and Rust.

The following table differentiates the three most common options for programming:

Parameter	Arduino IDE	MicroPython	ESP-IDF
Language	C++	Python	C
IDE support	Yes	No	No
Community support	High	Moderate	High
Low-level access	Limited	Limited	Full
Learning curve	Easy	Easy	Moderate

Table 1.1 – Comparison of programming options for ESP32

Table 1.1 compares the three most common options for programming ESP32. The Arduino IDE and MicroPython are beginner-friendly options, while ESP-IDF provides you complete access to the functionalities of ESP32. However, the absence of IDE support in ESP-IDF and MicroPython makes it difficult for beginners to get started.

The Arduino IDE 2.0

The Arduino IDE 2.0 is the latest version of the popular **open source software** (**OSS**) for programming Arduino boards. The IDE is an easy-to-use platform for programming microcontrollers and creating interactive electronic projects. It has many new features as compared to the previous versions, it is more user-friendly and powerful, and you can use and manage libraries (libraries are pre-written code modules that simplify the development of Arduino projects by providing functions for various tasks), boards, and projects in a single place, making it easier to find and organize your work.

It is an official software for programming Arduino boards, but you can add support for other boards such as ESP32, ESP8266, **Network Repository Function** (**NRF**) boards, and **Synchronous Transport Module** (**STM**) boards, and its user-friendly interface helps beginner-level developers get started easily.

Installing the Arduino IDE 2.0

Installing the Arduino IDE 2.0 is a very straightforward process that is like installing any other software. Following are summarized steps you can follow to install the Arduino IDE 2.0 on your system:

1. Go to the Arduino software page on the Arduino website (`https://www.arduino.cc/en/software`).

2. Scroll down to the download options and select an option based on your operating system:

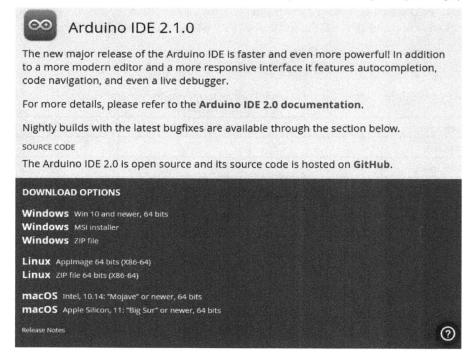

Figure 1.3 – Arduino IDE download options

3. For Windows, run the installer and follow the prompt. For Linux, extract the downloaded file and run the `arduino -ide` script. For macOS, open the downloaded `.dmg` file and drag the application's Arduino IDE 2.0 icon into the application folder.

> **Important note**
>
> Depending on your system configuration, you may need to install additional dependencies or drivers. Refer to the Arduino installation documentation (`https://docs.arduino.cc/software/ide-v2/tutorials/getting-started/ide-v2-downloading-and-installing`) or *Arduino Forum* for more details.

Hopefully, you have successfully installed the Arduino IDE, and in the next section, we will have an overview of the Arduino IDE user interface.

An overview of the Arduino IDE 2.0 user interface

The IDE 2.0 is divided into four main sections: the menu bar, the left sidebar, the editor area, and the bottom panel. The menu bar provides access to all functions and tools available in the IDE, including opening and saving files, compiling code, and uploading it to the board:

Figure 1.4 – Overview of the Arduino IDE 2.0 user interface

The left sidebar contains the project explorer, which shows the structure of the project, the board manager, which can help you install new boards' support, the library manager, which will help you to include, search for, and install new libraries, and debugger and search options, which help while writing code and debugging errors.

The editor area is where code is written and edited, and features such as syntax highlighting and autocompletion make it easy to write code.

The bottom panel displays the console output, debugging information, and serial monitor, which we will be using a lot in upcoming chapters for debugging our code.

Setting up the Arduino IDE 2.0 for ESP32

To use ESP32 in the Arduino IDE, we will first have to install the ESP32 board support, which helps us to compile, build, and upload the ESP32 program. The board support can be installed using the following steps:

1. Once the Arduino IDE is installed, launch **Arduino IDE**.

2. Go to **File | Preferences…**:

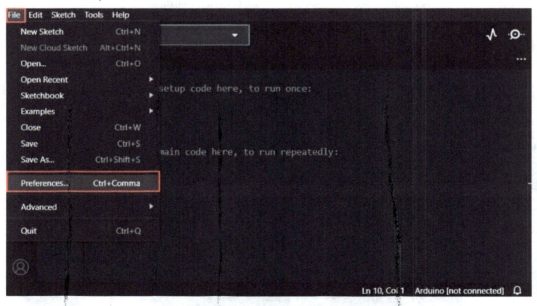

Figure 1.5 – Preferences in the Arduino IDE

3. Paste the following link into the **Additional boards manager URLs** section: `https://raw.githubusercontent.com/espressif/arduino-esp32/gh-pages/package_esp32_index.json`

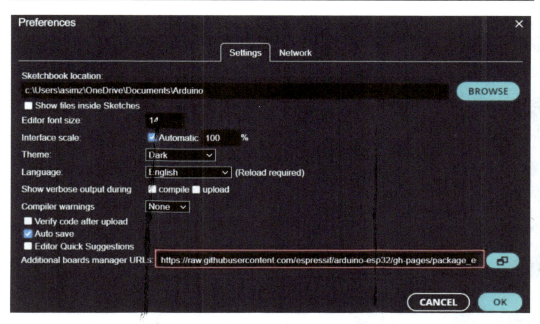

Figure 1.6 – Pasting URL into the Additional boards manager URLs section

4. After adding the URL to the **Additional boards manager URLs** section, go to **BOARDS MANAGER**, which can be accessed from the left-hand side menu, type `esp32`, and install the board support:

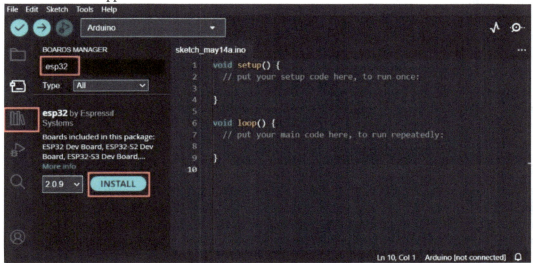

Figure 1.7 – Installing ESP32 board support in the Arduino IDE

5. It will be installed in a few minutes, and you will see the results in the output window:

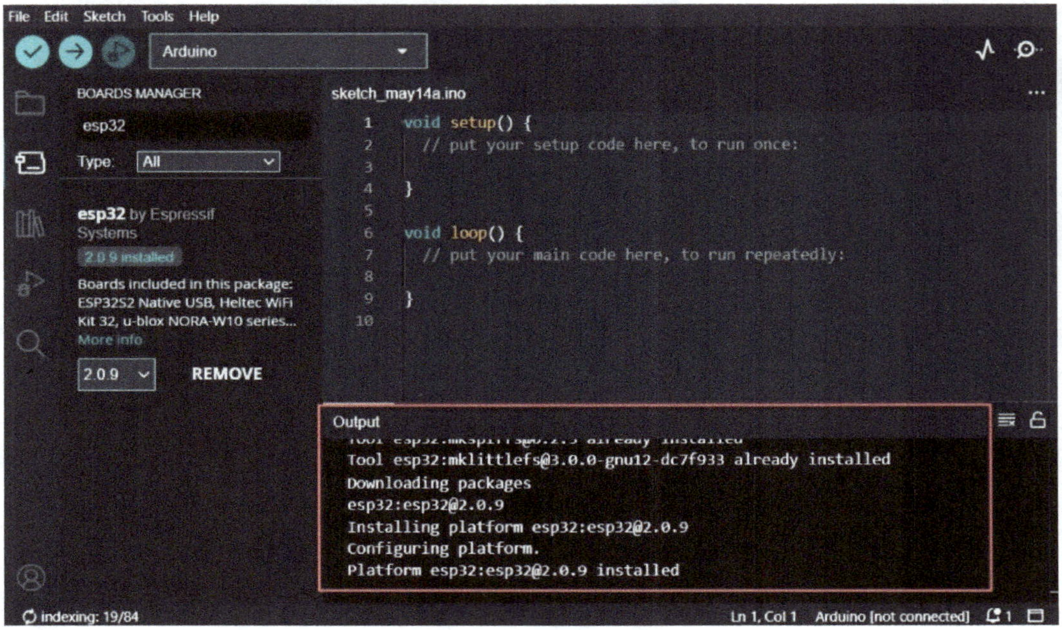

Figure 1.8 – ESP32 board support installed in the Arduino IDE

> **Important note**
>
> If you have multiple URLs in the **Additional boards manager URLs** section (for example, if you have ESP8266, NRF boards, or other boards support installed), you can separate the URLs using a comma between them.

You have now installed the board support for ESP32 and are ready to write and upload exciting IoT programs to ESP32 using the Arduino IDE. In the next part, we will write a "Hello World" example for ESP32.

ESP32 "Hello World" example using the Arduino IDE 2.0

In other programming languages, the Hello World program is the simplest program that serves as an introduction to the programming language and mostly prints "Hello World." In the case of ESP32 and the Arduino IDE, the equivalent to the Hello World program is a blinking LED as it is the simplest and most basic program to test the functionality of the board and its ability to communicate with the IDE. If the LED blink is successful, the developer can verify that the board and IDE are working as expected and can proceed to more complex projects.

You can follow the next steps to run the "Hello World" example:

1. Open a new sketch by clicking **File** | **New** in the Arduino IDE.

2. Type the following code in the new sketch:

```
void setup() {
  pinMode(LED_BUILTIN, OUTPUT);
}
void loop() {
  digitalWrite(LED_BUILTIN, HIGH);
  delay(1000);
  digitalWrite(LED_BUILTIN, LOW);
  delay(1000);
}
```

The Hello World code is made up of two parts or functions: the setup() function and the loop() function.

The setup() function runs only once when the ESP32 board is powered up or reset. In our previous code, we used the setup() function to initialize the LED pin as an output.

The loop() function runs continuously after the setup() function has been executed. In our last example, we first turn on the LED using the digitalWrite() function and set the digital pin to HIGH. Then, using the delay() function, we wait for 1000 milliseconds or 1 second before setting the state of the LED to OFF by setting the digital pin to LOW and wait for another short amount of time to use the delay() function. The process is repeated, resulting in the LED blinking.

3. Make sure you have selected the right version of the ESP32 board and the correct COM port.

4. Upload the sketch to the ESP32 board by clicking on the **Upload** button in the Arduino IDE and wait for the upload process to complete.

5. Once the upload is complete, you will see the built-in LED in ESP32 should start blinking:

Figure 1.9 – Built-in LED state OFF (left ESP32) and built-in LED state ON (right ESP32)

Congratulations! You have run your first project using ESP32 and the Arduino IDE. You are on the right track to build exciting IoT projects. In the next section, you will learn a bonus skill; that is, simulating your project in a browser.

Bonus – Simulating ESP32 projects

This book is written to give you practical knowledge of ESP32 and encourages you to build projects using real hardware, but simulating ESP32 projects can be advantageous in several ways as compared to using actual hardware. Simulation can save costs and allows you to do rapid testing and debugging without hardware damage, and it provides an interactive way for beginners to learn and experiment with ESP32 and the Arduino IDE.

Let's simulate the Hello World program in the ESP32 simulator. You could follow the next steps to simulate your ESP32 projects:

1. Visit `https://www.wokwi.com`, which is an Arduino and ESP32 simulator and is designed to simulate IoT projects in a browser:

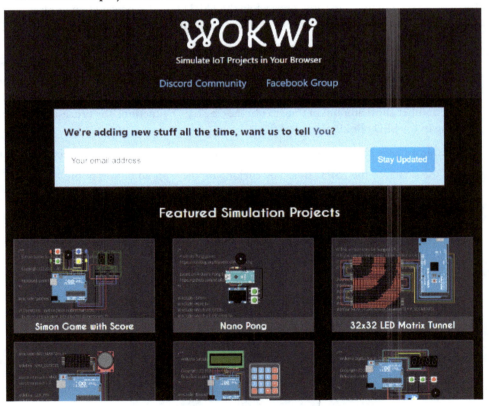

Figure 1.10 – Wokwi IoT simulator

2. Sign up for a new account and then log in:

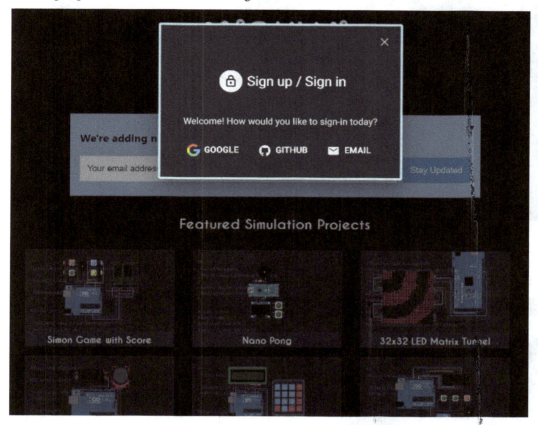

Figure 1.11 – Signing up for or signing in to Wokwi

3. After logging in, navigate to https://wokwi.com/dashboard/projects and click on + **NEW PROJECT**:

Figure 1.12 – Creating a new project in Wokwi

4. When it asks for boards, select **ESP32** if you want to simulate using the Arduino programming language:

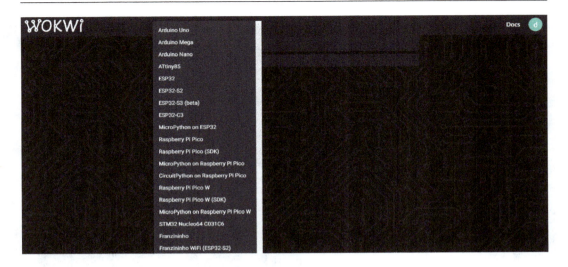

Figure 1.13 – Selecting the ESP32 board in Wokwi

5.   In the `sketch.ino` file, paste the Hello World code:

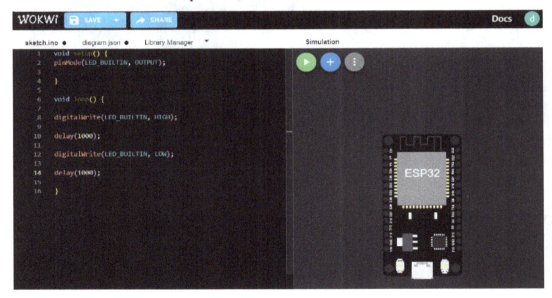

Figure 1.14 – Writing code in Wokwi

6.   Click on the green button that says **Start the simulation**, and you will see that the built-in LED will start blinking:

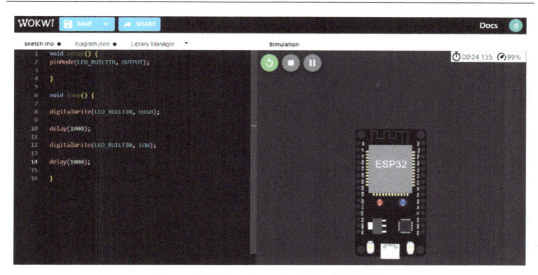

Figure 1.15 – Running a simulation in Wokwi

If you would like to add more parts, you can click on the blue + button, and you will see many peripheral options such as buttons, switches, LEDs, LCDs, different sensors, and so on:

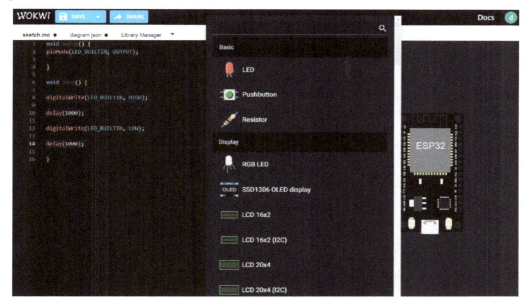

Figure 1.16 – Adding a new part in Wokwi

This simulation tool will help you debug code without actually making circuits. All the examples that we will perform in this book can be simulated using Wokwi.

Summary

In this chapter, we discussed the basics of IoT, including its main characteristics that distinguish it from other technologies, and we discussed the architecture of IoT and learned the directions of data flow and control flow in the IoT architecture. Then, we explored some common and popular applications of IoT such as smart homes, healthcare, industrial automation, transportation, logistics, and agriculture.

After discussing IoT, we discussed the ESP32 board, compared it with other microcontrollers, and discussed the different variants of ESP32 boards and how ESP32 can be programmed. We then discussed the Arduino IDE 2.0, which is the latest version of the Arduino official board programmer, installed the ESP32 board support to set it up for using ESP32, and finally, we ran a "Hello World" example on ESP32 and simulated it using an ESP32 simulator, which can help us in cost savings, testing, and debugging.

In the next chapter, we will be discussing how to interface sensors with ESP32.

2

Connecting Sensors and Actuators with ESP32

In this chapter, we will dive into the world of sensors and actuators with the ESP32, a highly versatile and powerful microcontroller. By exploring its built-in features and connectivity options, you will develop a fundamental understanding of how to interact with the physical world using advanced pieces of hardware.

We will start with the introduction to the ESP32's **general purpose input/output (GPIO)** pins and their functionality. Next, we will learn about **universal asynchronous receiver-transmitters (UART)** and serial communication, which will enable us to exchange data between devices. After mastering UART, we will turn our attention to the **serial peripheral interface (SPI)** communication protocol, a method commonly used to send data between microcontrollers and small peripherals. Finally, we will delve into I2C communication, a highly efficient two-wire protocol used for short-distance data transmission.

To truly understand these concepts, we will bring them to life using real-world sensor examples. By directly applying these communication protocols to tangible scenarios, you will be able to better understand and remember their functionality.

By the end of this chapter, you will not only have a deep understanding of these key communication methods, but you will also have hands-on experience using them with the ESP32. The practical skills acquired here will be invaluable, as they form the basis for creating a wide range of **internet of things (IoT)** devices and applications, from home automation systems to environmental sensors and beyond.

In this chapter, we are going to cover the following main topics:

- Getting hands-on with ESP32 GPIO pins and an overview of them
- Mastering UART and serial communication
- Understanding SPI communication
- I2C communication with ESP32

Through these topics, we will traverse from the basics of the ESP32 to more complex, real-world applicable sensor and actuator interfaces, shaping you into a capable ESP32 developer.

Technical requirements

For this chapter, we will need the following components:

- ESP32 dev kit
- Push button
- LED
- DS1307 RTC module
- PN532 RFID module

Getting hands-on with ESP32 GPIO pins and an overview of them

GPIO is a fundamental feature found in microcontrollers and other embedded systems. It refers to the ability of the microcontroller to interact with the external world by providing a flexible set of input and output pins. GPIO pins can be configured to either read or write digital signals, allowing the microcontroller to communicate with various devices and peripherals. As input, GPIO pins can detect the state of external sensors, switches, or digital signals. For example, we can read the temperature from temperature sensors. As outputs, they can drive LEDs, control motors, or interface with other electronic components. The versatility of GPIO pins makes them essential for a wide range of applications, enabling the microcontrollers to interact with and control the physical environment.

In this section, we will dive into ESP32 GPIO pins and explore their potential. By understanding this topic, you will be able to control various electronic components and devices. Let's take a moment to familiarize ourselves with the GPIO pins available in the ESP32 dev kit.

ESP32 peripherals

The peripherals available on the ESP32 microcontroller may vary depending on the specific version or variant of the ESP32 module. However, in general, almost all versions of the ESP32 contain a rich set of peripherals that greatly enhance the capabilities of the microcontroller. These commonly found peripherals include but are not limited to the following:

- **UART**: A hardware communication interface that allows serial data transmission between devices
- **Inter-Integerated Circuit (I2C)**: A synchronous, multi-master, multi-slave communication protocol used for connecting multiple devices on the same bus
- **SPI**: A synchronous, full duplex communication protocol for high-speed data exchange between a master and multiple slave devices

- **Analog-to-digital convertor** (**ADC**): A device or component that converts analog signals into digital values for processing

- **Digital-to-analog converters** (**DAC**): A device that converts digital values into corresponding analog signals

- **Pulse - width modulation** (**PWM**): A technique to control analog devices using digital signals by varying the duty cycle of a square wave

- **Timers and counters**: Components used to measure time and intervals and count events in embedded systems

We will start with a basic input/output example with the ESP32.

ESP32 basic input/output example

In this example, we will interface a push button and LED with the ESP32. We will write an Arduino program to read the button status. If the LED is on and the button is pressed, the LED will turn off. If the LED is off and the button is pressed, the LED will turn on. This means that we will be using the button as a toggle switch:

1. Firstly, we will interface the push button. We will connect one terminal of the push button to a GPIO pin (D12) on the ESP32 and connect the other terminal to the **ground** (**GND**) pin on the ESP32.

2. Next, we will interface the LED. Connect the anode (longer leg) of the LED to a GPIO pin (D13) on the ESP32 and connect the cathode (shorter leg) of the LED to the GND pin on the ESP32.

    The circuit diagram is shown in the following figure:

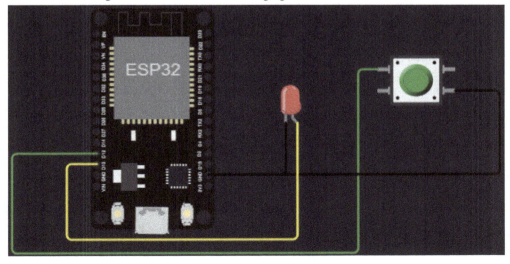

Figure 2.1 – Interfacing a button and LED with ESP32

3. Then, we will open Arduino IDE. Write the following code and upload it to the connected ESP32 board as explained in the `hello world` example in *Chapter 1*. The code can be found on GitHub at `https://github.com/PacktPublishing/Programming-ESP32-with-Arduino-IDE/tree/main/Chapter%202/ESP32_button_and_LED`:

```
// Digital input and output pin definitions
#define BUTTON_PIN 12
#define LED_PIN 13
void setup() {
  // Set the button pin as input
  pinMode(BUTTON_PIN, INPUT_PULLUP);
  // Set the LED pin as output
  pinMode(LED_PIN, OUTPUT);
}
void loop() {
  // Read the state of the button
  int buttonState = digitalRead(BUTTON_PIN);
  // If the button is pressed (LOW state), turn on the LED
  if (buttonState == LOW) {
    digitalWrite(LED_PIN, HIGH);
  } else {
    // Otherwise, turn off the LED
    digitalWrite(LED_PIN, LOW);
  }
}
```

In this code, we first define the pin numbers for the button input (BUTTON_PIN) and LED output (LED_PIN). For the `setup()` function, we set the button pin as input with a built-in pull-up resistor using the INPUT_PULLUP mode. A pull-up resistor is enabled for the specified input pin (BUTTON_PIN). It ensures that when the button is not pressed, the pin is pulled up to a high logic level (typically representing 1 or 3.3V, and when the button is pressed and connects the pin to the ground, it reads as a low logic level (typically representing 0 or 0V). This configuration helps avoid floating inputs and provides a known high-level voltage when the button is not pressed.

> **Important note**
>
> Alternatively, you could have used the pull-down configuration (INPUT_PULLDOWN) to achieve a similar result, where the pin would be pulled down to a low logic level ('0' or '0V') when the button is not pressed and read as high ('1' or '3.3V') when the button is pressed. The choice between pull-up and pull-down depends on the specific circuit requirements and design preferences.

Then, in the `loop()` function, it reads the state of the button. If it is pressed (LOW state), it turns on the LED by setting the LED pin to HIGH. Otherwise, it turns off the LED by setting the LED pin to LOW.

There are several sensors that act as normal switches and can be interfaced in a similar way as capacitive touch sensors, hall effect sensors, optical sensors, proximity sensors, and force sensing resistors.

Moving from the basic input-output example to the PWM example, let's explore a more advanced and efficient method of controlling electronic devices using varying duty cycles.

ESP32 PWM example

Pulse-width modulation (**PWM**) is a technique that allows for the control of the average power delivered to a load by varying the width of the pulses in a periodic signal. This is typically used to control the intensity of LEDs, the speed of motors, and other analog-like functions in digital systems.

To demonstrate the example, we will connect the LED with ESP32 and write a program to increase/decrease the intensity of the LED by changing the PWM values:

1. LEDs have two legs, with the longer leg being the anode (positive) and the shorter leg being the cathode (negative). Connect the anode of the LED to a digital output pin (D13) on the ESP32 board. Connect the cathode of the LED to a current-limiting resistor, which is required to protect the LED from excessive current and to ensure it operates within its specified voltage and current ratings. Connect the other end of the current-limiting resistor to the GND pin on the ESP32 board, as shown in the following figure:

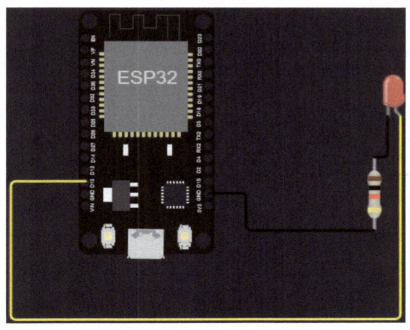

Figure 2.2 – Interfacing the LED with the ESP32

2. Then, we will write the following code in Arduino IDE and upload it to the selected ESP32 board as explained in the `hello world` example in *Chapter 1*. The code can be found on GitHub at `https://github.com/PacktPublishing/Programming-ESP32-with-Arduino-IDE/tree/main/Chapter%202/ESP32_PWM`:

```
#define PWM_PIN 13
void setup() {
  pinMode(PWM_PIN, OUTPUT);
}
void loop() {
  for (int dutyCycle = 0; dutyCycle <= 255; dutyCycle++) {
    analogWrite(PWM_PIN, dutyCycle);
    delay(10);
  }
}
```

This code uses PWM on the ESP32 to generate a varying duty cycle signal on pin 13.

The duty cycle can be represented mathematically as follows:

$$Duty\ cycle\ (\%) = \frac{Time\ on}{period} \times 100\%$$

The duty cycle is often represented using an 8-bit value, which can range from 0 to 255. This 8-bit value allows for 256 possible levels of duty cycle, where 0 represents fully off (0% duty cycle) and 255 represents fully on (100% duty cycle). In the preceding code, because of the `for` loop, the duty cycle value gradually increases in steps of one, resulting in a fading effect when connected to an output device such as an LED. The following diagram illustrates the intensity of the LED by varying the duty cycle:

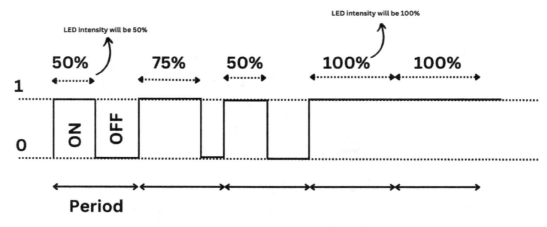

Figure 2.3 – Duty cycle and fading in and out of an LED

PWM could be used for LED dimming, motor speed control, audio generation, power control, and analog simulations.

Now that we have covered the basic input-output example and PWM example, let's take a step further into the basics of communication by exploring UART.

Mastering UART communication

A UART is a hardware device or a protocol that manages asynchronous serial communication between devices. It facilitates data transmission by converting bytes of data from the CPU into a continuous stream of bits suitable for transfer via communication links. One of the key features of UART is that it does not require a clock signal. This simplifies hardware, reduces power consumption, and allows flexible data rates but may also lead to potential timing and synchronization issues between the sender and receiver, requiring additional overhead for start and stop bits and making it less suitable for high-speed or long-distance communication. The absence of a clock signal makes this protocol asynchronous. This simple yet powerful communication protocol is commonly used in microcontroller-based projects for inter-device communication, making it an essential part of our ESP32 study.

In this section, we will cover the following topics related to UART in the context of ESP32 and Arduino IDE:

- How a UART protocol works
- UART communication between two ESP32 modules
- Sensors that use the UART protocol

By the end of this section, you will have a solid understanding of how the UART protocol works, how to utilize it with ESP32 using Arduino IDE, and how to establish communication between two ESP32 modules. Additionally, you will be familiar with some common sensors that employ UART and can be easily interfaced with ESP32 for various applications.

How the UART protocol works

As already mentioned, UART is a serial communication protocol that enables the transmission and reception of data between devices. Since it is an asynchronous protocol, no clock is involved in the transmission. Instead, UART uses two data lines: the receiver (Rx) line for receiving data and the Tx line for transmitting data.

The data format in UART consists of a start bit, data bits (typically 8 bits), an optional parity bit for error detection, and one or more stop bits. The start bits, which are always low (0), mark the beginning of the data frame. The data bits represent the actual information being transmitted, and the optional parity bit can be used for error checking by adding an extra bit (odd or even) to each transmitted byte. The parity bit is set in a way that ensures the total number of bits (including the parity bit) in each byte is either even or odd. Upon reception, the receiver checks the parity of the received byte; if it doesn't match the expected parity, an error is detected, allowing for basic error detection in the data transmission process. Finally, the stop bits, typically one or two bits high (1), indicate the end of the data frame. The data format of UART can be seen in *Figure 2.4*:

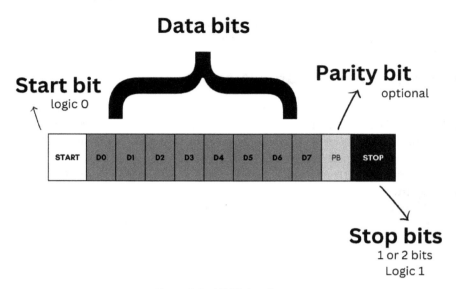

Figure 2.4 – UART data format

For example, if we would like to send the word IoT using UART, the transmission would take the following approach:

1. Convert each character of IoT to its ASCII equivalent:

Character	ASCII Code	Binary
"I"	73	01001001
"o"	111	01101111
"T"	84	01010100

Concatenate the ASCII codes together:

```
I O T
01001001 01101111 01010100
```

2. Add the start bit, parity bit (if applicable), and stop bit to the data:

  - Start bit: 0

  - Data bits: 01001001 01101111 01010100

  - Parity bits (if used): Not included in this example

  - Stop bits: 1

The complete UART data frame for IoT would be the following:

```
0 01001001 1 0 01101111 1 0 01010100 1
```

This data will be transmitted at a certain speed, which is called the **baud rate**. It represents the number of **bits per second (bps)** that can be transferred. Common baud rates include 9600, 115200, and 921600 bits per second.

UART communication between two ESP32s

In the context of working with UART in Arduino IDE and ESP32, the process of converting strings and handling start and stop bits is automated, relieving developers of manual conversion. The UART hardware module in the ESP32 and the accompanying software libraries in Arduino IDE take care of these tasks seamlessly. When transmitting data, you can simply provide the string or data to be sent, and the UART library takes care of converting it into the appropriate data format, including the start and stop bits. On the receiving end, the UART library receives the data frame, extracts the information, and provides it in a usable format, such as a string or individual bytes.

We will take the following steps to make two ESP32s communicate using the UART protocol:

1. Since we already discussed that UART uses the two data lines Rx and Tx, we will first create a circuit in which two ESP32s are connected to each other using these two datelines.

    The Rx of the first ESP32 should be connected to the Tx of the other ESP32. The Tx of the first ESP32 should be connected to the Rx of the other ESP32. To ensure the circuit is completed, the GND of both ESP32s should be common. *Figure 2.5* shows the circuit diagram:

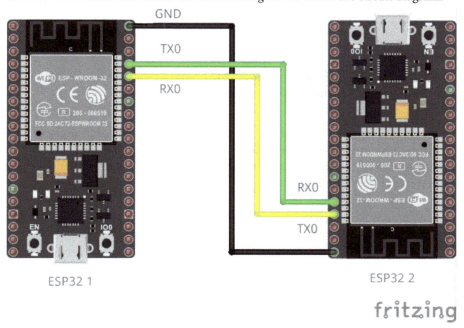

Figure 2.5 – ESP32-to-ESP32 UART communication

2.   Now, we will write the following code in the Arduino IDE to send the word IoT over the UART communication. The code can be found on GitHub at https://github.com/PacktPublishing/Programming-ESP32-with-Arduino-IDE/tree/main/Chapter%202/UART%20Communication/Sender:

```
void setup() {
  // Set UART baud rate to 9600
  Serial.begin(9600);
}

void loop() {
  // Send the string "IoT" over UART
  Serial.println("IoT");

  // Wait for a moment before sending again
  delay(1000);
}
```

In this code, the Serial.begin(baudrate) function helps us set the baud rate, the serial.println() function helps us send the data, and the delay function makes us wait a certain number of milliseconds (in this case 1000 ms) before sending data again.

3.   You will have to upload this code, using Arduino IDE, to the first ESP32. Make sure you have selected the right ESP32 variant and COM PORT.

> **Important note**
> While uploading the code, make sure that the ESP32 Rx and Tx pins are not connected to the other ESP32 because this can interfere with the uploading process.

4.   Once the code is uploaded successfully, you can open **Serial Monitor** by going to the **Tools** menu and clicking on **Serial Monitor** in Arduino IDE (or pressing *Ctrl* + *Shift* + *M* on Windows/Linux or *Cmd* + *Shift* + *M* on macOS). Set the baud rate to 9600 and you will see the output IoT, as seen in *Figure 2.6*:

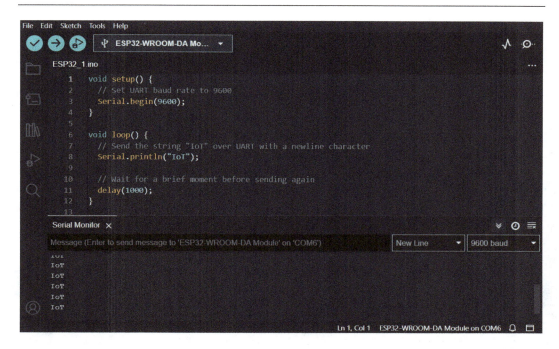

Figure 2.6 – The first ESP32 transmitting the word IoT using UART

5. Similarly, connect the second ESP32 and upload the following code, making sure that the board variant and COM PORT are selected properly. The code can be found on GitHub at https://github.com/PacktPublishing/Programming-ESP32-with-Arduino-IDE/tree/main/Chapter%202/UART%20Communication/Receiver:

```
void setup() {
  // Set UART baud rate to 9600
  Serial.begin(9600);
}

void loop() {
  if (Serial.available() > 0) {
    // If data is available to read
    String receivedData = Serial.readString();
    // Process or use the received data
    // Example: Print the received data
    Serial.print("Received Data: ");
    Serial.println(receivedData);
  }
}
```

In this code, we have set up the baud rate as in the code of the first ESP32. Make sure both boards use the same baud rate and the `Serial.available()` function to make sure that the data is being received. The `serial.readstring()` function helps us to read strings from the other ESP32. In the end, we are printing that data to the Serial Monitor. There are several other `Serial` functions, which you can learn about from the documentation (`https://reference.arduino.cc/reference/cs/language/functions/communication/serial/`).

6. After uploading the code, make sure both ESP32s are connected as described in the circuit diagram and open the serial port of the second ESP32. You will see the output in *Figure 2.7*:

Figure 2.7 – The second ESP32 receiving the word IoT using UART

Now you have learned how to send and receive data in the ESP32 using UART communication in Arduino IDE. In the following section, we will discuss some of the sensors that can be interfaced with the ESP32 and can use UART communication.

Sensors that use UART communication

Several sensors use UART communication and can be interfaced with ESP32:

- **GPS modules**: Many GPS modules use UART communication to send location data to ESP32. ublox NEO 6m and NEO 7m are examples.

- **RFID readers**: Some RFID readers use UART to communicate with ESP32, such as MFRC522 and PN532.

- **Bluetooth modules**: Certain Bluetooth modules, such as HC-05 and HC-06, use UART communication to enable wireless connectivity, but the ESP32 already has Bluetooth capabilities. Knowing this can help you with other microcontrollers that do not have Bluetooth capabilities.

- **GSM/GPRS modules**: UART can be used to interface the ESP32 with GSM/GPRS modules for cellular communication. Modules such as SIM800L and SIM900A can be connected to the ESP32 via UART to enable SMS, voice calls, internet connectivity, or NB-IoT.

- **Thermal printers**: Some thermal printers use UART for data transfer. By connecting a thermal printer, such as the popular Adafruit thermal printer or similar modules to the ESP32 via UART, you can print text, images, barcodes, and WR codes.

In this section, we have learned what the UART communication protocol is, how it works, and how to use the UART communication protocol to make two ESP32s communicate. We have also familiarized ourselves with some of the devices that use the UART communication protocol. In the next section, we will explore the I2C communication protocol.

I2C communication with ESP32

I2C is another serial communication protocol, but unlike the UART protocol, it is a synchronous communication protocol that is used for communications between integrated circuits or devices on a shared bus. Since it is a synchronous communication protocol, it requires a clock signal and works in the master-slave architecture. Therefore, it is commonly used in scenarios where multiple devices need to communicate with the master/central device.

In this section, we will explore the following topics related to I2C communication in the context of ESP32 and Arduino IDE:

- How I2C communication works
- I2C communication example using ESP32
- Sensors that use I2C communication

By the end of this section, you will be able to explain the I2C protocol, differentiate it from UART, use it with ESP32 using Arduino IDE, and understand some of the common sensors available on the market that can be interfaced using I2C.

How I2C communication works

As already discussed, I2C communication works through a master-slave architecture, where one device acts as the master and there can be one or multiple slave devices. Communication takes place using two wires, SDA and SCL:

- **Serial data line** (**SDA**): This is used for transmitting and receiving data between devices. It carries the actual data being transferred.

- **Serial clock line** (**SCL**): This is responsible for providing a clock signal that synchronizes the data transfer between devices.

The master-slave architecture of I2C can be seen in *Figure 2.8*.

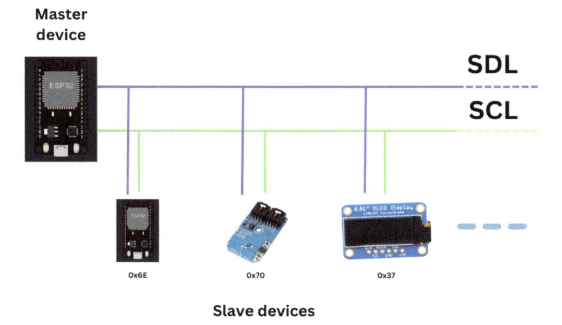

Figure 2.8 – I2C master-slave architecture

> **Important note**
> In addition to SDL and SCL connections, a common ground connection is required between devices using the I2C protocol. The GND connection provides a reference voltage level that ensures reliable and accurate data transfer between the devices. A pull-up resistor is also needed to keep the communication stable and prevent data clashes. Most modules have a built-in pull-up resistor.

The master device initiates communication with the slave devices. The following is a step-by-step explanation of how the I2C protocol works, which is also depicted in *Figure 2.9*:

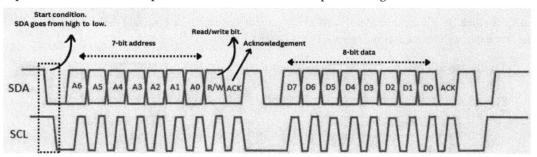

Figure 2.9 – I2C waveform

1. **Start condition**: The master device initiates communication by sending a start condition on the bus. It consists of a high-to-low transition on the SDA line while the SCL line remains high.

2. **Addressing**: After the start condition, the master sends the 7-bit or 10-bit address of the slave address it wants to communicate with. The address is sent with the **most significant bit** (**MSB**) first. In *Figure 2.8*, you will see the addresses of each device. These addresses help us identify the device.

3. **Read/write bit**: The master sends a read or write bit after the slave address. The read bit (1) indicates that the master wants to read the data from the slave device, while the write bit (0) indicates that the master wants to write the data to the slave.

4. **Data transfer**: Depending on the read/write bit, data transfer occurs between the master and slave. In a write operation, the master sends data bytes to the slave. In a read operation, the slave sends data bytes to the master. The data is sent in packets of eight bits, with each bit followed by an acknowledgment bit.

5. **Acknowledgment**: After each byte transfer, the receiving party (either the master or slave) sends an acknowledgment (ACK) bit. If the ACK bit is low, it indicates that the data byte was received successfully. If it is high, it indicates no acknowledgment (NACK), signaling an error.

6. **Stop condition**: To end the communication, the master sends a stop condition. This consists of a high-to-low transition on the SDA line while the SCL line remains high. The stop condition allows other devices on the bus to resume communication.

It is worth noting that, throughout the communication process, the SDA line carries the data while the SCL carries the clock signal generated by the master. The clock signal synchronizes the data transfer between devices. The sequence of the start condition, address, data transfer, acknowledgment, and stop condition repeats for each transaction on the I2C bus. I2C communication allows for multi-master configurations, which allow multiple master devices to share a common SPI bus, each capable of initiating communication independently. This makes it a versatile protocol for inter-device communication in various applications.

An I2C communication example using ESP32

To demonstrate how I2C communication works on ESP32, we will be using an example of the DS1307 **real-time clock (RTC)** module. An RTC is a hardware device that keeps track of the current date and time, even when the system is powered off or restarted:

1. Firstly, we will make a connection between the DS1307 RTC and the ESP32. RTC modules consist of five pins:

    - VCC: A power pin that requires 5V or 3.3V in the case of the ESP32

    - GND: Connect this pin to the GND of the ESP32

    - SDA: Connect this pin to the SDA pin of the ESP32

    - SCL: Connect this pin to the SCL pin of the ESP32

    - SQW/OUT: Provides square wave or interrupt output, though it is optional and we will not be using this pin in our example

Figure 2.10 shows the circuit diagram of an ESP32 and a DS1307 RTC module:

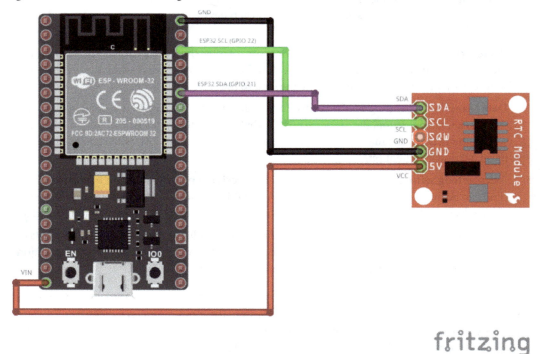

Figure 2.10 – ESP32 and DS1307 I2C circuit diagram

2. Now we will write code in the Arduino IDE for the ESP32 to read the date and time information from the RTC module. But first, we will have to install two libraries so we can access the pre-defined I2C and RTC functions:

- `Wire`

- `RTCLib` by Adafruit

You will have the `Wire` library already installed. You can install `RTCLib` from the library manager as follows:

I.   Go to the library manager

II.   Search for `RTClib`

III. Install `RTClib` by Adafruit

The steps are marked in the following figure:

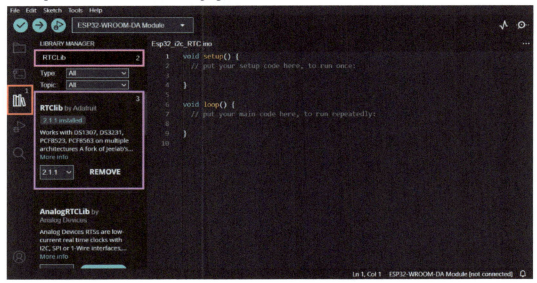

Figure 2.11 – How to install RTCLib in Arduino IDE

Once you have installed the library, you can write the code. The code can be found on GitHub at `https://github.com/PacktPublishing/Programming-ESP32-with-Arduino-IDE/tree/main/Chapter%202/I2C%20Communication/ESP32_RTC`:

1. We will start by importing two libraries, `Wire` and `RTClib`:

- The `Wire` library enables I2C communication and the `RTClib` library provides the necessary function to interface with the DS1307 RTC module

- The RTC_DS1307 rtc line initializes an instance of the RTC_DS1307 class, which represents the RTC module:

```
#include <wire.h>
#include <RTClib.h>
RTC_DS1307 rtc;
```

2. Then, we will initialize the setup function and initialize the serial communication at a baud rate of 9600 to show the current date time in the Serial Monitor:

```
void setup() {
  Serial.begin(9600);
  Wire.begin();
  // Uncomment the following line if the RTC has not been
initialized
  // rtc.adjust(DateTime(F(__DATE__), F(__TIME__)));
  if (!rtc.begin()) {
    Serial.println("Couldn't find RTC");
    while (1);
  }
  if (!rtc.isrunning()) {
    Serial.println("RTC is not running!");
    // Uncomment the following line to set the RTC to the date
and time at the moment of uploading the code
    // rtc.adjust(DateTime(F(__DATE__), F(__TIME__)));
  }
}
```

Let's briefly discuss the various functions used:

- Wire.begin(): Initializes the I2C communication.
- if (!rtc.begin()): Checks if the RTC module is detected and properly connected. If not, it prints an error message and enters an infinite loop.
- If (!rtc.isrunning): Checks if the RTC is running. If not, it prints a message that the RTC is not running. You can uncomment the rtc.adjust() line to set the RTC to the current date and time.

1. Now, we will write the loop function to read the date and time and print it on the serial monitor:

```
void loop() {
  DateTime now = rtc.now();
  Serial.print("Current Date and Time: ");
  Serial.print(now.year(), DEC);
```

```
    Serial.print('/');
    Serial.print(now.month(), DEC);
    Serial.print('/');
    Serial.print(now.day(), DEC);
    Serial.print(' ');
    Serial.print(now.hour(), DEC);
    Serial.print(':');
    Serial.print(now.minute(), DEC);
    Serial.print(':');
    Serial.print(now.second(), DEC);
    Serial.println();
    delay(1000);
}
```

- The `loop()` function, as discussed, is executed repeatedly.

- `DateTime now = rtc.now()` retrieves the current date and time from the RTC module and stores it in the now variable of type `DateTime`.

- The subsequent `Serial.print()` statement displays the current date and time in the serial monitor. DEC is used to specify the format in which the value should be printed, that is, decimal (base 10) format.

- The `delay(1000);` line adds a one-second delay before the next iteration of the loop.

2. Now, you can upload the code and open the serial monitor to see the results. You will see the following results:

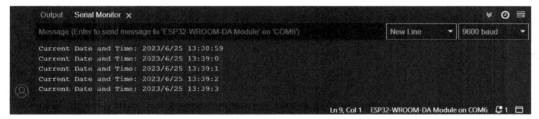

Figure 2.12 – Current Date and Time using the RTC module and ESP32

You could also simulate the project in the Wokwi simulator. *Figure 2.13* shows the simulation of this project in the Wokwi simulator and the results:

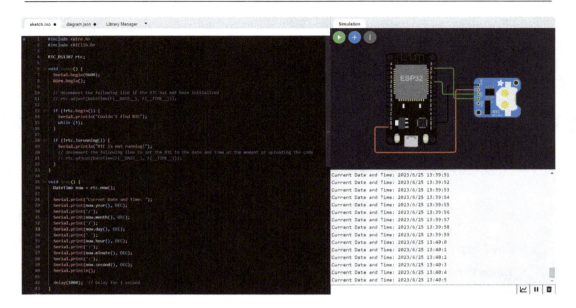

Figure 2.13 – Simulation of the project

In this example, we did not use the address of our slave device, which is the RTC module (0x68) in the code. It was taken care of by RTClib.

The RTC module will be a useful addition is some of your IoT projects. It can provide accurate timekeeping, allowing devices to synchronize actions, schedule tasks, and coordinate events within the IoT network. Also, it enables devices to maintain the correct date and time, ensuring data logging, event sequencing, and time-sensitive operations.

Devices that use I2C communication with ESP32

The following are some of the devices that utilize I2C communication with ESP32:

- **Sensors**: Examples include temperature and humidity sensors, barometric pressure sensors (BMP180, BMP280), accelerometers and gyroscopes (MPU6050, MPU9250), magnetometers (HMC5883L), ambient lights (TSL2561), proximity sensors (VL53L0X), gas and air quality sensors (CCS811, MQ Series Gas Sensor), and many more available on the market

- **Display modules**: Examples include LCD screens (16x2 LCD) and OLED displays (SSD1306)

- **RTC modules**: These maintain accurate timekeeping, even during power loss (DS1307, DS3231)

- **EEPROM and FRAM memory modules**: These provide non-volatile storage for data retention (24LC256 EERPROM)

- **I/O expanders**: These expand the number of input/output pins of the ESP32 (MCP23017)

In this section, we explored I2C communication. We learned how to use the I2C communication protocol in ESP32 and we learned about some of the devices that use I2C communication. In the next section, we will dive into SPI communication.

Understanding SPI communication

SPI is a synchronous serial communication protocol widely used for connecting microcontrollers or other digital devices with peripheral devices. It provides a straightforward and efficient means of data transfer, making it suitable for applications that require high-speed and full- duplex communication.

Like the I2C communication protocol, the SPI protocol uses a master-slave architecture, where one device acts as a master, controlling the communication, and one or more devices act as slaves, responding to commands from the master.

In this section, we will explore the following topics related to the SPI communication and ESP32:

- How SPI communication works
- SPI communication example using ESP32
- Sensors or devices that use SPI communication

By the end of this section, you will be able to understand what the SPI communication protocol is, how it works, how we can use it in ESP32-based projects, and some common peripherals in which we use the SPI protocol to communicate.

How does SPI communication work

SPI communication works through a master-slave architecture, where one device acts as the master and controls the communication while one or more devices act as slaves and respond to commands from the master. SPI uses four primary pins for communication:

- SCLK (serial clock): The clock signal generated by the master device
- MOSI (master out/slave in): The line through which the master sends data to the slave
- MISO (master in/slave out): The line through which the slave sends data back to the master
- SS/CS (slave select/chip select): The line used by the master to select the desired device for communication

Figure 2.14 shows the master-slave architecture of SPI communication between a master and multiple slaves:

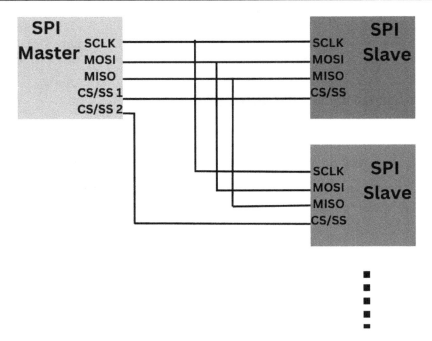

Figure 2.14 – SPI communication in a master-slave architecture

Here's a step-by-step explanation of how SPI communication works:

1. **Configuration**: The master device sets up the communication settings.

2. **Chip select**: The master selects the slave device to communicate with.

3. **Clock generation**: The master generates a clock signal.

4. **Clock polarity and phase: Clock polarity (CPOL)** and **clock phase (CPHA)** are crucial in SPI communication, as they determine the timing and synchronization between devices. CPOL sets the idle state of the clock, ensuring both devices agree on when data transmission begins. CPHA determines when data is sampled, ensuring that data bits are captured at the correct clock edges, maintaining synchronization between the sender and receiver.

5. **Frame format**: The number of bits and data format is defined.

6. **Data validity and synchronization**: Timing is synchronized for proper data interpretation.

7. **End of Communication**: The master deactivates the slave device's chip select line to indicate the end of communication. The following figure shows the waveform that illustrates the working of read and write requests in SPI communication:

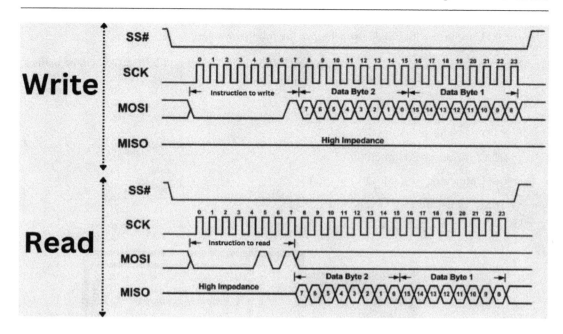

Figure 2.15 – SPI read and write waveform

In *Figure 2.15*, you can see that SS# goes from high to low when selecting the chip.

For the transmission of instructions and data, the **Master Output/Slave Input (MOSI)** line sends instructions to write, followed by the associated data. Meanwhile, the **Master Input/Slave Output (MISO)** line remains at high impedance during this phase.

Conversely, during the reading of data, the MOSI line sends an instruction to read, and the MISO line transmits the data back to the master.

Now you have learned how SPI communication works, let's apply it in ESP32 using Arduino IDE.

SPI communication example using ESP32

There are several peripherals that use SPI communication. For the sake of this example, we will be using a PN532 NFC reader and ESP32.

An NFC reader is a device that communicates with NFC tags or devices in proximity. It enables secure data exchange over short distances, typically a few centimeters. NFC readers are used in various applications such as access control, mobile payments, and IoT devices for contactless interactions and data transfer.

To use the NFC module with ESP32, we will take the following steps:

1. Firstly, let's make a connection between the PN532 NFC reader and ESP32. We will be using the following connections, as shown in *Figure 2.16*:

    -   SCK: Connected with GPIO 14

    -   MISO: Connected with GPIO 12

    -   MOSI: Connected with GPIO 13

    -   SS: Connected with GPIO 15 of the ESP32

    -   GND: Connected with GND of the ESP32

    -   VCC: Connected with the ESP32 VIN or 3.3V

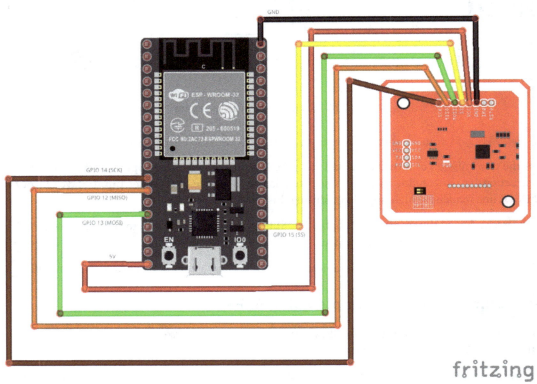

Figure 2.16 – ESP32 and PN532 circuit diagram

The PN532 module can be connected to the ESP32 using SPI, I2C, or UART communication, and the communication method can be configured using the switches on the module. The following table shows the switch configuration:

Communication protocol	Switch 1	Switch 2
UART(HST)	0	0
I2C	1	0
SPI	0	1

Table 2.1 – PN532 communication protocol settings

We are using SPI communication, therefore, the first switch should be set to 0 and the other should be set to:1.

Now we will write code to scan the RFID card and print the scanned card ID on the serial monitor. The code can be found on GitHub at https://github.com/PacktPublishing/Programming-ESP32-with-Arduino-IDE/tree/main/Chapter%202/SPI%20Communication/ESP32_NFC.

1. First, we will have to include a couple of libraries:

    ```
    #include <SPI.h>
    #include <Adafruit_PN532.h>
    ```

    We are using two libraries: SPI for using SPI communication and Adafruit_PN532 for using the functions of the NFC module. You will have to install the Adafruit_PN532 library. You can use this library by searching for the Adafruit_PN532 library in the library manager and then installing it.

2. Then, we define the pins specified for SPI communication with the PN532 NFC module:

    ```
    #define PN532_SCK  (14)
    #define PN532_MOSI (13)
    #define PN532_SS   (15)
    #define PN532_MISO (12)
    ```

3. Next, we create an instance of the Adafruit_PN532 class with the specified SPI pins:

    ```
    Adafruit_PN532 nfc(PN532_SCK, PN532_MISO, PN532_MOSI, PN532_SS);
    ```

4. In the `setup` function, we initialize the serial communication and NFC module using the `nfc.begin()` function. It checks for the firmware version of the PN532 module, and if the version data is not obtained (indicating a problem), it prints an error message and halts the program. If the version data is obtained successfully, it prints the chip type and firmware version and writes `Waiting for a card` to indicate that it is ready to detect a card:

```
void setup(void) {
  Serial.begin(115200);
  nfc.begin();
  uint32_t versiondata = nfc.getFirmwareVersion();
  if (! versiondata) {
    Serial.print("Didn't find PN53x board");
    while (1); // halt
  }
  // Got ok data, print it out!
  Serial.print("Found chip PN5"); Serial.
println((versiondata>>24) & 0xFF, HEX);
  Serial.print("Firmware ver. "); Serial.print((versiondata>>16)
& 0xFF, DEC);
  Serial.print('.'); Serial.println((versiondata>>8) & 0xFF,
DEC);
  Serial.println("Waiting for a Card ...");
}
```

5. Then, we define the `loop()` function, which will be executed repeatedly:

```
void loop(void) {
  uint8_t success;
  uint8_t uid[] = { 0, 0, 0, 0, 0, 0, 0 };
  uint8_t uidLength;
  success = nfc.readPassiveTargetID(PN532_MIFARE_ISO14443A, uid,
&uidLength);

  if (success) {
    Serial.println("Found a card");
    Serial.print("  UID Length: ");Serial.print(uidLength,
DEC);Serial.println(" bytes");
    Serial.print("  UID Value: ");
    nfc.PrintHex(uid, uidLength);
    if (uidLength == 4)
    {
      // We probably have a Mifare Classic card ...
      uint32_t cardid = uid[0];
      cardid <<= 8;
      cardid |= uid[1];
```

```
        cardid <<= 8;
        cardid |= uid[2];
        cardid <<= 8;
        cardid |= uid[3];
        Serial.print("Seems to be a Mifare Classic card #");
        Serial.println(cardid);
      }
      Serial.println("");
    }
  }
```

First, we declare the `success`, `uid`, and `uidLength` variables. `uid` is an array used to store the **unique identifier (UID)** of the detected card, and `uidLength` represents the length of the UID. Using the `nfc.readPassiveTargetID()` function, it attempts to read the UID and its length. If a card is successfully detected, it prints a message indicating the card's presence, the UID length, and the UID value. If the UID length is 4 bytes, it assumes it's a MIFARE Classic card and extracts the individual bytes to form a 32-bit card ID, which is then printed along with a descriptive message. Finally, it prints a blank line for separation before checking for the presence of the next card.

6. Now, you can upload the code to the ESP32 using Arduino IDE. Open the serial monitor, and once you scan an RFID or NFC card, you will see the output on the serial monitor, as shown in *Figure 2.17*:

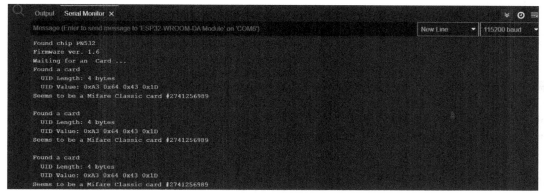

Figure 2.17 – PN532 NFC card read serial monitor result

Now you have learned how SPI communication works and how to use it with ESP32 using the SPI library. TheNFC and RFID modules will be very useful additions to your IoT-based projects for secure and contactless access control, allowing for the authentication and identification of users and devices. It can also be used to enable seamless data exchange and tracking in IoT applications, such as inventory management, supply chain, and asset tracking.

Devices that use SPI communication

There are several peripherals that can be interfaced with ESP32 using SPI communication. Some of the common devices are as follows:

- TFT LCD displays: ILI9341, ST7789, SSD1306

- SD card modules: MicroSD card adapter

- ADC chips: MCP3008, ADS1115

- RFID readers: MFRC522, PN532

- Ethernet controllers: ENC28J60

- LoRa transceivers: SX1276, SX1278

- DAC chips: MCP4922, MAX521

- Pressure sensors: BMP280, MS5611

- Accelerometers and gyroscopes: MPU9250, ADXL345

- Temperature sensors: MAX31855

In this section, we have learned how the SPI communication protocol works, how we can use it with ESP32, and what some of the commonly available devices that can be interfaced with ESP32 using SPI communication are.

Summary

In this chapter, we learned about ESP32 peripherals and the functions of those peripherals. We learned how to use the IOs of ESP32 and how to use PWM. Furthermore, we discussed the most common serial communication protocols, such as UART, I2C, and SPI, in detail to help you connect many peripherals not only with ESP32 but also with other microcontrollers. We also learned how we can make two ESP32s communicate and how to interface RTC modules and RFID/NFC modules. The learnings of this chapter will make a strong foundation for developing IoT.

In the next chapter, we will discuss how to interface displays and cameras with ESP32.

3

Interfacing Cameras and Displays with ESP32

In this chapter, we embark on an exciting journey of connecting cameras and displays to the ESP32 microcontroller. As we explore the features of ESP32 and the Arduino IDE, we will uncover the ability to capture and show visual information. This will enable us to create even more dynamic and interactive projects.

We will begin by familiarizing ourselves with the ESP32 camera module and its capabilities. We will explore how to program the ESP32 camera, enabling us to capture images. Additionally, we will delve into integrating a motion sensor with the ESP32 camera module and create a program that triggers image capture whenever motion is detected. This comprehensive approach will allow us to gain a thorough understanding of the ESP32 camera, program it effectively, and implement motion-based image capture functionality.

Following our exploration of the camera, we will shift our focus to display interfaces. We will discover the different types of display interfaces, including **Serial Peripheral Interface (SPI)**, **Inter-Integrated Circuit (I2C)**, and parallel, and gain insights into their respective advantages and complexities. By examining popular display modules compatible with ESP32, we are introduced to a wide range of options for visual output.

With this knowledge in hand, we will learn the process of interfacing displays with ESP32. We will explore display libraries specific to the EPS32 platform, learn how to configure display pins and connections, and how to initialize the display module. Displaying text and graphics on the screen becomes a more seamless process as we make ourselves familiar with the power of ESP32. We will also explore advanced display features such as touchscreen integration.

By the end of this chapter, you will have gained a solid foundation in the ESP32 camera module and displays with ESP32. The skills and knowledge acquired will empower you to create a wide range of projects.

In this chapter, we are going to cover the following main topics:

- Using the ESP32 camera module

- Interfacing displays with ESP32

- Comparison of displays

By covering these topics, we will advance from the fundamentals of camera and display interfaces to practical implementations that will enhance your skills as an ESP32 developer.

Technical requirements

In this chapter, for the projects that require a camera, we will be using the ESP32-CAM board, which has a built-in camera and SD card support. Furthermore, we will use the ESP32 DevKit board and 16x2 LCD, SSD1306 **organic light-emitting diode** (**OLED**), ILI9341 TFT Touchscreen, and e-paper displays.

All the code files used in this chapter will be available at `https://github.com/PacktPublishing/Programming-ESP32-with-Arduino-IDE/tree/main/Chapter3`.

Using the ESP32 camera module

The ESP32-CAM is a versatile and compact development board that combines an ESP32 microcontroller with a camera module, making it an ideal choice for projects involving image and video processing. This small yet powerful board offers a wide range of features, including built-in Wi-Fi and Bluetooth connectivity, which enable seamless communication with other devices. ESP32-CAM's camera module boasts a resolution of up to 2 megapixels and supports various image formats, allowing for the capture of high-quality photos and videos. Additionally, it features a microSD card slot for local storage, making it suitable for applications that require data logging or recording. With its rich set of capabilities, ESP32-CAM is a popular choice for projects such as surveillance systems, remote monitoring, IoT applications, and even robotics. Its open source nature and extensive community support further enhance its appeal, providing developers with a vast array of resources and libraries to accelerate their development process:

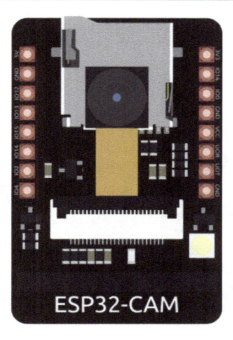

Figure 3.1 – ESP32-CAM

Next, let's understand how to use it.

How to use ESP32-CAM with the Arduino IDE

The ESP32-CAM board is distinct from the ESP32 development kit and requires a different approach to programming. Unlike the dev kit, the ESP32-CAM board does not have a built-in USB-to-serial converter, so an FTDI module is necessary to establish communication between the board and your computer. **FTDI**, which stands for **Future Technology Devices International**, is a company that specializes in USB interface technologies. Their FTDI modules act as bridges, allowing the conversion of USB signals into serial signals compatible with ESP32-CAM. To program the ESP32-CAM board, follow these steps:

1. Connect the FTDI module to your computer's USB port.

2. Identify the FTDI module's pinout, which typically includes TX (transmit), RX (receive), GND (ground), and VCC (power) pins.

3. Make the necessary connections between the FTDI module and the ESP32-CAM board. Connect the TX pin of the FTDI module to the RX pin of the ESP32-CAM board, the RX pin of the FTDI module to the TX pin of the ESP32-CAM board, and connect the GND and VCC pins appropriately. *Figure 3.2* shows the circuit.

4. Launch the Arduino IDE and select the ESP32-CAM board and port settings.

The program will be transferred to the ESP32-CAM board via the FTDI module, and once the upload is complete, the board will restart and begin executing the program:

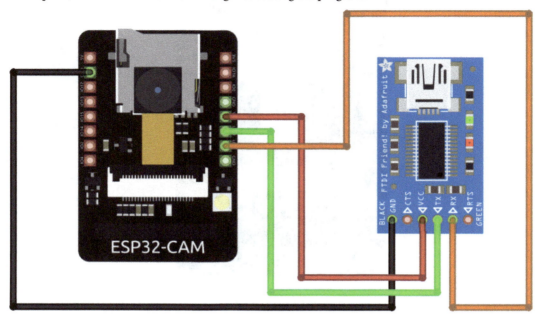

Figure 3.2 – Interfacing ESP32-CAM with FTDI module to program it using the Arduino IDE

Let's understand this with the help of an example.

ESP32 camera example

To demonstrate the use of the ESP32 camera, we will write a program to capture an image when there is motion. The example will involve a **passive infrared** (**PIR**) motion sensor, an SD card, and an ESP32-CAM board.

The ESP32 camera module is configured to capture images using the OV2640 camera sensor, which communicates with the ESP32 microcontroller over the **Serial Camera Control Bus** (**SCCB**). SCCB is a simple, two-wire serial protocol like I2C and is used to configure and control the camera module, setting parameters such as exposure, gain, and image size. The pixel data from the camera sensor is read out and processed, then the image is stored on an SD card. The communication between the ESP32 board and the camera sensor occurs through SCCB for control and configuration, but the actual image data transfer is handled by the camera module and ESP32's camera library, which abstracts these details and provides a convenient interface for capturing and saving images.

We will follow the following steps to use ESP32 camera module in this example,

1. Firstly, we will have to make the following connections:

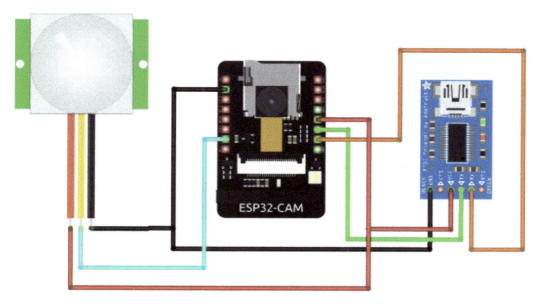

Figure 3.3 – Interfacing a PIR motion sensor with ESP32-CAM

2. The PIR motion sensor's data pin is connected to the IO2 pin on the ESP32-CAM board, while its VCC and GND pins are connected to the 3.3V and GND pins of the ESP32-CAM board, as shown in *Figure 3.3*. The FTDI module employs the same pin configuration as depicted in *Figure 3.2*. Connect the TX pin of the FTDI module to the RX pin of the ESP32-CAM board, the RX pin of the FTDI module to the TX pin of the ESP32-CAM board, and connect the GND and VCC pins appropriately.

3. After making the connections, we will have to install the `esp_camera` and `SD_MMC` libraries.

4. After installing the libraries, make sure the SD card is plugged into the board and then upload the following code (the code is available on GitHub at `https://github.com/PacktPublishing/Programming-ESP32-with-Arduino-IDE/tree/main/Chapter3/PIR%20motion%20Sensor%20and%20camera`):

```
#include "esp_camera.h"
#include <SD_MMC.h>
#define CAMERA_MODEL_AI_THINKER
#define PWDN_GPIO_NUM     -1
#define RESET_GPIO_NUM    -1
#define XCLK_GPIO_NUM     4
#define SIOD_GPIO_NUM     18
#define SIOC_GPIO_NUM     23
#define Y9_GPIO_NUM       36
#define Y8_GPIO_NUM       37
#define Y7_GPIO_NUM       38
```

```
#define Y6_GPIO_NUM        39
#define Y5_GPIO_NUM        35
#define Y4_GPIO_NUM        14
#define Y3_GPIO_NUM        13
#define Y2_GPIO_NUM        34
#define VSYNC_GPIO_NUM     5
#define HREF_GPIO_NUM      27
#define PCLK_GPIO_NUM      25

// Motion sensor configuration
#define MOTION_SENSOR_PIN 2
...

...

...

    Serial.println("Image captured and saved");
  }

  // Delay for a short time before checking for motion again
  delay(100);
}
```

This code sets up an ESP32-based camera module to capture images when motion is detected. It includes the necessary libraries and pin configurations.

In the setup() function, it initializes the serial communication, initializes the SD card using SD_MMC.begin(), and configures the camera module using camera_config_t. It also initializes the motion sensor using pinMode(MOTION_SENSOR_PIN, INPUT);.

In the loop() function, it checks whether motion is detected by calling if (digital-Read(MOTION_SENSOR_PIN) == HIGH). If motion is detected, it proceeds to capture an image. It retrieves the image using esp_camera_fb_get() and checks whether the capture was successful. If so, it opens a file named image.jpg on the SD card using SD_MMC.open(). If the file is opened successfully, it writes the image data to the file using file.write(), closes the file with file.close(), and releases the image buffer using esp_camera_fb_return(). Finally, it prints a message indicating that the image was captured and saved.

5. The code then waits for a short period (100 milliseconds) using delay(100) before checking for motion again. This loop continues indefinitely, monitoring for motion and capturing images accordingly.

In the following section, we will learn about the different visual options available for ESP32 and learn how to use them.

Interfacing displays with ESP32

Displays are beneficial for IoT projects involving ESP32 due to their ability to provide visual feedback and enhance user interaction. With displays, real-time sensor data, system status, and notifications can be easily conveyed, improving user experience. Additionally, displays enable the creation of intuitive user interfaces, allowing users to interact with the IoT system directly and access information conveniently.

In this section, we will discuss various display options that can be interfaced with ESP32 and cover the following topics:

- 16x2 LCD display
- OLED display
- TFT display with touch integration
- E-paper display
- Comparison of all the aforementioned displays

By the end of this section, you will have a solid understanding of how displays are interfaced with ESP32, and you will be able to select a suitable display for your next project.

Interfacing a 16x2 LCD with ESP32 using I2C

A 16x2 LCD with an I2C interface is a commonly used and versatile device for displaying information in embedded systems and microcontroller-based projects. It consists of an LCD with two rows, each capable of displaying up to 16 characters. The 16x2 LCD I2C is widely used in applications such as temperature monitoring, data logging, menu interfaces, and system status displays, providing a convenient and compact solution for visual information output in embedded projects.

This type of LCD relies on an integrated controller, often the HD44780, to facilitate character display on its two rows. In operation, the microcontroller sends commands and data via I2C to the LCD, allowing it to display alphanumeric characters, numbers, and symbols as needed.

How to interface a 16x2 LCD with ESP32

A 16x2 LCD could be interfaced with ESP32 using I2C communication, which we discussed in *Chapter 2*. We will make use of the **Serial Clock Line (SCL)** and **Serial Data Line (SDA)** pins of our LCD and make the connections explained in *Table 3.1*:

LCD Pins	ESP32 Pins
VCC	3.3V or 5V
GND	GND

LCD Pins	ESP32 Pins
SDA	D21 (SDA)
SCL	D22 (SCL)

Table 3.1 – How to interface a 16x2 LCD with ESP32

The connections defined in the preceding table are depicted in *Figure 3.4*:

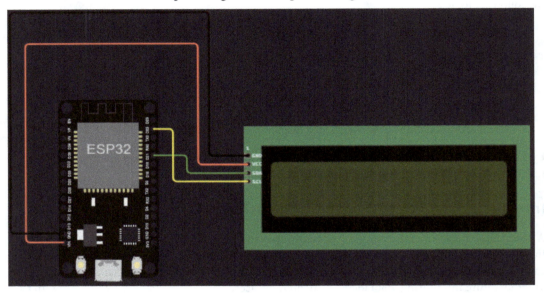

Figure 3.4 – Interfacing a 16x2 LCD with ESP32 using I2C

After making the connection, we will install the LiquidCrystal_I2C library and upload the following code, in which we will show text on the LCD, scroll text, and show customized icons on the LCD.

The code is available on GitHub at https://github.com/PacktPublishing/Programming-ESP32-with-Arduino-IDE/tree/main/Chapter3/16x2%20LCD:

```
#include <Wire.h>
#include <LiquidCrystal_I2C.h>

const int LCD_ADDRESS = 0x27;
const int LCD_COLS = 16;
const int LCD_ROWS = 2;

LiquidCrystal_I2C lcd(LCD_ADDRESS, LCD_COLS, LCD_ROWS);
```

```
void setup() {
  lcd.init();
  lcd.backlight();
  lcd.setCursor(0, 0);
  lcd.print("Hello, ESP32!");
  lcd.setCursor(0, 1);
  lcd.print("LCD Example");
  delay(3000);
  lcd.clear();
  lcd.print("Scrolling Text:");
  lcd.autoscroll();
  for (int i = 0; i < 16; i++) {
    lcd.scrollDisplayLeft();
    delay(500);
  }
  lcd.noAutoscroll();
  lcd.clear();
  byte heart[8] = {
    B00000,
    B01010,
    B11111,
    B11111,
    B01110,
    B00100,
    B00000,
  };
  lcd.createChar(0, heart);
  lcd.setCursor(0, 0);
  lcd.print("I ");
  lcd.write(byte(0));
  lcd.print(" ESP32!");
}

void loop() {
  // Do nothing in the loop
}
```

The code begins by defining constants for the LCD address (0x27) and the number of columns (16) and rows (2) of the LCD. An instance of the LiquidCrystal_I2C class named lcd is created, specifying the LCD address and dimensions.

In the `setup()` function, the LCD is initialized with `lcd.init()`. The backlight of the LCD is turned on using `lcd.backlight()`. The cursor is positioned at the beginning of the first row using `lcd.setCursor(0, 0)`, and the text `"Hello, ESP32!"` is printed using `lcd.print()`. The cursor is then moved to the beginning of the second row, and the text `"LCD Example"` is printed. A delay of 3 seconds is introduced with `delay(3000)`. The result is shown in *Figure 3.5 (a)*.

Next, the `lcd.clear()` function is called to clear the LCD. The text `"Scrolling Text:"` is printed using `lcd.print()`. The `lcd.autoscroll()` function is called to enable the automatic scrolling of text. A `for` loop is used to scroll the text to the left by one position at a time, with a delay of 500 milliseconds between each scroll. After scrolling 16 positions, the `lcd.noAutoscroll()` function is called to disable automatic scrolling. The `lcd.clear()` function is called again to clear the display. The output is shown in *Figure 3.5 (b)*.

A custom character representing a heart shape is defined using an array of bytes. The `lcd.createChar()` function is used to create a custom character at index 0 using the heart array. The cursor is positioned at the beginning of the first row, and the text `"I "` is printed using `lcd.print()`. The custom character representing a heart is displayed using `lcd.write(byte(0))`. Finally, the text `" ESP32!"` is printed. The output is shown in *Figure 3.5 (c)*.

In the `loop()` function, nothing is done, and the program remains idle, effectively creating an infinite loop:

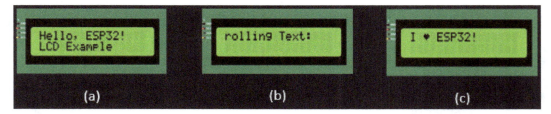

Figure 3.5 – (a) Text on 16x2 LCD, (b) Scrolling text, and (c) showing customized characters

In the next section, we will explore and learn how to use an I2C OLED display with ESP32, which offers better contrast and visibility than the 16x2 LCD.

Interfacing an OLED with ESP32 using I2C

An OLED display is a compact and versatile device for visual output in various electronic projects. We will be using the SSD1306 OLED display. It features a small OLED screen that offers high contrast and excellent visibility, even in low-light conditions. The I2C interface makes it easy to integrate the SSD1306 OLED display with a wide range of microcontrollers, including popular ones such as Arduino and ESP32. By using libraries such as `Adafruit_SSD1306`, developers can easily control the display, allowing for tasks such as displaying text, graphics, icons, and even animations. The SSD1306 OLED display with an I2C interface is commonly used in applications such as wearable devices, IoT projects, digital meters, and portable electronic gadgets, providing a compact, energy-efficient, and visually appealing solution for displaying information.

The SSD1306 OLED works by emitting light from individual LEDs to create a visible image. Each pixel in the OLED display emits its own light and can be controlled individually. The SSD1306 is a display driver chip that controls the OLED display, taking in data from a microcontroller and translating it into signals that instruct the individual pixels to emit light at varying intensities, creating text, images, and graphics. It communicates with the microcontroller using communication protocols such as I2C or SPI to receive data and commands for pixel control.

How to interface the SSD1306 OLED with ESP32

The SSD1306 OLED can be interfaced with ESP32 using I2C communication, which we discussed in *Chapter 2* and used in the previous section to interface the 16x2 LCD. We will make use of the SCL and SDA pins of our OLED and make the following connections explained in *Table 3.1* and *Figure 3.6*:

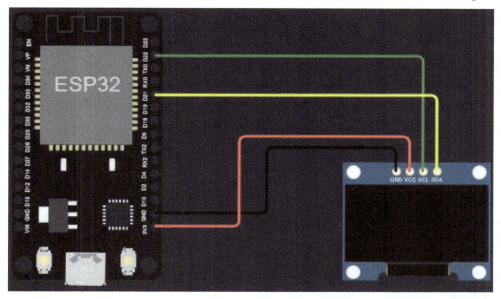

Figure 3.6 – Interfacing SSD1306 with ESP32 using I2C

After making the circuit, we will install the `Adafruit_GFX` and `Adafruit_SSD1306` libraries. Then, we will upload the following code, which will show text, change the font size of text, draw shapes, and draw bitmap images on the OLED.

The code is available on GitHub at `https://github.com/PacktPublishing/Programming-ESP32-with-Arduino-IDE/tree/main/Chapter3/SSD1306%20OLED`:

```
#include <Wire.h>
#include <Adafruit_GFX.h>
#include <Adafruit_SSD1306.h>
```

```
#define SCREEN_WIDTH 128
#define SCREEN_HEIGHT 64

Adafruit_SSD1306 display(SCREEN_WIDTH, SCREEN_HEIGHT, &Wire, -1);

const unsigned char logo [] PROGMEM = {
...

...

...
  display.clearDisplay();
  display.drawBitmap(0, 0, logo, 128, 64, SSD1306_WHITE);
  display.display();
  delay(2000);
}
```

This code demonstrates the usage of the Adafruit_SSD1306 library to control a 128x64 OLED display using an ESP32 microcontroller. It includes the necessary libraries, a Wire.h file for I2C communication, and Adafruit_GFX.h and Adafruit_SSD1306.h files for graphics functions and OLED display control. Make sure to install these libraries from the library manager.

The code sets the screen width and height constants based on the display's dimensions. An instance of the Adafruit_SSD1306 class named display is created, specifying the screen width, height, Wire object, and I2C address (-1 for the default).

In the setup() function, display initialization is performed. If the initialization fails, an error message is printed, and the program enters an infinite loop. After successful initialization, the display is cleared, the text size is set to 1, and the text color is set to white. Text is printed on the screen using the display's println() function, as can be seen in *Figure 3.7 (a)*. The display is then updated with display.display(), and a 2-second delay is introduced.

The loop() function is where the main display operations occur. First, the display is cleared. Text size is increased to 2, and ESP32 is printed at the specified position. Text size is reset to 1, and OLED Display is printed at a different position, as can be seen in *Figure 3.7 (b)*. The display is updated with display.display(), and a delay is introduced.

The process is repeated for several other graphical operations. These include drawing a rectangle (*Figure 3.7 (c)*), filling a circle (*Figure 3.7 (d)*), drawing a line, and displaying a bitmap in *Figure 3.7 (e)*. Each operation involves clearing the display, performing the specific graphical action using the appropriate function, updating the display, and introducing a delay before moving on to the next operation.

> **Important note**
>
> You could convert your BMP image to an array using this online tool: https://javl.github.io/image2cpp/.

This loop of displaying different graphics on the OLED display continues indefinitely, with each operation being displayed for 2 seconds before transitioning to the next:

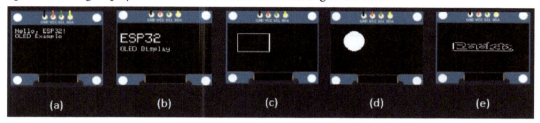

Figure 3.7 – (a) Text on OLED, (b) changing text size, (c) drawing a rectangle,
(d) drawing a circle, and (e) showing Packt bitmap logo

In this section, we have learned how to interface an OLED with ESP32 and show text, draw shapes, and show bitmap images. In the next section, we will explore the **thin-film-transistor** (TFT) display, which will enable us to interact with our projects using a touch interface.

Interfacing a TFT display with ESP32 using SPI and I2C

The ILI9341 SPI TFT display with I2C touch interface combines the benefits of both SPI and I2C communication protocols to provide a comprehensive visual and touch input solution. The display utilizes the SPI protocol for fast and efficient data transfer between the microcontroller and the display module. This enables high refresh rates and smooth graphics rendering on the TFT screen. Additionally, the touch input is facilitated through an I2C interface allowing for precise and responsive touch interaction. By employing libraries such as Adafruit_ILI9341 and Adafruit_FT6206, developers can easily control both the display and the touch functionality. This combination of SPI for display communication and I2C for touch input provides seamless integration of visual output and user interaction in projects ranging from embedded systems and portable devices to interactive displays and user interfaces.

How to interface ILI9341 with ESP32

As mentioned previously, the ILI9341 TFT display uses SPI communication for display functions and I2C communication for touch integration. To interface ILI9341 with ESP32, follow the connection guide in *Table 3.2*:

Touchscreen Pins	ESP32 Pins (SPI)
VCC	3.3V or 5V
GND	GND
CS	D15
RST	D4
DC/RS	D2

Touchscreen Pins	ESP32 Pins (SPI)
SDI/MOSI	D23 (MOSI)
SCK	D18 (SCK)
LED	NC
SDO/MISO	D19 (MISO)
SCL	D22 (SCL)
SDA	D21 (SDA)

Table 3.2 – Connection guide for ESP32 and ILI9341 TFT display

The same connections are depicted in *Figure 3.8*:

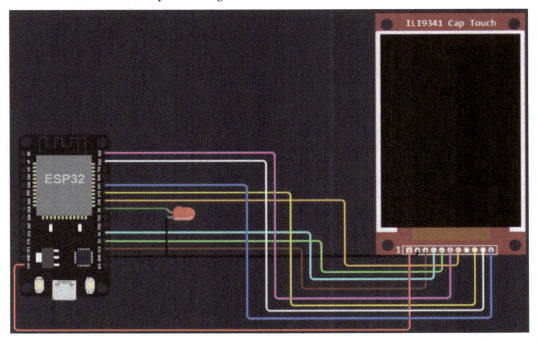

Figure 3.8 – Interfacing ILI9341 TFT display with ESP32

After making the circuit, make sure to install the `Adafruit_ILI9341`, `Adafruit_GFX`, and `Adafruit_FT6206` libraries and upload the following code, which shows a menu; on clicking a certain item, it performs actions.

The code is available on GitHub at `https://github.com/PacktPublishing/Programming-ESP32-with-Arduino-IDE/tree/main/Chapter3/TFT%20Touchscreen`:

```
#include <Adafruit_ILI9341.h>
#include <Adafruit_GFX.h>
#include <Adafruit_FT6206.h>
#define TFT_CS 15
#define TFT_DC 2
#define SCREEN_WIDTH 320
#define SCREEN_HEIGHT 240

#define BACKGROUND_COLOR ILI9341_BLACK
#define TEXT_COLOR ILI9341_WHITE
#define HIGHLIGHT_COLOR ILI9341_YELLOW
...
...

...
  tft.setTextSize(5);
  tft.setCursor(30, 100);
  tft.setTextColor(TEXT_COLOR);
  tft.print(temperature, 1);
  tft.setTextSize(3);
  tft.setCursor(200, 105);
  tft.print("C");
  tft.setTextSize(2);
}
```

The preceding code uses several libraries: Adafruit_ILI9341, Adafruit_GFX, and Adafruit_FT6206. Make sure to install them using the library manager before uploading the code. The TFT_CS and TFT_DC constants represent the chip's select and data/command pins, while SCREEN_WIDTH and SCREEN_HEIGHT define the dimensions of the display.

The code defines some additional constants for colors, such as BACKGROUND_COLOR, TEXT_COLOR, and HIGHLIGHT_COLOR. It also sets minimum and maximum touch coordinates for the x and y directions using TS_MINX, TS_MAXX, TS_MINY, and TS_MAXY.

The ts object is used to handle the touch input, and the tft object controls the display. The menuOption array holds the text for different menu options. The currentOption and numOption variables keep track of the currently selected option and the total number of options.

In the setup() function, the display is initialized, its rotation is set to 0, and the screen is filled with the specified background color. Text-related settings, such as text size and color, are configured. The LED pin is set as an output, and if the touchscreen fails to initialize, the code enters an infinite loop.

The `loop()` function continuously checks whether the touchscreen is touched. If a touch is detected, the coordinates are mapped to the screen dimensions. If the touch falls within the range of the menu options, the corresponding option is identified, and the menu is redrawn with the selected option highlighted. The code then performs a specific action based on the selected option, such as toggling an LED, showing the temperature, changing the background color (shown in *Figure 3.9 (c)*), and rotating the screen, as can be seen in *Figure 3.9 (d)*, or restarting ESP32.

The `drawMenu()` function is responsible for drawing the menu options on the screen. It clears the screen, iterates through the menu options, sets the text color based on the current option, and prints the menu text at the appropriate position. The menu is shown in *Figure 3.9 (a)*.

The `Toggle_LED()` function toggles the state of an LED connected to pin 5. It updates the LED_ state variable and sets the digital output of the LED accordingly.

The `showTemp()` function displays a temperature reading on the screen. It fills the screen with background color, sets the text size and color, and prints the text `Temperature` at a specific position. It then displays a temperature value (`25.5` in this case) with one decimal place, followed by the `C` unit at another position on the screen, as can be seen in *Figure 3.9 (b)*:

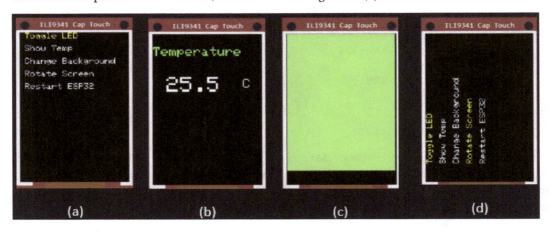

Figure 3.9 – (a) Main menu on the TFT screen, (b) showing temperature
on the TFT, (c) changing colors, and (d) rotating screen

In this section, you have learned how to use the visual and touch interface of the TFT touchscreen. In the next section, we will interface an e-paper display, which is a very popular display for reading devices, such as Amazon Kindle.

Interfacing an e-paper display with ESP32

An e-paper display, also known as an electronic paper display or e-ink display, is a unique type of display technology that mimics the appearance of traditional ink on paper. E-paper displays such as e-ink work by manipulating charged pigment particles within tiny microcapsules to create visible text or images. It offers several advantages, including low power consumption and a wide viewing angle. An e-paper display is particularly well suited for applications where static or slowly changing content is sufficient, such as e-readers, electronic shelf labels, and signage. It operates by manipulating charged particles within microcapsules, resulting in a visible change in the display's appearance. One popular variant is an e-paper display with a 2.9" size, which provides a compact yet readable screen area. It can be interfaced with microcontrollers such as ESP32, enabling control over the display's content and appearance. With the help of libraries such as GxEPD2, developers can easily update the e-paper display with new information, create simple graphics, and showcase text-based content. An e-paper display offers a unique and eye-friendly visual experience, making it a popular choice in applications where power efficiency, readability, and durability are key requirements.

How to interface an e-paper display with ESP32

To interface an e-paper display with ESP32, we will use the SPI communication protocol. Follow the connection guide in *Table 3.3*:

E-Paper Display Pins	ESP32 Pins
VCC	3.3V
GND	GND
DIN	D23
CLK	D18
CS	D5
DC	D17
RST	D16
BUSY	D4

Table 3.3 – Connection guide to interface an e-paper display with ESP32

The same connections are depicted in *Figure 3.10*:

Figure 3.10 – Interfacing an e-paper display with ESP32

After making the connection, make sure to install the GxEPD2_BW and Adafruit_GFX libraries and the required fonts and then upload the code, which will print Hello World on the e-paper displays.

The code is available on GitHub at https://github.com/PacktPublishing/Programming-ESP32-with-Arduino-IDE/tree/main/Chapter3/E-paper:

```
#include <GxEPD2_BW.h>
#include <Adafruit_GFX.h>
#include <Fonts/FreeMonoBold12pt7b.h>
#include <Fonts/FreeSerif9pt7b.h>

GxEPD2_BW<GxEPD2_290, GxEPD2_290::HEIGHT> display(GxEPD2_290(/*CS=*/
5, /*DC=*/ 17, /*RST=*/ 16, /*BUSY=*/ 4));

void setup() {
  Serial.begin(115200);
  display.init();
  display.setRotation(1);
}
void loop() {
  display.fillScreen(GxEPD_WHITE);
  display.setFont(&FreeMonoBold12pt7b);
```

```
  display.setTextColor(GxEPD_BLACK);
  display.setCursor((display.width() - 11) / 2, display.height() / 2);
  display.println("Hello World");
  display.display();
  delay(10000);
}
```

The code uses several libraries to control an e-paper display. The `GxEPD2_BW` library is used to interface with the display, and the `Adafruit_GFX` library provides graphics functions. Two different fonts are included for text rendering. The `display` object is initialized with the necessary pins for communication with the e-paper display. In the `setup()` function, serial communication is initiated, and the display is initialized and set to a specific rotation. The `loop()` function continuously clears the screen, sets the font and text color, positions the cursor, prints the text `Hello World` (as can be seen in *Figure 3.10*), updates the display, and adds a delay of 10 seconds before repeating the process.

In the next section, we will compare all the displays we have interfaced with ESP32.

Comparison of displays

This section compares all the displays you have learned about in previous chapters and interfaced with ESP32. *Table 3.4* will help you understand which display will fit your needs for a certain type of project. These displays are compared based on type, resolution, communication protocol, power consumption, price, and applications:

Feature	16x2 LCD I2C	SSD1306 OLED I2C	ILI9341 TFT Touchscreen	2.9" E-Paper Display
Display Type	LCD	OLED	TFT	E-paper
Resolution	16x2	128x64	320x240	296x128
Communication Protocol	I2C	I2C	SPI	SPI
Touch Capability	No	No	Yes	No
Color Support	Monochrome	Monochrome	Color	Monochrome
Power Consumption	Low	Low	Medium	Ultra-low
Refresh Rate	N/A	N/A	High	Medium
Visibility in Bright Light	Good	Poor	Good	Excellent
Price	Low	Low	Medium	High
Memory Requirement	Low	Low	Medium	Low
Suitable for Battery-Powered Projects	Yes	Yes	Yes	Highly recommended

Feature	16x2 LCD I2C	SSD1306 OLED I2C	ILI9341 TFT Touchscreen	2.9" E-Paper Display
Application	Simple text-based display	Small graphical displays	Larger touch-enabled displays	Low-power and high-contrast displays for e-books, signage, and so on

Table 3.4 – Comparing different display options that can be interfaced with ESP32

The table shows that the 16x2 LCD and SSD1306 OLED are cheap options and will provide a reasonable monochrome display for ESP32 projects, but if you are willing to add a touch interface and would like to show colorful graphics, a TFT touchscreen will be the best option, and for ultra-low power applications, an e-paper display will be the most suitable choice.

Summary

In this chapter, we explored the capabilities of the ESP32 microcontroller when it comes to connecting cameras and displays. We began by understanding the ESP32 camera module and its features. We learned how to program the ESP32 camera to capture images and integrate a motion sensor for triggering image capture based on motion detection.

Moving on to display interfaces, we discussed various types of display interfaces, such as SPI, I2C, and parallel. We examined popular display modules compatible with ESP32 and the options they offer for visual output. With this knowledge, we learned how to interface displays with ESP32, configure display pins and connections, and initialize the display module. We also delved into advanced display features such as touchscreen integration.

In the next chapter, we will take our first step toward IoT development with ESP32 by learning about network-based protocols.

Part 2 – IoT Protocols and ESP32

In this part, you will familiarize yourself with IoT protocols, and you will learn the theory of these protocols from an ESP32 perspective. By the end of this part, you will be able to select the appropriate network and data-based protocol for your IoT projects.

This part has the following chapters:

- *Chapter 4, Implementing Network-Based Protocols with ESP32*
- *Chapter 5, Choosing the Right Data-Based Protocols for Your ESP32 Project*

4

Implementing Network-Based Protocols with ESP32

In this chapter, we will climb the first stairs toward **internet of things** (**IoT**) development and explore network-based protocols with the versatile ESP32 microcontroller. Throughout this journey, we will uncover the power of wireless communication and its potential to transform your IoT projects into dynamic connected systems.

Our exploration begins by diving into the ESP32's built-in Wi-Fi capabilities. We'll learn how to harness the potential of Wi-Fi by configuring the ESP32 as both a client and an access point. This will enable us to connect to existing networks and create personalized local networks for our IoT devices. But our exploration doesn't stop there; we will also venture into more advanced features, such as Wi-Fi Direct and peer-to-peer communication, to make our devices communicate seamlessly.

Next, we'll delve into **Bluetooth Low Energy** (**BLE**), a crucial technology for short-range communication. By enabling BLE on the ESP32, we can create personal area networks, connecting our devices to smartphones and sensors. We'll cover BLE server and client modes, mastering the art of establishing connections and exchanging data efficiently.

The world of IoT is not confined to local networks; it extends to vast cellular networks. In this chapter, we'll show you how to utilize the ESP32's capabilities to connect to 4G networks, opening a world of possibilities for remote and mobile IoT applications.

Moreover, we'll uncover the potential of **narrowband IoT** (**NB-IoT**), a low-power, wide-area network technology perfect for specific IoT use cases. By integrating NB-IoT communication with the ESP32, we can take advantage of its energy efficiency and wide coverage, making our projects more sustainable and far-reaching.

But our exploration doesn't stop at cellular networks; we'll also understand LoRaWAN. Each of these protocols brings unique strengths, catering to specific IoT applications. With the ESP32, we will explore how to integrate these protocols, understand their characteristics, and leverage their advantages to create a diverse range of IoT solutions.

As with every chapter, we will provide comprehensive examples and step-by-step instructions to guide you through the implementation of Wi-Fi and BLE protocols. For other protocols, we will provide a general overview. By the end of this chapter, you will have acquired a solid foundation in network-based protocols, expanding your skills as an ESP32 developer.

In this chapter, we will cover the following topics:

- Types of networks
- Exploring wireless capabilities with Wi-Fi
- Creating a personal area network with BLE
- Expanding ESP32 connectivity beyond Wi-Fi and BLE

By covering these topics, you will understand the fundamental differences between these protocols and be able to select the best protocols according to the requirements of their projects.

Technical requirements

For this chapter, we will need the following components:

- ESP32 x 2
- A smartphone
- A BG95 shield
- A LoRaWAN module

The code files for this chapter are available at `https://github.com/PacktPublishing/Programming-ESP32-with-Arduino-IDE/tree/main/Chapter4`.

First, let's explore the types of networks.

Types of networks

Networks can be categorized into various types based on their geographical coverage and communication characteristics. **Local area networks (LANs)** cover a small area, such as homes or offices, enabling devices within the network to communicate directly. **Wide area networks (WANs)** span across large geographical areas and connect distant locations, such as the via the internet. **Personal area networks (PANs)** are small, localized networks that typically span a person's immediate surroundings. **Metropolitan area networks (MANs)** cover larger cities or metropolitan regions, and **campus area networks (CANs)** link multiple LANs within educational institutions or large organizations. **Storage area networks (SANs)** are specialized networks for data storage and retrieval.

In our book, we will be focusing on three main types of networks:

- **LAN**: LANs are crucial for connecting devices within a limited geographic area, such as homes, offices, or schools. They allow for the seamless sharing of resources such as files, printers, and internet access among connected devices. In our exploration of LANs, we will utilize protocols such as Wi-Fi, BLE, and Zigbee.

- **WAN**: WANs play a vital role in connecting networks over large geographical distances, enabling global communication. The internet itself is a prime example of a WAN, linking devices and networks worldwide. We will delve into WANs using protocols such as cellular (4G, 5G), NB-IoT, and LoRaWAN.

- **PAN**: PANs focus on connecting devices within a small personal space, such as a person's workspace or immediate surroundings. We will explore PANs using technologies such as Bluetooth and **near-field communication** (**NFC**), which enable seamless connections between smartphones, tablets, and wearable devices.

By understanding these network types and their associated protocols, you will be well-equipped to create a wide range of projects, empowering you to develop innovative IoT applications and communication solutions. Now let's explore Wi-Fi.

Exploring wireless capabilities with Wi-Fi

Wi-Fi, short for **wireless fidelity**, is a wireless communication technology that allows devices to connect to the internet and local networks without using physical cables. It operates on radio frequency signals, typically in 2.4 GHz and 5 GHz bands, and enables data transmission between devices such as smartphones, laptops, and IoT devices. Wi-Fi provides high-speed and reliable internet access, facilitating seamless connectivity and enabling users to access online resources, stream media, and communicate with other devices within the network range. In this section, we will explore how Wi-Fi protocols work, the capabilities of ESP32 Wi-Fi, and a few practical examples of using ESP32 as an access point and client. But first, let's see how the Wi-Fi protocol works.

How the Wi-Fi protocol works

TheWi-Fi protocol, based on IEEE 802.11 standards, works by enabling devices to communicate wirelessly over radio frequencies. When a Wi-Fi-enabled device (such as a smartphone or laptop) wants to connect to a Wi-Fi network, it first sends a probe request to discover available networks. The **access point** (**AP**), acting as the network's base station, responds with a probe response containing network details.

Once the device chooses a network and requests to join, a process called authentication and association takes place. The device and AP exchange authentication frames to establish trust, followed by association frames to finalize the connection. After successful association, data frames are used to transfer information between the device and the AP, allowing internet access and communication within the local network. The Wi-Fi request and response flow is shown in *Figure 4.1*:

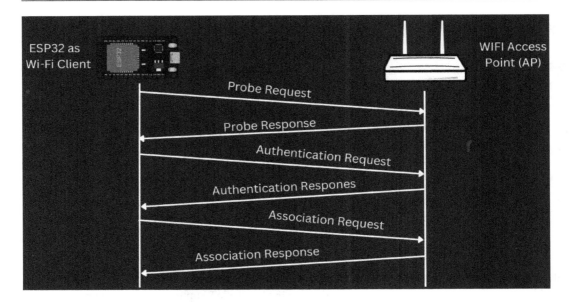

Figure 4.1 – How the Wi-Fi protocol works

The Wi-Fi protocol handles data integrity, flow control, and error correction to ensure reliable and efficient wireless communication between devices and access points.

Now that we understand how the Wi-Fi protocol works, let's explore the features offered by the built-in Wi-Fi module in ESP32.

ESP32 built-in Wi-Fi capabilities

One of the key features that sets ESP32 apart is its built-in Wi-Fi capabilities, making it a popular choice for IoT projects that require wireless connectivity.

The ESP32's built-in Wi-Fi module supports the 802.11b/g/n Wi-Fi standard and allows it to act both as a Wi-Fi client and an access point. As a client, it can connect to existing Wi-Fi networks, enabling it to access the internet and communicate with other devices on the network. This makes it possible for the ESP32 to retrieve data from online servers, send sensor data to cloud platforms, and interact with web services.

Additionally, the ESP32 can be set up as a Wi-Fi access point, allowing other devices to connect directly to it. In this mode, it acts as a hub, enabling devices to communicate with each other and access resources hosted by the ESP32. This feature is particularly useful for creating a LAN in IoT applications, where devices need to interact without accessing the internet.

The ESP32's Wi-Fi implementation supports various security protocols, such as WPA2, WPA3, and WEP, ensuring that data transmitted over the network is encrypted and secure. This is crucial for protecting sensitive information and preventing unauthorized access to connected devices.

Furthermore, the ESP32's Wi-Fi stack offers several advanced features, such as Wi-Fi Direct, which enables direct communication between devices without the need for a traditional Wi-Fi network infrastructure. This feature is useful for scenarios where devices need to establish peer-to-peer connections quickly and efficiently.

First, let's look at how we could use the ESP32 as an access point.

ESP32 as Wi-Fi access point

In this example, we will create our own access point using the ESP32. An access point, commonly referred to as an AP, is a wireless communication device that functions as a central hub for connecting other devices to a local network. In this scenario, the ESP32 will act as an access point, allowing other devices to connect to it directly for communication and data exchange.

To enable Wi-Fi functionalities on the ESP32, the WiFi library is essential. This library integrates seamlessly into Arduino IDE when we set up support for the ESP32 board, as we accomplished in *Chapter 1*.

We will upload the following code to the ESP32 using Arduino IDE, which will help us create a Wi-Fi access point:

```
#include <WiFi.h>
const char* ssid = "MyESP32AP";
const char* password = "password123";

void setup() {
  Serial.begin(115200);
  WiFi.softAP(ssid, password);
  IPAddress apIP(192, 168, 4, 1);
  IPAddress subnet(255, 255, 255, 0);
  WiFi.softAPConfig(apIP, apIP, subnet);
  Serial.print("Access Point IP Address: ");
  Serial.println(WiFi.softAPIP());
}
void loop() {
  // Your code goes here
}
```

In this code, the WiFi.softAP() function is used to set up the ESP32 as an access point. The ssid variable represents the name of the access point (SSID = MyESP32AP), and the password variable is the password required to connect to the access point. You can change these values to set your desired SSID and password.

After setting up the access point, the code configures a static IP address for the access point using WiFi.softAPConfig(). In this example, the access point IP address is set to 192.168.4.1.

When the ESP32 is powered on with this code, it will start broadcasting the specified SSID, and other devices can connect to it using the provided password. Once connected, devices will be assigned IP addresses from the specified subnet, allowing them to communicate with the ESP32 acting as the access point.

Once the code has been uploaded, you will be able to see the `MyESP32AP` Wi-Fi on your laptop, mobile phone, or any device that supports a Wi-Fi connection, as seen in the following figure:

Figure 4.2 – MyESP32 as a Wi-Fi access point

If we connect to the `MyESP32AP` network, we will not be able to access the internet. However, we will still be able to connect to the services and devices within the local network. Now, let's understand using an example how we can utilize the ESP32 as a Wi-Fi client.

ESP32 as a Wi-Fi client

In this example, we will write code to use the ESP32 as a Wi-Fi client. A Wi-Fi client is a device that connects to an existing wireless network, such as your home Wi-Fi network, a public hotspot, or the access point we just made using ESP32. As a Wi-Fi client, the ESP32 will be able to access the internet and interact with services outside of its local network, if the AP provides internet connectivity. This mode allows the ESP32 to join an existing network, just like your smartphone or laptop does, enabling it to browse the web, send data to online servers, and perform various internet-related tasks.

Like in the previous example, we will utilize the Wi-Fi library for the demonstration.

We will upload the following code in the second ESP32 using Arduino IDE:

```
#include <WiFi.h>
const char* ssid = "MyESP32AP";
const char* password = "Password123";

void setup() {
```

```
  Serial.begin(115200);

  WiFi.begin(ssid, password);

  Serial.print("Connecting to WiFi...");
  while (WiFi.status() != WL_CONNECTED) {
    delay(500);
    Serial.print(".");
  }

  Serial.println();
  Serial.print("Connected to WiFi network with IP address: ");
  Serial.println(WiFi.localIP());
}

void loop() {
  // Your code goes here
}
```

In this code, replace YourWiFiSSID with the name of your Wi-Fi network (SSID) and YourWiFiPassword with the password required to connect to your Wi-Fi network.

For this example, we can use SSID = "MyESP32AP" and Password = "Password123", which we set in the ESP32 as an AP example. But, if you would like to connect your ESP32 to the internet, you could replace the SSID and password with the SSID and password of your home Wi-Fi network, which in most cases will be printed on the back of your Wi-Fi router.

The WiFi.begin() function is used to initiate the connection to the Wi-Fi network using the specified SSID and password. The code then waits until the connection is established, checking the connection status with WiFi.status(). Once the connection is successful, the ESP32 will print the local IP address obtained from the Wi-Fi router.

When you upload this code to your ESP32, it will act as a Wi-Fi client and attempt to connect to the specified Wi-Fi network. After connecting successfully, you will be able to see the results on **Serial Monitor**, as seen in *Figure 4.3*:

Figure 4.3 – ESP32 as a Wi-Fi client

A Wi-Fi client can be used in both LANs and WANs to enable devices to connect to the internet and communicate with other devices. In a LAN, a Wi-Fi client connects to a local Wi-Fi router or access point, allowing devices such as smartphones, laptops, and IoT devices to access resources and share data within the network. In a WAN, the Wi-Fi client connects to a remote Wi-Fi router or access point, enabling devices to access the internet and communicate with other devices across long distances.

Using Wi-Fi Direct for P2P connections

Now let's utilize the two examples to create a **peer-to-peer** (**P2P**) connection and share data.

We will upload the following code in the first ESP32 to create a Wi-Fi server using Arduino IDE:

```
#include <WiFi.h>
WiFiServer server(80);
const char* ssid = "MyESP32Direct";
const char* password = "password123";

void setup() {
  Serial.begin(115200);
  WiFi.softAP(ssid, password);

  IPAddress apIP(192, 168, 4, 1);
  IPAddress subnet(255, 255, 255, 0);
  WiFi.softAPConfig(apIP, apIP, subnet);

  server.begin();

  Serial.print("WiFi Direct Group Owner IP Address: ");
  Serial.println(WiFi.softAPIP());
}

void loop() {
  WiFiClient client = server.available();
  if (client) {
    Serial.println("Client connected.");
    client.println("Hello from Group Owner!");
    while (client.connected()) {
      if (client.available()) {
        String message = client.readStringUntil('\n');
        Serial.print("Received message: ");
        Serial.println(message);
      }
    }
    client.stop();
```

```
      Serial.println("Client disconnected.");
    }
  }
}
```

In the `setup` function, the code starts by initializing the serial communication for debugging purposes. It then configures the ESP32 to function as a Wi-Fi Direct access point using the `WiFi.softAP()` function. The SSID (network name) and password are set using the `ssid` and `password` variables.

An IP address (`apIP`) and subnet (`subnet`) are defined for the access point using the `WiFi.softAPConfig()` function. These settings establish the IP configuration for devices connecting to this access point.

The code initializes a `WiFiServer` object named `server` on port `80`. This server will handle incoming client connections and requests.

The serial output displays the IP address of the Wi-Fi Direct access point, which will be used by connected devices to communicate.

In the `loop` function, the code continually checks for incoming client connections using the `server.available()` function. If a client connects, it enters a loop that handles the client's communication.

Upon client connection, the code prints a message indicating that a client has connected. The server sends a simple `Hello from Group Owner!` message to the connected client.

Inside the inner loop for the connected client, the code checks if there's data available from the client using `client.available()`. If data is available, it reads the incoming message until it encounters a newline character.

The received message is then printed to **Serial Monitor** to display the content of the message.

Once the client has finished transmitting data or disconnected, the code stops the client connection using `client.stop()` and prints a message indicating that the client has been disconnected.

Then, we will upload the following code to the second ESP32 using Arduino IDE so we can use ESP32 as a Wi-Fi client and connect to the Wi-Fi server we just created and share the data:

```
#include <WiFi.h>

const char* ssid = "MyESP32Direct";
const char* password = "password123";

void setup() {
  Serial.begin(115200);
  WiFi.begin(ssid, password);

  Serial.print("Connecting to WiFi Direct Group Owner...");
```

```
  while (WiFi.status() != WL_CONNECTED) {
    delay(500);
    Serial.print(".");
  }

  Serial.println();
  Serial.print("Connected to WiFi Direct Group Owner with IP address:
");
  Serial.println(WiFi.localIP());
}

void loop() {
  // Check if there is a connection to the server
  if (WiFi.status() == WL_CONNECTED) {
    WiFiClient client;

    // Connect to the server on the Group Owner's IP address and port
80
    if (client.connect("192.168.4.1", 80)) {
      // Read and print the message from the Group Owner
      while (client.connected()) {
        if (client.available()) {
          String message = client.readStringUntil('\n');
          Serial.print("Received message: ");
          Serial.println(message);

          // Send a response message to the Group Owner
          client.println("Hello from Client!");
        }
      }
      client.stop();
    } else {
      Serial.println("Connection to server failed.");
    }
  } else {
    Serial.println("WiFi connection failed.");
  }
}
```

In this example, the first ESP32 acts as a group owner in SoftAP mode, and the second ESP32 connects to it as a client. The group owner waits for the client to connect and then sends a `Hello from Group Owner!` message. The client then reads the message and sends a `Hello from Client!` response message back to the group owner.

> **Note**
>
> Please make sure you have the correct Wi-Fi credentials (SSID and password) for both ESP32 boards and upload the corresponding code to each board. Additionally, ensure that both boards are within range and can communicate with each other over Wi-Fi.

After uploading the code, you will see the following outputs on **Serial Monitor**. The following screenshot shows the serial output of the Wi-Fi server:

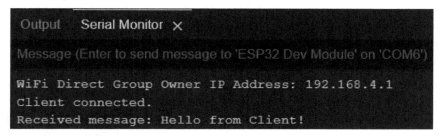

Figure 4.4 – ESP32 P2P connection using Wi-Fi server or AP Serial Monitor

The following figure shows the serial output of the Wi-Fi client and the received message from the server:

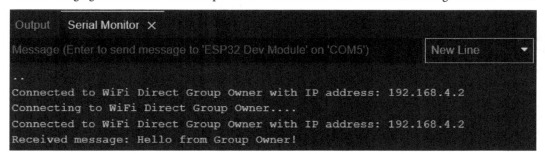

Figure 4.5 – ESP32 P2P connection using Wi-Fi client Serial Monitor

In this section, we have explored how the Wi-Fi protocol works, what the capabilities of ESP32 built-in Wi-Fi are, and how we can use ESP32 as an access point and Wi-Fi client. In the next section, we will explore the Bluetooth Low Energy protocol.

Creating a personal area network with BLE

BLE stands for **Bluetooth Low Energy**, which is a wireless communication technology designed for low-power, short-range data exchange between devices. It is a subset of the classic Bluetooth technology, optimized for battery-powered devices and applications that require intermittent data transmission. BLE enables devices such as smartphones, smartwatches, and IoT sensors to establish connections and exchange data efficiently, making it ideal for applications such as fitness tracking, home automation, and proximity-based interactions. Its low energy consumption allows devices to operate for extended periods on small batteries, making BLE a popular choice for various wireless applications.

To get started with BLE, let's see how the BLE protocol works on a fundamental basis.

How the BLE protocol works

This initial explanation gives you a general understanding of the concepts and mechanisms behind BLE. The actual implementation and functioning of BLE involve intricate technical details and processes. This explanation will provide you with a foundational understanding of how BLE works, serving as a starting point for your exploration of the BLE protocol.

The BLE protocol works based on a master-slave architecture, where one device acts as the master and one or more devices act as slaves. The master initiates communication and controls data exchange with the slaves. BLE uses small packets of data, called *advertising packets*, to broadcast information about the device's presence and capabilities. When a slave device receives an advertising packet from the master, it can request a connection, and the master can accept or reject the request. Once connected, devices can exchange data in small packets, minimizing power consumption. BLE uses quick connection and disconnection cycles to save energy, making it ideal for low-power applications such as smart home devices, wearables, and beacons.

Now, let's explore the capabilities of the BLE module present in the ESP32.

ESP32 BLE capabilities

The ESP32 microcontroller has excellent capabilities for BLE communication, making it a popular choice for IoT projects that require wireless connectivity. Here are some key features and capabilities of the ESP32 for BLE:

- **Dual-mode Bluetooth**: The ESP32 supports both Bluetooth Classic (BR/EDR) and BLE. This dual-mode capability allows it to communicate with a wide range of devices, including smartphones, Bluetooth audio devices, and other BLE-enabled IoT devices.

- **BLE central and peripheral**: The ESP32 can operate as both a central device and a peripheral device in a BLE network. As a central device, it can scan for and connect to other BLE devices. As a peripheral, it can advertise its services and data, allowing other central devices to connect to it.

- **High-level APIs**: The ESP32's BLE stack comes with high-level APIs that simplify the development process. This allows developers to focus on application logic rather than dealing with low-level Bluetooth protocol intricacies.

- **Generic Attribute Profile (GATT) support**: The ESP32 supports GATT, which is a key feature of BLE that defines how devices exchange data and interact with each other. GATT profiles allow the ESP32 to define its services, characteristics, and attributes, making it easy to create custom data exchange protocols.

- **Low-power capabilities**: The ESP32's BLE implementation is optimized for low power consumption. It supports various power-saving modes, allowing the device to operate efficiently on small batteries and prolonging the battery life of battery-powered devices.

- **BLE security features**: The ESP32 provides various security mechanisms for BLE communication, such as encryption, authentication, and pairing. These features help ensure the confidentiality and integrity of data exchanged between BLE devices.

- **Beacon support**: The ESP32 can act as a BLE beacon, broadcasting advertising packets to nearby devices. BLE beacons are commonly used for location-based services and proximity marketing.

With its powerful BLE capabilities, the ESP32 offers a flexible and efficient solution for developing BLE-enabled IoT applications. Whether you need to create a BLE peripheral to collect sensor data or a BLE central to interact with other devices, the ESP32's BLE features provide the necessary tools to build innovative and connected solutions.

With a grasp of how BLE operates and an understanding of ESP32's BLE capabilities, let's dive into the practical aspects of utilizing BLE as both a server and a client on the ESP32 platform.

BLE server and client using ESP32

In this section, we will delve into the concepts of the BLE server and client using the ESP32 microcontroller platform in conjunction with Arduino IDE. The ESP32's built-in Bluetooth capabilities allow us to create robust wireless communication setups. Let's start with a BLE server. The following figure shows a BLE server and client communication:

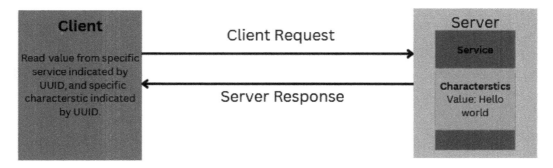

Figure 4.6 – BLE client request and server response

BLE server

A BLE server is a fundamental component of the Bluetooth ecosystem that plays a pivotal role in enabling efficient and low-power wireless communication between devices. In essence, a BLE server is a device or software entity that offers specific services and data to other devices, referred to as BLE clients, within its proximity. These services encapsulate various functionalities, with each service containing characteristics that represent specific data points or attributes. The BLE server's role is to respond to read and write requests from clients, allowing them to retrieve data or modify settings.

The applications of BLE servers span across a wide spectrum of industries and use cases. In the realm of IoT, BLE servers facilitate seamless communication between smart home devices, enabling users to control lights, thermostats, and locks from their smartphones. In healthcare, BLE servers can be integrated into wearable health trackers to transmit real-time data, such as heart rate and activity levels, to monitoring apps. Retail environments leverage BLE servers for location-based services, offering tailored promotions to customers as they move through stores. Moreover, BLE servers are vital in asset tracking systems, enabling efficient monitoring and management of inventory in warehouses. From automotive to logistics, and from entertainment to industrial automation, BLE servers provide the foundation for creating interconnected and efficient systems that enhance user experiences, optimize processes, and conserve energy.

We will use the following BLE server code to demonstrate an example BLE server. Note that this code is the modified version of the BLE library example code:

```
#include <BLEDevice.h>
#include <BLEUtils.h>
#include <BLEServer.h>

#define SERVICE_UUID        "4fafc201-1fb5-459e-8fcc-c5c9c331914b"
#define CHARACTERISTIC_UUID "beb5483e-36e1-4688-b7f5-ea07361b26a8"

void setup() {
  Serial.begin(115200);
  Serial.println("Starting BLE work!");
  BLEDevice::init("Long name works now");
  BLEServer *pServer = BLEDevice::createServer();
  BLEService *pService = pServer->createService(SERVICE_UUID);
  BLECharacteristic *pCharacteristic = pService->createCharacteristic(
                                         CHARACTERISTIC_UUID,
                                         BLECharacteristic::PROPER-
TY_READ |
                                         BLECharacteris-
tic::PROPERTY_WRITE);
  pCharacteristic->setValue("Hello World");
  pService->start();
  BLEAdvertising *pAdvertising = BLEDevice::getAdvertising();
  pAdvertising->addServiceUUID(SERVICE_UUID);
  pAdvertising->setScanResponse(true);
  pAdvertising->setMinPreferred(0x06);  // functions that help with
iPhone connections issue
  pAdvertising->setMinPreferred(0x12);
```

```
  BLEDevice::startAdvertising();
  Serial.println("Characteristic defined! Now you can read it in your
phone!");
}

void loop() {
  // put your main code here, to run repeatedly:
  delay(2000);
}
```

At the start of the code, the necessary BLE libraries are imported: BLEDevice.h, BLEUtils.h, and BLEServer.h. These libraries provide essential functions and classes for handling BLE communication.

The code defines two important **Universally Unique Identifiers (UUIDs)**. SERVICE_UUID and CHARACTERISTIC_UUID are used to uniquely identify the service and characteristic provided by the BLE server. UUIDs are crucial for ensuring proper communication between BLE devices.

Moving to the setup() function, the serial communication is initialized with a baud rate of 115200, which is a common speed for debugging and communication with the Serial Monitor in Arduino IDE.

The BLE device is initialized using BLEDevice::init("Long name works now"). Here, a name is assigned to the BLE device to allow other devices to identify it during discovery processes.

A BLE server is then created using BLEDevice::createServer(), and a corresponding service is instantiated using the createService(SERVICE_UUID) method of the server instance.

Inside the service, a characteristic is defined using pService->createCharacteristic(C HARACTERISTIC_UUID, ...). This characteristic is configured to have both read and write properties, enabling bi-directional data exchange.

The value of the characteristic is set to "Hello World" using pCharacteristic->setValue("Hello World"). This initial value represents the data that can be read from the characteristic by a client device.

Once the characteristic is defined and configured, the service is started using pService->start().

The BLE server's advertising parameters are configured, including the service UUID, scan response, and preferred connection parameters. After the setup is complete, the server initiates advertising with BLEDevice::startAdvertising().

To provide additional information for debugging and user feedback, a message is printed to the serial monitor, indicating that the characteristic is ready for interaction by client devices.

The loop() function, though currently empty, is where repeated tasks can be placed. In this example, it includes a delay of two seconds between iterations using delay(2000).

Now, you can upload the code using Arduino IDE and open **Serial Monitor**. You will be able to see the following results in **Serial Monitor**:

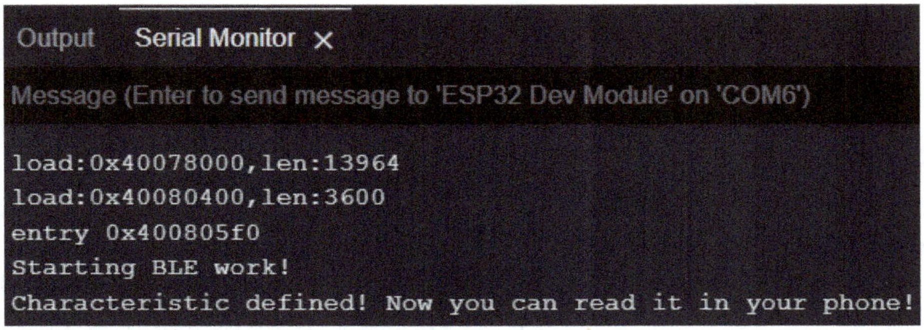

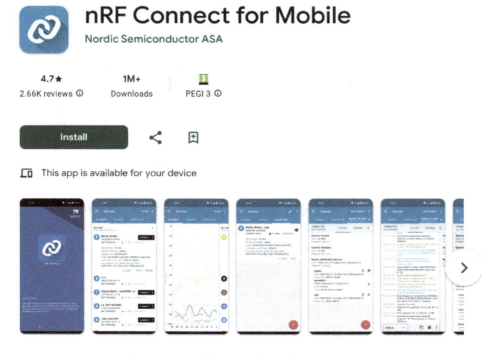

```
Output    Serial Monitor  ×

Message (Enter to send message to 'ESP32 Dev Module' on 'COM6')

load:0x40078000,len:13964
load:0x40080400,len:3600
entry 0x400805f0
Starting BLE work!
Characteristic defined! Now you can read it in your phone!
```

Figure 4.7 – ESP32 BLE server Serial Monitor

Now that the server has been started, let's connect our mobile to the server and read the message.

Testing it on the mobile app

To test our ESP32 server, we will install the *nRF Connect for Mobile* app on our smartphone. You will be able to find this app in the Google Play Store or Apple App Store, as shown in *Figure 4.8*:

Figure 4.8 – nRF Connect for Mobile application

Once the app has been installed, take the following steps:

1. Turn on Bluetooth.

2. Open the application.

3. Give the necessary permission to the application when it asks you to access Bluetooth.

4. Navigate to the device, and find the `Long Name works now` device, as shown in the first screenshot in *Figure 4.9*.

5. Click on **CONNECT**.

6. You will be able to see the data from the device, such as generic attributes, access, and the service UUID. The service UUID is the same as we defined in the code in the second screenshot in *Figure 4.9*.

7. Clicking on the service will open the characteristic. The UUID of the characteristic will be shown, which we defined in the code, as shown in the third screenshot in *Figure 4.9*.

8. Click on the read (down arrow) button, as marked in the third screenshot.

9. You will see the properties and value in the form of a hex and the string `"Hello World"`, as shown in the fourth screenshot in *Figure 4.9*.

Figure 4.9 – Using the nRF Connect application to see BLE server data

The mobile application connects to the ESP32 as a client where the ESP32 was acting as a server. Now let's see how we can use ESP32 as a BLE client in the next example.

BLE client

A BLE client is a key participant in the Bluetooth ecosystem that plays a vital role in establishing communication with BLE servers. A BLE client is typically a device or software component that initiates connections to BLE servers to retrieve data, interact with services, and control various functionalities. Unlike traditional Bluetooth connections, BLE clients are designed to consume minimal power, making them ideal for scenarios where energy efficiency is a priority.

BLE clients interact with BLE servers by discovering available services and their corresponding characteristics. Once a connection is established, a BLE client can perform several actions:

- **Service discovery**: The BLE client can scan for nearby BLE devices and discover the services they offer. Each service represents a specific set of features or capabilities.

- **Characteristic interaction**: Within each service, there are characteristics that contain data or provide control points. A BLE client can read data from characteristics, write data to them, and sometimes enable notifications or indications to receive real-time updates.

- **Data exchange**: BLE clients can exchange data with BLE servers, enabling applications such as health monitoring, home automation control, and remote device management.

- **Remote control**: BLE clients can control various aspects of BLE servers. For instance, a BLE client might control the brightness of smart lighting or adjust settings on a wearable device.

- **Background interaction**: BLE clients can perform tasks even when they are not actively connected to a BLE server, allowing for periodic data synchronization or background updates.

BLE clients are commonly found in a wide range of devices and applications, including smartphones, tablets, smartwatches, fitness trackers, medical devices, IoT devices, and more. Their lightweight nature and ability to efficiently communicate with BLE servers have enabled the proliferation of innovative solutions that rely on low-power, short-range wireless communication.

We will use the following BLE client code to demonstrate an example of ESP32 as a BLE client, which is a modified version of examples provided by the BLE library:

```
#include "BLEDevice.h"
static BLEUUID serviceUUID("4fafc201-1fb5-459e-8fcc-c5c9c331914b");
static BLEUUID    charUUID("beb5483e-36e1-4688-b7f5-ea07361b26a8");

static boolean doConnect = false;
static boolean connected = false;
static boolean doScan = false;
static BLERemoteCharacteristic* pRemoteCharacteristic;
static BLEAdvertisedDevice* myDevice;
...
...
...
```

```
  if (connected) {
    String newValue = "Time since boot: " + String(millis()/1000);
    Serial.println("Setting new characteristic value to \"" + newValue
+ "\"");
        pRemoteCharacteristic->writeValue(newValue.c_str(), newValue.
length());
  }else if(doScan){
    BLEDevice::getScan()->start(0);   // this is just example to start
scan after disconnect, most likely there is better way to do it in
arduino
  }
  delay(1000); // Delay a second between loops.
} // End of loop
```

You can find the entire code in the chapter's GitHub repository.

The provided code exemplifies an Arduino-based BLE client application. Its purpose is to establish communication with a targeted BLE server, facilitating interactions with its services and characteristics. The code employs the BLEDevice library and adopts a modular structure with predefined UUIDs, callback functions, and control flags.

Initially, the script defines essential UUIDs (serviceUUID and charUUID) to uniquely identify the remote service and characteristic the client intends to connect with and manipulate. Subsequently, the code initializes Boolean flags such as doConnect, connected, and doScan to manage the application's logical flow.

Two callback functions are introduced: notifyCallback and MyClientCallback. The former handles notifications received from the remote characteristic, while the latter extends the BLEClientCallbacks class to manage connection and disconnection events.

The connectToServer() function encapsulates the procedure of establishing a connection with the remote BLE server. It creates a BLE client, establishes a connection, retrieves references to the desired service and characteristic, reads the characteristic's value if permitted, and registers a notification callback if applicable.

The setup() function initializes serial communication and the BLE device and configures a BLE scanner to actively search for devices advertising the target service UUID. Scanning parameters are set, and scanning is initiated for a brief period.

In the loop() function, the code checks the doConnect flag. If set, it invokes the connectToServer() function to establish a connection with the desired BLE server. Upon successful connection, the code updates a remote characteristic with the current time since boot. Disconnected clients initiate scanning again if doScan is set.

A brief delay is inserted between iterations of the loop to manage processing frequency.

Now, we will upload the code to ESP32 using Arduino IDE and open **Serial Monitor**. We will see the following results in **Serial Monitor**:

Figure 4.10 – ESP32 BLE client Serial Monitor

Since we already defined in our code which service and characteristics we would like to read, this code reads that and prints it in **Serial Monitor**. This code could be modified to write the characteristics as well.

ESP32 as BLE Beacon advertiser

Beacon advertising is a fundamental feature of BLE technology that enables devices to broadcast their presence and information to nearby devices in a power-efficient manner. A BLE beacon is a small, battery-operated device that periodically emits short packets of data, known as advertisements, which can be detected by other BLE-enabled devices, such as smartphones, tablets, or other beacon receivers. These advertisements contain information about the beacon itself, such as its identity, location, and additional data. The data is typically organized into a specific format, including fields such as the beacon's UUID and major and minor values for more **refined identification and signal strength information (RSSI)**. This data is usually broadcast using a low transmission power to minimize power consumption, allowing beacons to operate for extended periods on a single battery.

BLE beacon advertising serves various purposes and applications:

- **Proximity sensing**: Beacons enable devices to detect their proximity to specific locations or objects. This is widely used in retail environments for location-based marketing, guiding customers to specific products, or offering personalized promotions based on their location within a store.

- **Indoor navigation**: Beacons can assist in indoor navigation by providing contextual information to users within large indoor spaces such as malls, airports, and museums. Apps on users' smartphones can use beacon data to help navigate them through complex indoor environments.

- **Asset tracking**: Organizations can use beacons to track the movement of assets within a confined area, such as in warehouses or factories. This improves inventory management and optimizes processes.

- **Attendance and check-ins**: Beacons enable automated attendance tracking in classrooms, conferences, and events. Attendees' devices can automatically check in when they come within range of a beacon.

- **IoT integration**: Beacons facilitate interaction with IoT devices. For instance, a beacon near a smart home device could trigger actions such as turning on lights or adjusting thermostats when a user's smartphone comes into proximity.

- **Location analytics**: Businesses and organizations can gather data on user behavior and movement patterns by analyzing the interactions between users' devices and beacons. This data can be used to make informed decisions for improving user experiences.

A BLE client actively connects to and communicates with BLE peripherals (such as beacons) to exchange data, while a BLE beacon is a passive device that broadcasts data for nearby BLE clients to receive and use, such as for location or sensor information.

For the BLE beacon example, we will use the following code, which is a modified version of the example code provided in the BLE library:

```
#include <BLEDevice.h>
#include <BLEServer.h>
#include <BLEUtils.h>
#include <BLE2902.h>
#include <BLEBeacon.h>
#define DEVICE_NAME "ESP32"
#define SERVICE_UUID "7A0247E7-8E88-409B-A959-AB5092DDB03E"
#define BEACON_UUID   "2D7A9F0C-E0E8-4CC9-A71B-A21DB2D034A1"
#define BEACON_UUID_REV "A134D0B2-1DA2-1BA7-C94C-E8E00C9F7A2D"
#define CHARACTERISTIC_UUID "82258BAA-DF72-47E8-99BC-B73D7ECD08A5"
BLEServer *pServer;
BLECharacteristic *pCharacteristic;
bool deviceConnected = false;
uint8_t value = 0;
class MyServerCallbacks: public BLEServerCallbacks {
    void onConnect(BLEServer* pServer) {
      deviceConnected = true;
...
...
...
void loop() {
  if (deviceConnected) {
    Serial.printf("*** NOTIFY: %d ***\n", value);
    pCharacteristic->setValue(&value, 1);
    pCharacteristic->notify();
    value++;
```

```
    }
    delay(2000);
}
```

You can find the entire code in the chapter's GitHub repository.

What follows is a detailed explanation of the code's functionality.

At the beginning of the code, various UUIDs are defined, such as DEVICE_NAME, SERVICE_UUID, BEACON_UUID, BEACON_UUID_REV, and CHARACTERISTIC_UUID. These UUIDs are crucial for uniquely identifying the device, the service, and the characteristic being created.

The sketch establishes a BLE server instance, pServer, and defines a boolean variable, device-Connected, to track whether a device is connected to the server.

Two callback classes are created:

- MyServerCallbacks: This class extends BLEServerCallbacks and includes methods to manage device connections and disconnections. Upon a device connecting, the onConnect() method sets deviceConnected to true, and upon disconnection, the onDisconnect() method sets deviceConnected to false and restarts advertising to make the device visible and connectable again.

- MyCallbacks: This class extends BLECharacteristicCallbacks and defines an onWrite() method to handle incoming data when the characteristic is written to.

The init_service() function is responsible for creating the BLE service and characteristic, as well as the associated descriptor and starting advertising. It constructs the service, defines the characteristic with read, write, and notify properties, attaches callback functions, and starts both the service and advertising.

The init_beacon() function configures the BLE advertising data to create an iBeacon using the BLEBeacon class. It sets the iBeacon's manufacturer ID, major and minor values, signal power, and proximity UUID. This function stops the previous advertising and starts a new one with the updated iBeacon data.

In the setup() function, serial communication is initialized, and the BLE device and server are initialized using BLEDevice::init() and BLEDevice::createServer(), respectively. Callbacks are assigned, and the init_service() and init_beacon() functions are called to initialize the BLE service and iBeacon.

Finally, in the loop() function, if a device is connected (deviceConnected is true), the code sends notifications to the connected device using the characteristic's notify() method. The characteristic's value is updated incrementally, and a delay of two seconds is introduced between iterations.

Now, we will upload the code using Arduino IDE and open **Serial Monitor**. We will see the following results in **Serial Monitor**:

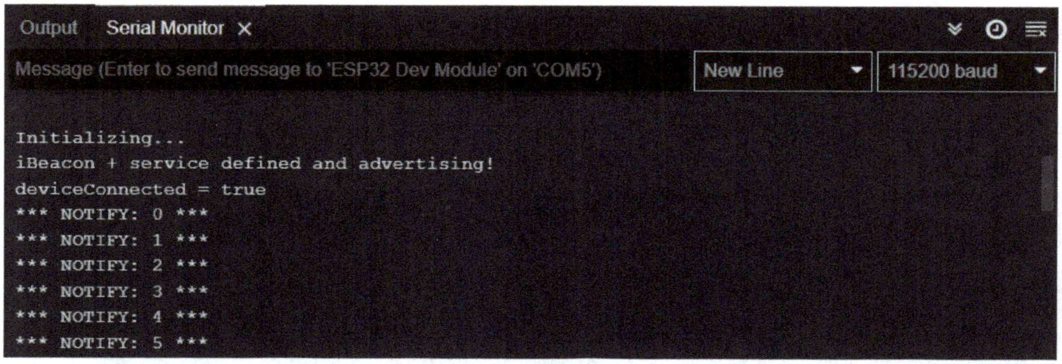

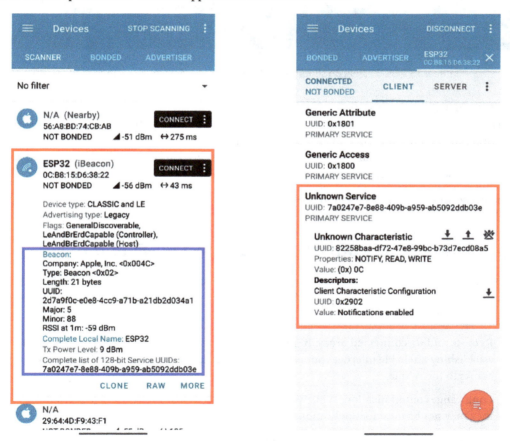

Figure 4.11 – ESP32 beacon service started

Now, we can open the nRF Connect app to read the advertised data:

Figure 4.12 – Reading the beacon advertised data in the nRF Connect application

In the first screenshot, you can see the advertised data under the beacon, such as the UUID and list of services. In the case of multiple BLE devices, this information will be useful to see which services are being advertised so we can connect only to the device we need data from. When we connect to the device, the ESP32 will start notifying. You will observe the value changing, as in the second screenshot of *Figure 4.12*, and observe the following results in **Serial Monitor**:

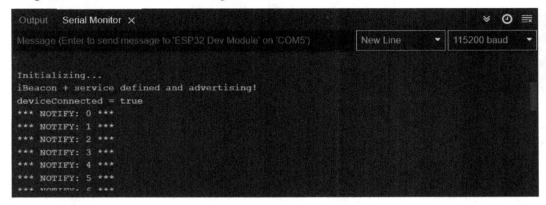

Figure 4.13 – ESP32 beacon sending notifications to the device after connection

In this section, we have learned the fundamentals of BLE and how we can use BLE as a server, client, and beacon using ESP32. Considering that BLE is quite extensive, information on it could fill a whole book. However, these examples provide a starting point for your BLE journey. If you're interested in diving deeper into BLE, you can explore additional examples available in the BLE library to expand your understanding further.

In the next section, we will explore how we can expand ESP32 connectivity beyond built-in Wi-Fi and BLE.

Expanding ESP32 connectivity beyond Wi-Fi and BLE

We have already explored ESP32 Wi-Fi and BLE capabilities. While the built-in Wi-Fi and BLE capabilities of the ESP32 offer robust connectivity options, there are scenarios where these technologies alone may not suffice:

- **Remote and disconnected areas**: In remote or rural areas with limited Wi-Fi infrastructure, establishing a reliable internet connection can be challenging. Here, cellular communication comes to the rescue.

- **Long-range communication**: While Wi-Fi and BLE are suitable for short-range communication, they may not be ideal for applications requiring long-range connectivity.

- **Contactless and close proximity interaction:** In scenarios where physical contact or proximity is not feasible, NFC presents an excellent option.

In each of these scenarios, the ESP32, when combined with additional communication modules, can overcome the limitations of Wi-Fi and BLE and enable connectivity in diverse and challenging environments.

In this section, we explore the exciting realm of alternative communication protocols that can be integrated with the ESP32 to transcend the limitations of Wi-Fi and BLE. We will see how these protocols work and how they can be interfaced with ESP32 without going into much detail. These communication protocols are dependent on the module used and the code, and the interfacing depends on the type of module being used.

Cellular communication with ESP32

Cellular communication offers a compelling solution for extending the connectivity of the ESP32 microcontroller beyond the limitations of traditional Wi-Fi and Bluetooth. By integrating a cellular module, such as a 2G, 3G, or 4G/LTE modem, the ESP32 gains the ability to access the internet and transmit data over cellular networks. This capability is particularly valuable in scenarios where Wi-Fi connectivity is unavailable or impractical, such as in remote areas or mobile applications. With cellular communication, the ESP32 can seamlessly communicate with cloud services, exchange data with remote servers, and enable real-time monitoring and control of IoT devices from virtually anywhere. Moreover, the ubiquity of cellular networks ensures that ESP32-based devices can remain connected and operational across vast geographic regions, making cellular communication an essential enabler for a wide range of IoT applications, including asset tracking, smart agriculture, and remote monitoring systems.

Different generations of cellular networks

- **1G**: The first generation of cellular networks, 1G, was an analog-based system that enabled basic voice communication.

- **2G**: The second generation, 2G, brought digital cellular networks. 2G enabled text messaging (SMS) and provided improved voice quality and security.

- **3G**: The third generation, 3G, marked a significant leap in mobile data capabilities. It offered faster data transfer rates, enabling basic internet access, email, and multimedia messaging.

- **4G**: The fourth generation, 4G, brought **long-term evolution** (LTE) technology. 4G networks provided high-speed data transmission, enabling seamless video streaming, mobile app functionality, and enhanced mobile internet experiences.

- **5G**: The fifth generation, 5G, is continuing to expand globally and represents a significant advancement in cellular technology. 5G offers ultra-fast data rates, ultra-low latency, and massive device connectivity. 5G is expected to power transformative applications such as augmented reality, smart cities, autonomous vehicles, and advanced industrial automation.

Then, there is a specific variant of cellular technology designed to cater to the unique requirements of IoT applications. NB-IoT operates within the licensed cellular spectrum and provides long-range, low-power communication for IoT devices.

NB-IoT

NB-IoT is a **low-power wide area network (LPWAN)** technology designed to enable efficient and low-cost communication for IoT devices. It is a part of the **3rd Generation Partnership Project (3GPP)** standards, specifically developed for IoT applications that require long-range connectivity, low power consumption, and support for a massive number of connected devices.

Key characteristics of NB-IoT include the following:

- **Low power consumption**: NB-IoT is optimized for low -power operation, allowing IoT devices to operate on batteries for extended periods, often lasting several years, without frequent recharging or replacement.

- **Long range**: NB-IoT provides excellent coverage and penetration capabilities, enabling communication over long distances and through obstacles such as buildings and walls, making it suitable for applications in urban and rural environments.

- **Narrowband transmission**: As the name suggests, NB-IoT uses narrowband transmission, which allows it to operate in a limited frequency range. This narrow bandwidth optimizes the network's capacity, making it ideal for IoT applications that transmit small amounts of data infrequently.

- **Low cost**: Due to its simplified architecture and use of existing cellular infrastructure, NB-IoT offers cost-effective solutions for IoT connectivity, making it attractive for a wide range of applications.

- **Massive connectivity**: NB-IoT supports a massive number of connected devices within a single cell, accommodating the anticipated growth of IoT devices in the future.

NB-IoT is particularly well-suited for applications that involve remote monitoring, smart metering, asset tracking, agricultural monitoring, and other scenarios where devices need to be deployed over large areas and operate with minimal power consumption. It co-exists with other cellular technologies, such as 2G, 3G, and 4G/LTE, making it a versatile choice for IoT deployments across different regions and networks.

As a result of these advantages, NB-IoT has gained significant traction in the IoT industry and is being adopted by telecommunication operators and device manufacturers to build robust and scalable IoT networks.

How to connect ESP32 with a cellular network

To connect the ESP32 with cellular networks such as 3G, 4G, or LTE technology, the first step is to select a compatible cellular module from popular options such as SIM800, QuectelEC25, or QuectelBG95. Once chosen, the cellular module needs to be connected to the ESP32 using the appropriate hardware interfaces, such as UART, SPI, or I2C, with specific pin connections and communication protocols outlined in the module's datasheet.

For the sake of a practical example, we will use a QuectelBG-95 shield, which can be attached to an ESP32 board. The BG95 shield is an advanced cellular communication module that offers seamless integration with the ESP32 microcontroller, providing reliable and high-speed data connectivity over 2G, 3G, 4G, and LTE-M/NB-IoT networks.

The BG95 shield offers compatibility with the ESP32 HUZZAH board, allowing for easy integration by simply placing it on top of the ESP32. We will also have to use a 4G-enabled SIM card to access the 4G cellular network.

Figure 4.14 – ESP32 connected to a BG95 shield

Connecting ESP32 to cellular networks (4G/NB-IoT)

Once the shield has been connected to the ESP32, we will need AT commands to send signals to the BG95 module. **AT commands**, short for **ATtention commands**, are a set of instructions used to communicate with and control modems, cellular modules, and other communication devices. The name AT originates from the two-character prefix AT that is added before each command to get the attention of the device.

AT commands follow a specific syntax, typically starting with AT. This is followed by a command name and optional parameters and ends with **carriage return** (**CR**) and **line feed** (**LF**) characters (\r\n). Here's an example:

```
AT+CGATT=1\r\n
```

This command instructs the device to attach to the GPRS service.

AT commands are usually sent over a serial communication interface (such as UART) to the device, and the device responds with a corresponding result or status. The response typically includes an OK message to indicate the command was successful or an error code if there was an issue.

You will find the specific commands for connecting to the 2G, 3G, 4G, and LTE networks in the datasheets of the modules, but for the sake of this simple example, here is how to send AT commands using Arduino IDE:

```
#include <SoftwareSerial.h>
SoftwareSerial BG95Serial(2, 3); // RX, TX pins for BG95 Shield
const int baudRate = 9600;
void setup() {
  Serial.begin(115200);
  BG95Serial.begin(baudRate);

  // Wait for the BG95 module to initialize
  delay(1000);

  Serial.println("Initializing BG95...");
  sendATCommand("AT");
  sendATCommand("AT+CPIN?");
}
void loop() {
  // Your code goes here
}
void sendATCommand(String command) {
  BG95Serial.println(command);
  delay(500);
  while (BG95Serial.available()) {
    Serial.write(BG95Serial.read());
  }
}
```

In this code, we use the SoftwareSerial library to communicate with the BG95 module through its Rx and Tx pins (pins 2 and 3 on the ESP32). We establish a serial connection at a baud rate of 9600, which is the default baud rate for the BG95 module.

The sendATCommand() function sends AT commands to the BG95 module and prints the response to **Serial Monitor** for debugging purposes. The AT commands used in the setup function are basic commands to initialize and configure the BG95 module to connect to the 4G network.

> **Note**
> The preceding code only establishes the connection to the 4G network. To perform other operations, such as sending and receiving data, making HTTP requests, or configuring the BG95 module further, you will need to send additional AT commands as per the BG95 module's documentation and specifications.

The LoRaWAN protocol

The **long range wide area network** (**LoRaWAN**) protocol is a low-power, long-range wireless communication technology designed to connect battery-operated devices over large distances. LoRaWAN operates using unlicensed **industrial, scientific, and medical** (**ISM**) bands, allowing for global deployment without the need for cellular network subscriptions. The protocol's strength lies in its ability to provide long-range communication while maintaining a low data rate and ultra-low power consumption, making it suitable for IoT applications in smart cities, agriculture, asset tracking, environmental monitoring, and more. LoRaWAN operates in a star-of-stars topology, where end devices communicate with one or more gateways, which, in turn, forward data to a central network server. This architecture allows for efficient and scalable data transmission over large geographic areas. LoRaWAN's robustness in challenging environments, low cost, and ease of deployment have contributed to its growing popularity, fostering the expansion of IoT networks and unlocking new possibilities for innovative and connected solutions across various industries.

ESP32 with LoRaWAN: the general process

To use the ESP32 with LoRaWAN, you'll need to follow a few steps to set up the hardware and software components:

1. **Hardware**: We will need ESP32 and a LoRa transceiver module that supports the LoRaWAN protocols, and we will need an antenna for the LoRa module.

2. **LoRaWAN network provider**: LoRaWAN devices need to connect to a LoRaWAN network server. Choose a LoRaWAN network provider (such as The Things Network, ChirpStack, etc.) and create an account. You will need to set up your device on their platform.

3. **Hardware Connectivity**: Connect the LoRa module to the ESP32 using appropriate pins. Refer to your module's documentation for pin connections. Attach the antenna to the LoRa module.

4. **Libraries and code**: You could use libraries such as `lmic` for LoRaWAN and libraries for your specific LoRa module. Write code using the installed libraries to configure the LoRaWAN parameters, such as keys, frequency, data rate, and so on. The exact code will depend on the library you're using and the LoRaWAN provider.

It's important to note that this is a general example intended to provide you with an overview of the various connectivity options available when using the ESP32. Your specific project requirements and goals will influence the choice of connectivity protocol and implementation details.

Now let's compare different network protocols in terms of technology, range, data rate, power consumption, and application.

Comparison of protocols

The following table provides a comparison between different connectivity options for IoT using ESP32 protocols:

Protocol	Technology	Range	Data rate	Power consumption	Application
Wi-Fi	IEEE 802.11	Short (Up to 100m)	High (Mbps)	Moderate to high	Internet connectivity, local area networks
BLE	Bluetooth Low Energy	Short (up to 100m)	Low (Kbps)	Low	Wearables, IoT devices, proximity-based apps
Cellular (4G)	LTE	Long (up to several kilometers)	High (Mbps)	Moderate to high	Mobile internet, voice, video streaming
NB-IoT	LTE	Long (up to several kilometers)	Low (Kbps)	Ultra-low	IoT devices, smart metering, agriculture
Zigbee	IEEE 802.15.4	Moderate (up to 100m)	Low (Kbps)	Low	Smart home automation, industrial automation
LoRaWAN	LoRa	Long (several kilometers to tens of kilometers)	Low (Kbps)	Ultra-Low	Smart agriculture, asset tracking, smart cities
NFC	Near-field communication	Very Short (Up to 10cm)	Low (Kbps)	Low	Contactless payment, access control

Table 4.1 – Different connectivity options for ESP32

From *Table 4.1*, you will get an idea of which network protocol is suitable for certain applications. While BLE and Wi-Fi are built into ESP32, and we will be focusing more on these two in the projects, having a general idea of other protocols will help you take on the next steps.

Summary

In this chapter, we delved into various connectivity options that allow us to establish connections between the ESP32 and diverse networks. We delved deep into the Wi-Fi and BLE protocols, performing hands-on exercises to grasp their practical applications.

However, there are scenarios where these options might not suffice or are unavailable. To address such situations, we expanded our knowledge to encompass cellular communication and the LoRaWAN protocol. These additional protocols empower us to broaden the ESP32's connectivity by leveraging external modules.

In the forthcoming chapter, we'll take a closer look at data-based protocols. This exploration will shed light on how we can effectively exchange data across different devices using these network protocols.

5

Choosing the Right Data-Based Protocols for Your ESP32 Projects

In this chapter, we embark on a pivotal journey to empower your ESP32 projects with the most suitable data-based protocols. This chapter delves into the fundamental understanding of essential protocols that drive the communication backbone of IoT systems. We will explore key protocols such as **Hypertext Transfer Protocol (HTTP)**, **Message Queuing Telemetry Transport (MQTT)**, and webhooks, equipping you with the knowledge to make informed decisions in selecting the right protocol for your ESP32 projects.

Our exploration begins with a comprehensive exploration of HTTP. You will gain insights into HTTP's request-response mechanism for seamless communication between ESP32 devices and web servers.

The journey continues with a deep dive into the MQTT protocol. We will delve into MQTT's **publish-subscribe (pub-sub)** architecture for real-time IoT communication and implement MQTT on ESP32 devices, enabling dynamic network creation and responsive IoT apps.

Webhooks emerge as another vital aspect of this chapter. We will uncover the potential of webhooks as a mechanism to trigger actions in response to specific events.

Throughout this chapter, our approach remains consistent: providing step-by-step instructions, real-world examples, and hands-on guidance. By the conclusion of this chapter, you will have gained a profound understanding of HTTP, MQTT, and webhooks.

In this chapter, we will cover and understand the following topics with their applications:

- Exploring HTTP with ESP32 – enabling IoT devices to communicate with web servers

- Exploring MQTT for IoT communication with ESP32

- Adding real-time notifications using webhooks

- A real-life analogy of HTTP, MQTT, and webhooks

- Comparing HTTP, webhooks, and MQTT

By covering these topics, readers will understand the fundamental differences between these protocols and can select the best protocols or use them together according to the requirements of the project.

Technical requirements

For this chapter, we will require the following hardware and software components:

- ESP32

- An LED

- OLED SSD1306 display

- Servo motor

- Push button

- OpenWeather API

- HiveMQ public MQTT broker

Now, let's explore the most common protocol widely used by web applications: the HTTP protocol.

Exploring HTTP with ESP32 – enabling IoT devices to communicate with web servers

In the interconnected world of IoT, efficient communication between devices and web servers is paramount. One of the foundational protocols that has powered the internet since its beginning is HTTP. In the context of IoT, HTTP plays a pivotal role in facilitating communication between resource-constrained devices, such as the ESP32 microcontroller, and remote web servers. This section dives into the details of HTTP communication, specifically tailored for ESP32 projects. We'll explore how ESP32 can seamlessly interact with web servers, enabling IoT devices to exchange data, retrieve information, and contribute to the ever-expanding landscape of IoT. First, let's explore what the HTTP protocol is and how it works.

What is HTTP?

HTTP is the foundation of data communication on the World Wide Web. It is an application layer protocol that defines how clients (typically web browsers) request resources from servers and how servers respond to these requests. HTTP enables the exchange of various types of data, including text, images, videos, and more, making it the backbone of web communication.

How does HTTP work?

HTTP uses the request-response model for data transfer. *Figure 5.1* shows the request, response, and server processing involved in the HTTP protocol:

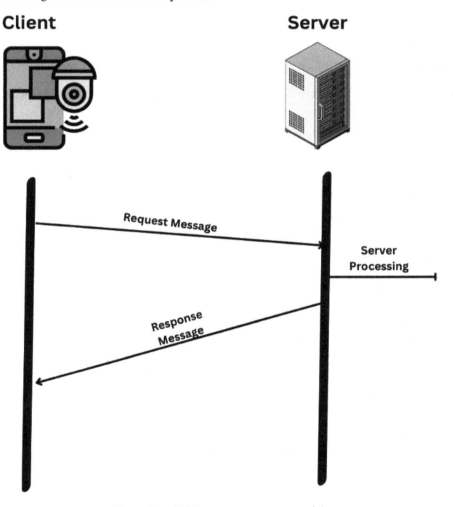

Figure 5.1 – HTTP request-response model

Let's understand how it works:

1. **Client-server interaction**: Communication in HTTP revolves around a client-server model. The client, often a web browser or an IoT device in the case of IoT projects, initiates a request for a specific resource located on a server.

2. **Request**: The client sends an HTTP request to the server. This request contains several components:

   - **HTTP method**: Specifies the action the client wants to perform (for example, GET to retrieve data, POST to submit data, or PUT to update data)

   - **Uniform Resource Identifier (URI)**: A unique address that identifies the resource the client wants to access

   - **Headers**: Additional information about the request, such as user-agent, accept-encoding, and more

   - **Body (optional)**: Used in methods such as POST to send data to the server

3. **Server processing**: Upon receiving the request, the server processes it. It identifies the requested resource, performs any necessary server-side actions, and prepares a response.

4. **Response**: The server sends an HTTP response back to the client. This response also includes several components:

   - **Status code**: A numerical code indicating the outcome of the request (for example, 200 OK, 404 Not Found, or 500 Internal Server Error)

   - **Headers**: Metadata about the response, including content type, length, and server information

   - **Body**: The actual data being sent back to the client – for example, in the case of a web page, the HTML content

5. **Client rendering**: The client (web browser or IoT device) receives the response. If the response includes HTML content, the client renders it into a human-readable format. Other resources such as images, style sheets, and scripts referenced in the HTML are subsequently requested by the client using additional HTTP requests.

6. **Resource retrieval**: The client may need to retrieve additional resources linked in the original response. This involves sending more HTTP requests for each resource and receiving corresponding HTTP responses.

HTTP is a stateless protocol, meaning each request-response cycle is independent, and the server doesn't inherently retain information about previous interactions. To maintain state and enable more complex interactions (for example, user authentication), techniques such as cookies and session management are used.

In the context of ESP32 projects, understanding HTTP is crucial for enabling IoT devices to interact with web servers, retrieve data, send data, and contribute to the larger network of interconnected devices and services.

Now, we will learn how we can use ESP32 as an HTTP web server.

ESP32 as an HTTP web server

An HTTP web server is a software application that receives and processes HTTP requests from clients (typically web browsers) and responds by delivering web content such as HTML pages, images, and other resources. It acts as an intermediary between clients and the requested resources, facilitating the transfer of data over the internet. By interpreting incoming HTTP requests and generating appropriate responses, an HTTP web server enables the hosting and access of web content, forming the foundation of the World Wide Web and supporting seamless interaction between users and online resources.

In the following example, we will create a simple web server to control an LED attached to ESP32. Users can access ESP32's IP address from their web browser, view the LED's status, and toggle it on and off using the provided button on the web page.

For this example, we will use the same circuit that we used in the ESP32 basic input/output example in *Chapter 2*. The circuit diagram can be found in *Figure 2.1*. Then, we will upload the following code to ESP32 using the Arduino IDE. The code is available at https://github.com/PacktPublishing/ Programming-ESP32-with-Arduino-IDE/tree/main/Chapter%205/ESP32_ webserver:

```
#include <WiFi.h>
#include <WebServer.h>
const char* ssid = "YourWiFiSSID";
const char* password = "WIFIPASSWORD";
WebServer server(80);
const int ledPin = 13;
const int buttonPin = 12;
bool ledState = false;
void setup() {
  Serial.begin(115200);
  pinMode(ledPin, OUTPUT);
  pinMode(buttonPin, INPUT_PULLUP);
  digitalWrite(ledPin, ledState);
  WiFi.begin(ssid, password);
  while (WiFi.status() != WL_CONNECTED) {
    delay(1000);
    Serial.println("Connecting to WiFi"…");
  }
  Serial.print"n("WiFi connec"ed");
```

```
    Serial.print"n("IP addres": ");
    Serial.println(WiFi.localIP());
    server."n""/", HTTP_GET, handleRoot);
    server."n("/tog"le", HTTP_GET, handleToggle);
    server.begin();
}
void loop() {
    server.handleClient();
    int buttonState = digitalRead(buttonPin);
    if (buttonState == LOW) {
        ledState = !ledState;
        digitalWrite(ledPin, ledState);
    }
}
void handleRoot() {
    String html"= "<html><bo"y>";
    html "= "<h1>ESP32 LED Control</"1>";
    html "= "<p>LED Statu": " + String(ledState)"+ "<"p>";
    html "= "<form meth'd=''et' acti'n='/tog'l'"'>";
    html "= "<button ty'e='sub'it'>Toggle LED</butt"n>";
    html "= "</fo"m>";
    html "= "</body></ht"l>";
    server.send(20", "text/h"ml", html);
}
void handleToggle() {
    ledState = !ledState;
    digitalWrite(ledPin, ledState);
    server.send(20", "text/pl"in", "LED togg"ed");
}
```

At the beginning of the preceding code, the necessary libraries, WiFi.h and WebServer.h, are included. These libraries empower ESP32 to handle Wi-Fi connectivity and web server functionalities.

The code establishes the credentials for connecting to a Wi-Fi network by setting the ssid and password variables. Make sure to enter your Wi-Fi details.

The WebServer instance, initialized on port 80, serves as the backbone for processing incoming HTTP requests and providing appropriate responses.

The assignment of pins to control the LED and read the button input follows. The LED is linked to pin 13, while the button is connected to pin 12. The ledState Boolean variable is introduced to keep track of the LED's on/off status.

In the `setup()` function, serial communication is initiated for debugging purposes. The `pinMode()` function is used to configure the LED pin as an output and the button pin as an input with a pull-up resistor enabled. The LED is set to its initial state based on the `ledState` variable. ESP32 begins connecting to the specified Wi-Fi network, and a loop waits until a successful connection is established. Once connected, ESP32's local IP address is printed, signifying successful network integration. The `server.on()` statements define the route handlers for the root (`/`) and `/toggle` routes. The `server.begin()` function initiates the web server.

In the `loop()` function, the server continuously processes client requests using `server.handleClient()`. Additionally, the code monitors the button's state using `digitalRead(buttonPin)`. If the button is pressed (indicated by a LOW state), the `ledState` variable is toggled, and the LED is updated accordingly.

The `handleRoot()` function generates an HTML response when the root (`/`) route is accessed. This response displays the current LED status and offers a button to toggle it. The `handleToggle()` function responds to the `/toggle` route, toggling the LED's state and sending a confirmation message.

Once the code has been uploaded, and ESP32 is successfully connected to the Wi-Fi network, you will see an IP address in the serial monitor, as shown in *Figure 5.2*:

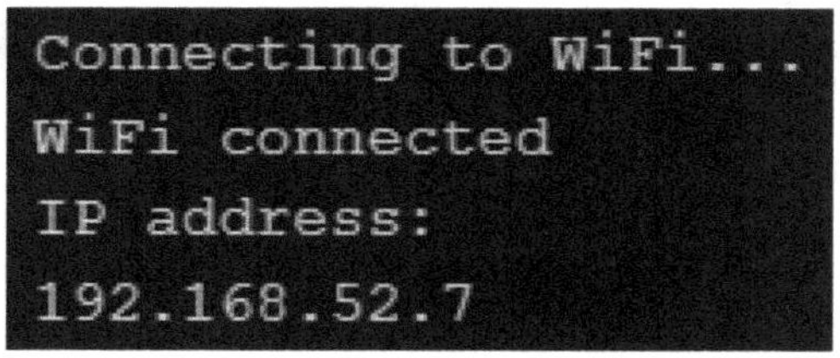

```
Connecting to WiFi...
WiFi connected
IP address:
192.168.52.7
```

Figure 5.2 – ESP32 connected to the Wi-Fi network

When you enter this IP address in any browser, such as Chrome, you will see a web page hosted by ESP32:

ESP32 LED Control

LED Status: 1

Toggle LED

Figure 5.3 – Web server hosted by ESP32

If you press the toggle LED button, the LED will change its state; if it is off, it will turn on or vice versa. The LED could be controlled by the physical button; in this case, you will be able to see the status on the web page.

Next, we will see how we can use ESP32 as an HTTP client.

ESP32 as an HTTP client

An HTTP client is a software application or a program that initiates HTTP requests to interact with web servers and retrieve information or resources from them. Acting as a client-side component, it sends specific HTTP requests, typically in the form of URLs, to designated servers. These requests can include commands to retrieve web pages, images, videos, or other data. Upon receiving the requested data from the server, the HTTP client processes and utilizes the received information for display, processing, or further interaction within the application or user interface.

For this example, we will read the temperature, humidity, and pressure values using the web API:

1. To carry out this example, you'll need to register on the **OpenWeatherMap** website and obtain an API key from `https://openweathermap.org/`:

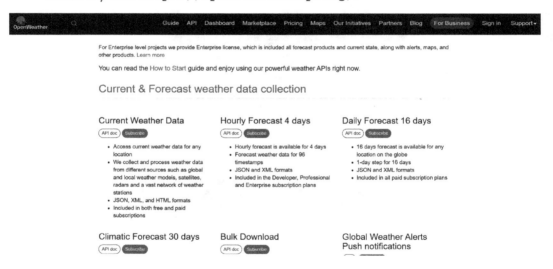

Figure 5.4 – OpenWeatherMap dashboard

2. You will have to create an account to access the API, so click on **Sign in** to sign in or create a new account.

3. It will show you different plans; for this example, we can use the free plan. We will click on the **Get API key** under the **Free** option, as shown in *Figure 5.5*:

Current weather and forecasts collection

Free	Startup	Developer	Professional	Enterprise
	35 EUR/ month	160 EUR/ month	410 EUR/ month	1750 EUR/ month
Get API key	Subscribe	Subscribe	Subscribe	Subscribe
60 calls/minute 1,000,000 calls/month	600 calls/minute 10,000,000 calls/month	3,000 calls/minute 100,000,000 calls/month	30,000 calls/minute 1,000,000,000 calls/month	200,000 calls/minute 5,000,000,000 calls/month
Current Weather	Current Weather	Current Weather	Current Weather	Current Weather
3-hour Forecast 5 days	3-hour Forecast 5 days	3-hour Forecast 5 days	3-hour Forecast 5 days	3-hour Forecast 5 days
Hourly Forecast 4 days	Hourly Forecast 4 days	Hourly Forecast 4 days	Hourly Forecast 4 days	Hourly Forecast 4 days
Daily Forecast 16 days	Daily Forecast 16 days	Daily Forecast 16 days	Daily Forecast 16 days	Daily Forecast 16 days
Climatic Forecast 30 days	Climatic Forecast 30 days	Climatic Forecast 30 days	Climatic Forecast 30 days	Climatic Forecast 30 days
Bulk Download	Bulk Download	Bulk Download	Bulk Download (global cities)	Bulk Download (global cities + ZIPs of US, EU, UK)
Basic weather maps	Basic weather maps	Advanced weather maps	Advanced weather maps	Advanced weather maps
Historical maps	Historical maps	Historical maps	Historical maps	Historical maps
Global Precipitation Map - Historical data	Global Precipitation Map - Historical data	Global Precipitation Map - Historical data	Global Precipitation Map - Historical data	Global Precipitation Map - Historical data
Weather Dashboard	Weather Dashboard	Weather Dashboard	Weather Dashboard	Weather Dashboard
Road Risk API (basic configuration)	Road Risk API (basic configuration)	Road Risk API (basic configuration)	Road Risk API (basic configuration)	Road Risk API (basic configuration)
Air Pollution API	Air Pollution API	Air Pollution API	Air Pollution API	Air Pollution API

Figure 5.5 – OpenWeatherMap API pricing options

4. It will ask you to sign up, so enter your details and click on **Create Account**:

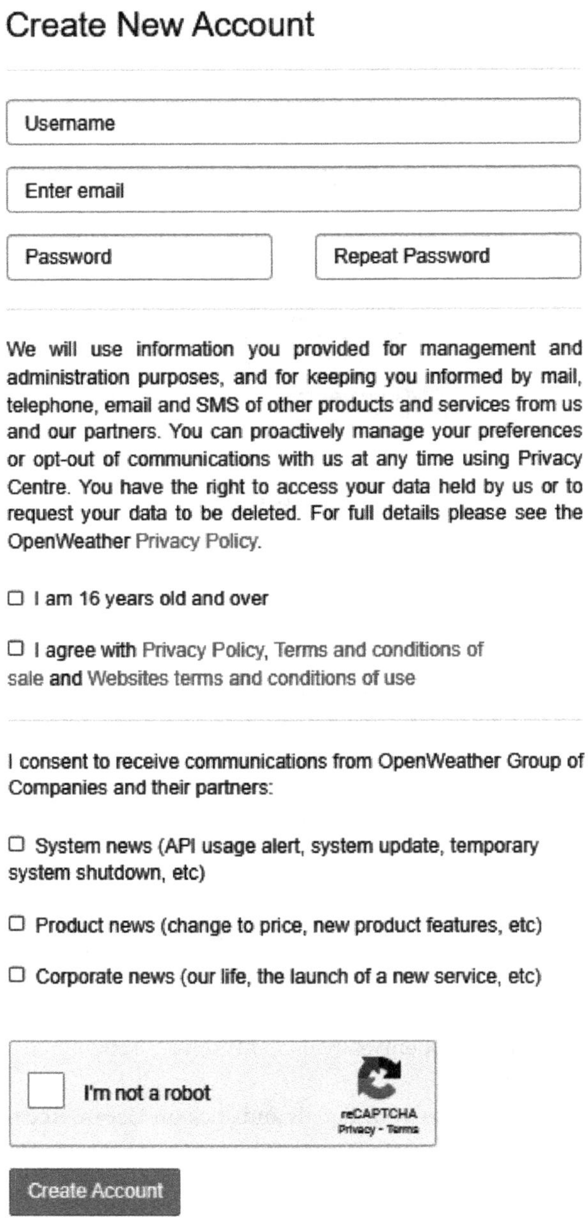

Create New Account

Username

Enter email

Password   Repeat Password

We will use information you provided for management and administration purposes, and for keeping you informed by mail, telephone, email and SMS of other products and services from us and our partners. You can proactively manage your preferences or opt-out of communications with us at any time using Privacy Centre. You have the right to access your data held by us or to request your data to be deleted. For full details please see the OpenWeather Privacy Policy.

☐ I am 16 years old and over

☐ I agree with Privacy Policy, Terms and conditions of sale and Websites terms and conditions of use

I consent to receive communications from OpenWeather Group of Companies and their partners:

☐ System news (API usage alert, system update, temporary system shutdown, etc)

☐ Product news (change to price, new product features, etc)

☐ Corporate news (our life, the launch of a new service, etc)

☐ I'm not a robot   reCAPTCHA
                         Privacy - Terms

Create Account

Figure 5.6 – Creating a new account

5.   After creating a new account, you will have to sign in, and after signing in, you will see a dashboard. Click on the **API keys** tab. It will show the following screen:

Figure 5.7 – Getting the API key from OpenWeatherMap

6.   Copy the key as we will need this in our code. *Figure 5.8* shows how we could use the API request:

Built-in API request by city name

You can call by city name or city name, state code and country code. Please note that searching by states available only for the USA locations.

API call

```
https://api.openweathermap.org/data/2.5/weather?q={city
name}&appid={API key}
```

```
https://api.openweathermap.org/data/2.5/weather?q={city
name},{country code}&appid={API key}
```

```
https://api.openweathermap.org/data/2.5/weather?q={city
name},{state code},{country code}&appid={API key}
```

Parameters

`q`	required	City name, state code and country code divided by comma, Please refer to ISO 3166 for the state codes or country codes. You can specify the parameter not only in English. In this case, the API response should be returned in the same language as the language of requested location name if the location is in our predefined list of more than 200,000 locations.
`appid`	required	Your unique API key (you can always find it on your account page under the "API key" tab)
`mode`	optional	Response format. Possible values are `xml` and `html`. If you don't use the `mode` parameter format is JSON by default. Learn more
`units`	optional	Units of measurement. `standard`, `metric` and `imperial` units are available. If you do not use the `units` parameter, `standard` units will be applied by default. Learn more
`lang`	optional	You can use this parameter to get the output in your language. Learn more

Figure 5.8 – API request by city name

7. To test our API key, go to the web browser and enter the following URL (make sure to enter your city and API key): `https://api.openweathermap.org/data/2.5/weather?q={City}&appid={API-key}`.

You will see a weather report in the form of JSON data, as in the following figure:

```
←  →  C    api.openweathermap.org/data/2.5/weather?q=London&appid=5ae492edb5f4610f94bc7406f01ee0e2
1    // 20230828120233
2    // https://api.openweathermap.org/data/2.5/weather?q=London&appid=5ae492edb5f4610f94bc7406f01ee0e2
3
4  ▾  {
5  ▾      "coord": {
6            "lon": -0.1257,
7            "lat": 51.5085
8        },
9  ▾      "weather": [
10 ▾        {
11            "id": 803,
12            "main": "Clouds",
13            "description": "broken clouds",
14            "icon": "04d"
15          }
16        ],
17        "base": "stations",
18 ▾      "main": {
19          "temp": 290.79,
20          "feels_like": 290.46,
21          "temp_min": 289.1,
22          "temp_max": 292.18,
23          "pressure": 1012,
24          "humidity": 71
25        },
26        "visibility": 10000,
27 ▾      "wind": {
28          "speed": 3.09,
29          "deg": 310
```

Figure 5.9 – API response in the browser

It shows that our API request has been responded to, and now our task is to read this data using ESP32 and show it on the OLED display.

8. We will upload the following code in our ESP32 project using the Arduino IDE to read the weather data in ESP32. The code is available at `https://github.com/PacktPublishing/Programming-ESP32-with-Arduino-IDE/tree/main/Chapter%205/ESP32_as_HTTP_client`:

```
#include <WiFi.h>
#include <HTTPClient.h>
#include <Arduino_JSON.h>
```

```
#include <Adafruit_GFX.h>
#include <Adafruit_SSD1306.h>
#include <Wire.h>
#define SCREEN_WIDTH 128
#define SCREEN_HEIGHT 64
#define OLED_RESET     -1
Adafruit_SSD1306 display(SCREEN_WIDTH, SCREEN_HEIGHT, &Wire,
OLED_RESET);
const char* wifiSSID =  "WIFI SSID";
const char* wifiPassword = "WIFI PASSWORD";
String openWeatherMapApiKey = "Your API Key";
String city = "London"; //change city name
String jsonBuffer;
void setup() {
  Serial.begin(115200);
  …
  …
  …
  http.end();
  return payload;
}
```

The preceding code uses several libraries, including WiFi.h for Wi-Fi connectivity, HTTPClient.h for making HTTP requests, Arduino_JSON.h for JSON parsing, and Adafruit_SSD1306.h for driving an OLED display.

After initializing the necessary constants and variables, the code's setup() function establishes a connection to a Wi-Fi network. It then initializes the OLED display and clears any existing content.

In the loop() function, if a Wi-Fi connection is established, the code constructs an API request URL specific to the desired city and country. It uses the httpGETRequest() function to make an HTTP GET request to the OpenWeatherMap API using the constructed URL. The response, which contains weather data in JSON format, is parsed using the Arduino JSON library.

The parsed JSON data is extracted to obtain temperature, pressure, humidity, and wind speed information. This data is both printed to the serial monitor and displayed on the OLED screen using the Adafruit_SSD1306 library.

If the Wi-Fi connection is lost, the code indicates WiFi Disconnected in the serial monitor. The loop continues to execute, fetching and displaying weather data at regular intervals.

The httpGETRequest() function is responsible for making HTTP GET requests to the specified server. It uses the HTTPClient library to establish a connection and retrieve data. The response is processed, and the payload is returned.

9. Upon uploading the code to ESP32, the device effectively accesses the OpenWeatherMap API, extracts relevant weather data, and seamlessly presents this information on both the serial monitor and the connected OLED screen, as shown in the following figure:

```
Connecting to WiFi...
..
Connected to WiFi network. IP Address: 10.10.0.2
HTTP Response code: 200
{"coord":{"lon":-0.1257,"lat":51.5085},"weather":
[{"id":804,"main":"Clouds","description":"overcast
clouds","icon":"04d"}],"base":"stations","main":
{"temp":16.26,"feels_like":15.95,"temp_min":14.92,"temp_max":18.21,"pressure":1013,"humidity"
:77},"visibility":10000,"wind":{"speed":4.63,"deg":300},"clouds":
{"all":100},"dt":1693213083,"sys":
{"type":2,"id":2075535,"country":"GB","sunrise":1693199174,"sunset":1693249077},"timezone":36
00,"id":2643743,"name":"London","cod":200}
JSON object = {"coord":{"lon":-0.1257,"lat":51.5085},"weather":
[{"id":804,"main":"Clouds","description":"overcast
clouds","icon":"04d"}],"base":"stations","main":
{"temp":16.26,"feels_like":15.95,"temp_min":14.92,"temp_max":18.21,"pressure":1013,"humidity"
:77},"visibility":10000,"wind":{"speed":4.63,"deg":300},"clouds":
{"all":100},"dt":1693213083,"sys":
{"type":2,"id":2075535,"country":"GB","sunrise":1693199174,"sunset":1693249077},"timezone":36
00,"id":2643743,"name":"London","cod":200}
Temperature: 16.26
Pressure: 1013
Humidity: 77
Wind Speed: 4.63
```

Figure 5.10 – API request and response in the serial monitor

10. Now, we could add an OLED using I2C communication, which we learned about in *Chapter 3*, as in *Figure 5.11*. The OLED shows the weather data:

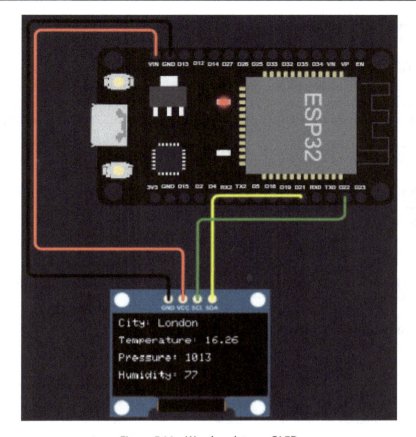

Figure 5.11 – Weather data on OLED

This practical illustration highlights the combination of IoT capabilities, HTTP communication, and data visualization in a succinct and coherent manner. Now, let's go through another bonus example that uses the HTTP protocol and will be helpful in other IoT projects.

Configuring and managing Wi-Fi using the HTTP protocol in ESP32

In the previous examples, when we were making IoT devices connect to Wi-Fi, we were putting the Wi-Fi details directly into the device's code. However, this could be a problem if we wanted to use the device in different places with different Wi-Fi networks. We would have to change the code each time, which can be tricky. Here's where the `WiFiManager` library comes in. It's like a helpful tool that lets us set up Wi-Fi for our device using a website so that we don't need to change the code every time. `WiFiManager` uses HTTP to talk to our device and make sure it connects to the right Wi-Fi network.

The following example will show you how `WiFiManager` uses HTTP to make connecting to Wi-Fi super easy, even if we move our device around:

1.   We will upload the following code in ESP32 using the Arduino IDE. Make sure to install the `WiFiManager` library by *tzapu* using the Arduino library manager, as we did in *Chapter 2*. The code is available at `https://github.com/PacktPublishing/Programming-ESP32-with-Arduino-IDE/tree/main/Chapter%205/ESP32_WiFiManager`:

```
#include <WiFi.h>
#include <WiFiManager.h>

void setup() {
  Serial.begin(115200);
  WiFiManager wifiManager;
  // Uncomment the following line to reset Wi-Fi settings and
enter configuration mode
  //wifiManager.resetSettings();
  wifiManager.autoConnect("ESP32-Config"); // Access point name
  Serial.println("Connected to Wi-Fi!");
  Serial.print("IP Address: ");
  Serial.println(WiFi.localIP());
}
void loop() {
  // Your code goes here
}
```

This code showcases the utilization of the `WiFiManager` library to simplify the process of connecting an ESP32 device to a Wi-Fi network. `WiFiManager` employs the HTTP protocol to establish communication between the device and a web-based configuration page, ensuring seamless Wi-Fi setup without requiring manual code modifications.

Upon initiating the code, the `setup()` function commences with serial communication setup for debugging purposes. An instance of the `WiFiManager` class is created, effectively initializing the `WiFiManager` tool.

Within the `setup()` function, you can uncomment the `wifiManager.resetSettings();` line if needed. This line instructs the `WiFiManager` class to reset any previous Wi-Fi settings and enter *configuration* mode. This can be useful when you want to change the Wi-Fi network the device connects to.

The core of the Wi-Fi configuration process is carried out by the `wifiManager.autoConnect("ESP32-Config");` line. This line prompts ESP32 to automatically connect to the saved Wi-Fi network if the credentials are available. If not, ESP32 enters configuration mode, creating an **access point (AP)** named `ESP32-Config` to which a user can connect. The user can then access a web page served by ESP32 through their web browser to enter the required Wi-Fi details without needing to modify the device's code.

After a Wi-Fi connection is successfully established, the serial monitor prints out a message indicating the connection status along with the assigned IP address.

In the `loop()` function, which is currently empty, you can add your own code for further functionality.

2. When you upload the code to ESP32, if it is not connected to the Wi-Fi network, it will open a Wi-Fi AP, which we discussed in the previous chapter. We will connect to the AP opened by ESP32 (in this case, **ESP32-Config**), as shown in *Figure 5.12*:

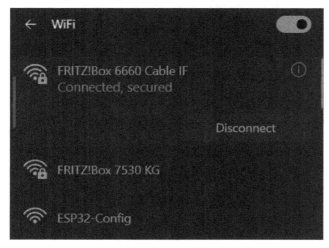

Figure 5.12 – ESP32 as AP

3. After connecting to the **ESP32-Config** AP, we will see the following data in the serial monitor:

```
Connected to Wi-Fi!
IP Address: 192.168.178.26
*wm:resetSettings
*wm:SETTINGS ERASED
*wm:AutoConnect
*wm:No wifi saved, skipping
*wm:AutoConnect: FAILED for  20 ms
*wm:StartAP with SSID:  ESP32-Config
*wm:AP IP address: 192.168.4.1
*wm:Starting Web Portal
*wm:[ERROR] scan waiting
*wm:.
*wm:.
*wm:.
```

Figure 5.13 – Starting the ESP32 web portal

4. Also, a web portal as shown in *Figure 5.14* will be opened automatically in the web browser; you can click on **Configure WiFi**:

Figure 5.14 – ESP32 WiFiManager portal

5. It will show you a list of all the Wi-Fi networks available. Click on the one you would like to connect to, enter a password, and click on **Save**:

OnePlus Nord2 5G	🔒 .ɪɪ
FRITZ!Box 7530 KG	🔒 .ɪɪ
FRITZ!Box 6660 Cable IF	🔒 .ɪɪ
WLAN-189230	🔒 .ɪɪ
BROADCOM_GUEST_1_EAD01	.ɪɪ
Bibanu28	🔒 .ɪɪ
PYUR Community	🔒 .ɪɪ
WLAN-572077	🔒 .ɪɪ
DIRECT-80-HP ENVY 4520 series	🔒 .ɪɪ
Cauchy	🔒 .ɪɪ
WLAN-L5R2AX	🔒 .ɪɪ
PS4-ABBA3F64B306	🔒 .ɪɪ

SSID

OnePlus Nord2 5G

Password

••••••••

☐ Show Password

Save

Refresh

Figure 5.15 – Connecting to a Wi-Fi network

6. After clicking on **Save**, you will be able to see in the serial monitor that you are connected to the Wi-Fi network, as shown in *Figure 5.16*:

```
*wm:-2 networks found
*wm:13 networks found
*wm:12 networks found
*wm:Connecting to NEW AP: OnePlus Nord2 5G
*wm:connectTimeout not set, ESP waitForConnectResult...
*wm:Connect to new AP [SUCCESS]
*wm:Got IP Address:
*wm:192.168.52.7
*wm:config portal exiting
Connected to Wi-Fi!
IP Address: 192.168.52.7
```

Figure 5.16 – Connected to the Wi-Fi network

7. Once you are connected to the Wi-Fi device, the Wi-Fi AP will be closed.

In summary, this code exemplifies how `WiFiManager` employs the HTTP protocol to facilitate the setup of Wi-Fi connections for an ESP32 device. By allowing users to access a web page served by ESP32 to input Wi-Fi credentials, the process of configuring Wi-Fi becomes hassle-free, eliminating the need to modify code when changing network environments. This approach enhances user-friendliness and adaptability, making it particularly useful for IoT devices that may be relocated or used in various settings.

In the next section, we will explore the MQTT protocol, which works on the pub-sub model.

Exploring MQTT for IoT communication with ESP32

Among the many different protocols used in IoT, MQTT stands out as a powerful option. MQTT, with its lightweight and pub-sub messaging paradigm, has found its place as a go-to protocol for enabling efficient communication between resource-constrained devices such as ESP32 and remote servers.

This section takes an in-depth journey into the domain of MQTT communication, purposefully tailored for ESP32 projects. We will explore the mechanisms through which ESP32 can seamlessly engage with MQTT brokers, granting IoT devices the capability to share data, receive updates, and actively participate in the dynamic ecosystem of IoT.

What is MQTT?

MQTT is a lightweight and efficient messaging protocol designed for the efficient exchange of data between devices, especially in scenarios where bandwidth and resources are limited. It was originally developed by IBM in the late 1990s and has since become a widely adopted protocol in the realm of IoT and **machine-to-machine (M2M)** communication.

Key characteristics of MQTT include the following:

- **Pub-sub model**: MQTT follows a pub-sub model, where devices communicate through a central broker. Devices that want to share information (publishers) send messages to specific "topics" on the broker, and other devices interested in that information (subscribers) can subscribe to those topics to receive messages.

- **Quality-of-service (QoS) levels**: MQTT supports different levels of QoS (that is, QoS 0, 1, and 2) for message delivery, which are explained in the next section of this chapter:

  - **Retained messages**: MQTT allows publishers to mark a message as "retained." This means that the last message sent on a topic will be stored on the broker and sent to new subscribers immediately upon subscription.

  - **Last will and testament (LWT)**: Clients can specify a "last will" message that will be sent by the broker if the client unexpectedly disconnects. This can be used to indicate the client's status or take appropriate actions.

- **Low overhead**: MQTT is designed to be lightweight, making it suitable for scenarios where bandwidth and resources are limited, such as IoT devices. The reason for the low overhead in MQTT is a small packet header (2 bytes) and pub-sub model.

- **Persistent connections**: Clients can establish long-lived connections to the broker, reducing the overhead of repeatedly establishing new connections for each message.

- **Security**: MQTT can be used with SSL/TLS encryption for secure communication, ensuring the confidentiality and integrity of the data exchanged.

- **Topic-based filtering**: Subscribers can use wildcard characters to subscribe to multiple topics that match a certain pattern.

MQTT has found widespread use in IoT applications where devices need to exchange information and control messages efficiently and reliably. It is commonly used for scenarios such as remote device monitoring, home automation, industrial automation, and more. To implement MQTT communication, devices need an MQTT broker that acts as a message hub, routing messages between publishers and subscribers.

Overall, MQTT's efficiency, simplicity, and flexibility make it a popular choice for IoT communication, especially in resource-constrained environments.

How does MQTT work?

The MQTT protocol operates on the principles of a pub-sub messaging model, facilitating efficient communication between devices in the IoT ecosystem. At its core, MQTT comprises three key components: *publishers*, *subscribers*, and a *central broker*. Let's look at this in more detail:

- *Publishers* are devices that generate data and wish to share it with other devices. To initiate communication, a publisher sends a message to a specific "topic" on the MQTT broker. This topic acts as a channel through which information is categorized and organized.

- *Subscribers* are devices interested in receiving specific types of data. They subscribe to topics on the broker to indicate their interest in particular information. When a publisher sends a message to a topic, the broker ensures that all relevant subscribers are notified.

- The *MQTT broker* plays a pivotal role in this architecture. It serves as an intermediary, receiving messages from publishers and forwarding them to the appropriate subscribers. It manages the routing of messages, allowing devices to communicate without needing to know the identities or addresses of individual recipients.

When a publisher sends a message to a topic, the broker receives it and evaluates which subscribers are interested in that topic. The broker then forwards the message to all subscribers of that topic. Subscribers can choose the level of QoS they desire for message delivery:

- **QoS 0**: The message is delivered at most once, and no acknowledgment is required.

- **QoS 1**: The message is delivered at least once, and an acknowledgment is sent back to the publisher.

- **QoS 2**: The message is delivered exactly once, utilizing a four-step handshake to ensure reliability. The four-step handshake involves the following:

  - The publisher sends a `PUBLISH` message

  - The receiver acknowledges the message

  - The publisher resends the `PUBLISH` message

  - The receiver confirms with a final acknowledgment

Furthermore, MQTT supports "retained" messages. When a publisher sends a retained message, the broker stores it as the "last-known value" for that topic. New subscribers immediately receive this retained message upon subscribing, ensuring they have the latest data.

Additionally, MQTT provides the concept of LWT. Clients can specify a message that the broker will send on their behalf if they disconnect unexpectedly. This feature is useful for conveying the status or availability of a device.

Overall, MQTT's operation is centered on the broker, which orchestrates the flow of messages between publishers and subscribers. This lightweight protocol excels in scenarios with limited bandwidth and resources, making it a preferred choice for IoT communication, where devices need to exchange information seamlessly and efficiently.

Figure 5.17 shows how we can use the MQTT protocol:

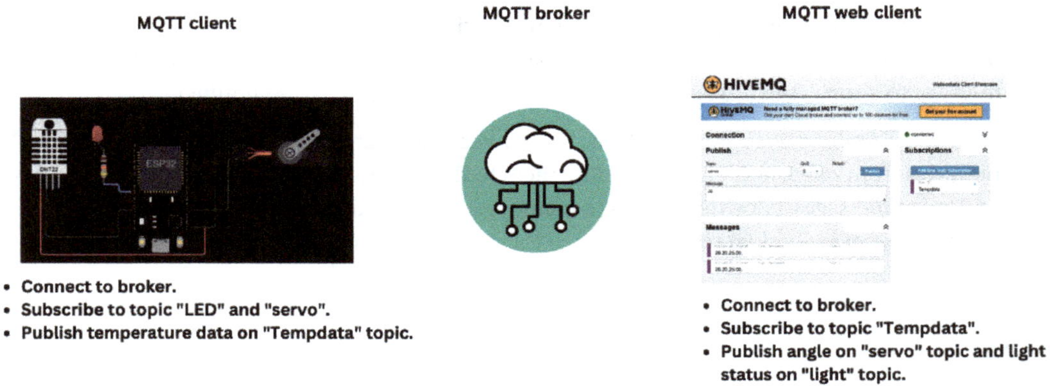

MQTT client

- Connect to broker.
- Subscribe to topic "LED" and "servo".
- Publish temperature data on "Tempdata" topic.

MQTT broker

MQTT web client

- Connect to broker.
- Subscribe to topic "Tempdata".
- Publish angle on "servo" topic and light status on "light" topic.

Figure 5.17 – How the MQTT protocol works

There are two clients: one uses ESP32 with other devices and sensors, while the other is a web client for MQTT. In the center, there's something called an MQTT broker. The ESP32 MQTT client subscribes to the LED and `servo` topics. Whenever a message shows up on these topics, ESP32 does things such as turning the LED on/off and moving the servo. Additionally, ESP32 regularly sends temperature data to the `Tempdata` topic. In the next example, we'll write code and do the same thing shown in *Figure 5.17*.

MQTT pub-sub example

Firstly, we will need an MQTT broker for the communication using the MQTT protocol. You could install the MQTT broker on your laptop or Raspberry Pi, or you could use the free public cloud MQTT brokers. We will be using the HiveMQ free MQTT cloud broker.

You can get details of the free MQTT broker at `https://www.hivemq.com/public-mqtt-broker/`, as shown in the following figure:

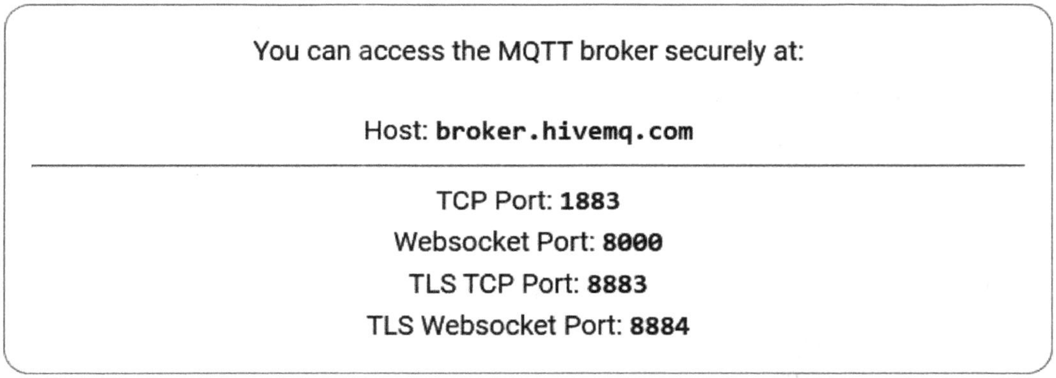

You can access the MQTT broker securely at:

Host: **broker.hivemq.com**

TCP Port: **1883**
Websocket Port: **8000**
TLS TCP Port: **8883**
TLS Websocket Port: **8884**

Figure 5.18 – HiveMQ free public broker

Now, we will use these details in our ESP32 code to connect to the MQTT broker and pub/sub messages. But first, let's make a circuit diagram:

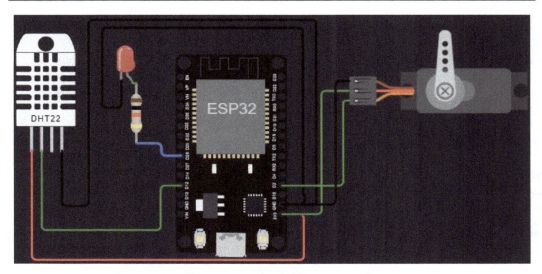

Figure 5.19 – ESP32 connected to DHT22 sensor and servo motor

We've set up the connections like this:

- The SDA pin of the DHT22 sensor is linked to the D12 pin of ESP32

- The data pin of the servo is connected to D2 on ESP32

- The negative (cathode) side of the LED is attached to the GND pin

- The positive (anode) side of the LED is connected to the D2 pin

- Both the servo and DHT22 use the VIN or 3.3V pin for their power, and their GND pins are connected to the ground

You can see this arrangement in *Figure 5.19*. Let's move to the next stage:

1. Now, we will upload the following code in our ESP32 project using the Arduino IDE. Make sure to change the Wi-Fi details. The code is available at https://github.com/PacktPublishing/Programming-ESP32-with-Arduino-IDE/tree/main/Chapter%205/ESP32_MQTT:

    ```
    #include <Adafruit_Sensor.h>
    #include <DHT_U.h>
    #include <WiFi.h>
    #include <PubSubClient.h>
    #include <Servo.h>
    #define DHTPIN 12
    #define LED 26
    #define SERVO_PIN 2
    ```

```
#define DHTTYPE     DHT22
DHT_Unified dht(DHTPIN, DHTTYPE);
...
...
...
    msgStr = String(temp) + "," + String(hum) + ",";
    byte arrSize = msgStr.length() + 1;
    char msg[arrSize];
    msgStr.toCharArray(msg, arrSize);
    client.publish(topic, msg);
    msgStr = "";
    delay(1);
  }
}
```

Let's break down the code step by step:

- **Library inclusions**: The code begins by including necessary libraries for different functionalities. Make sure to install them using the library manager. The libraries include the following:

  - `Adafruit_Sensor.h` and `DHT_U.h` for using the DHT temperature and humidity sensor

  - `WiFi.h` for connecting to a Wi-Fi network

  - `PubSubClient.h` for MQTT communication

  - `Servo.h` for controlling a servo motor

- **Pin definitions**: Various pins are defined using constants. These pins are used to connect different components such as the DHT sensor, LED, and servo motor

- **Sensor and actuator initialization**: The code initializes the DHT sensor and a servo motor using the defined pins

- **Wi-Fi and MQTT configuration**: In this part, we configure Wi-Fi and MQTT as follows:

  - Wi-Fi credentials (`ssid` and `password`) are set to connect ESP32 to a Wi-Fi network

  - The MQTT broker's address (`mqttServer`) and the client ID (`clientID`) are defined

  - A topic name (`topic`) is specified for publishing data to the MQTT broker

- **Wi-Fi setup function**: The `setup_wifi()` function is defined to establish a Wi-Fi connection. It waits for ESP32 to successfully connect to the network and then prints the local IP address.

- **MQTT reconnect function**: The `reconnect()` function handles MQTT reconnection. If the client is not connected to the broker, it attempts to reconnect. Subscriptions to MQTT topics (`lights` and `servo`) are done upon successful reconnection.

- **MQTT callback function**: The `callback()` function is called when a message is received on subscribed topics. It processes incoming messages to control the LED and servo motor based on the received commands.

- **Setup function**: In this function, we set up the inputs and outputs as follows:

  - Serial communication is initiated

  - The DHT sensor is initialized, and its sensor details are retrieved

  - The LED pin is set as an output and turned off

  - The servo motor is attached to its pin and set to the initial position

  - A Wi-Fi connection is established using the `setup_wifi()` function

  - The MQTT client's server address and callback function are set using the `client.setServer()` and `client.setCallback()` functions

- **Loop function**: In the `loop()` function, we connect to the MQTT broker and perform the following tasks:

  - If the MQTT client is not connected, the `reconnect()` function is called to attempt reconnection

  - The MQTT client's `loop()` function is called to handle MQTT communication

  - The code periodically reads the temperature and humidity values from the DHT sensor

  - If valid temperature and humidity values are obtained, they are printed

  - The temperature and humidity values are concatenated as a string and published to the specified MQTT topic

  - A non-blocking delay is used to control the timing of data publication

2. After uploading the code, you will see the following results in the serial monitor:

```
..
WiFi connected
IP address:
10.10.0.2
MQTT connected
Topic Subscribed
Temperature: 26.20°C
Humidity: 25.00%
PUBLISH DATA: 26.20,25.00,
Temperature: 26.20°C
Humidity: 25.00%
PUBLISH DATA: 26.20,25.00,
Temperature: 26.20°C
Humidity: 25.00%
PUBLISH DATA: 26.20,25.00,
```

Figure 5.20 – ESP32 publishing DHT22 data

3. Now, we will set up the web client to see the results. We will open the free MQTT web client provided by HiveMQ by going to `https://www.hivemq.com/demos/websocket-client/`. You will see a dashboard, as shown in *Figure 5.21*:

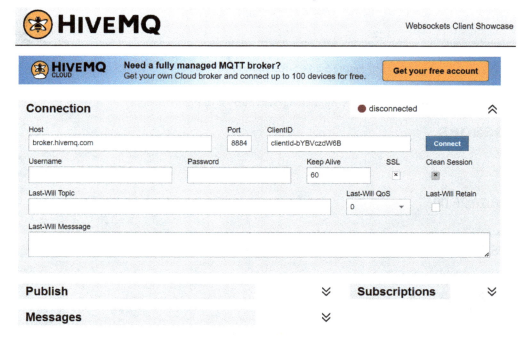

Figure 5.21 – HiveMQ free MQTT web client

4. We will enter the host (`broker.hivemq.com`) and port (`8883`) details and click on **Connect**. Once we are connected, we will add a new topic subscription by clicking on the button shown in *Figure 5.22*:

Figure 5.22 – Adding a new topic subscription

5. We will subscribe to the `Tempdata` topic on which we are publishing temperature and humidity values, as shown in *Figure 5.23*, and we will keep **QoS** at **0**:

Figure 5.23 – Subscribing to a topic

6. After a while, you will start seeing messages, as shown in *Figure 5.24*:

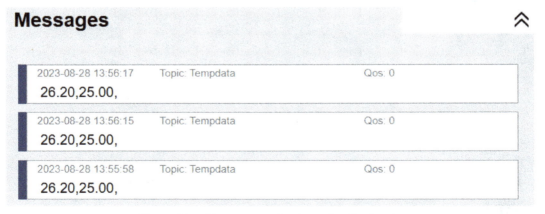

Figure 5.24 – Messages received on subscribed topic

7. Now, let's publish some messages. We will send **52** messages to the **servo** topics with QoS **0**, as shown in *Figure 5.25*:

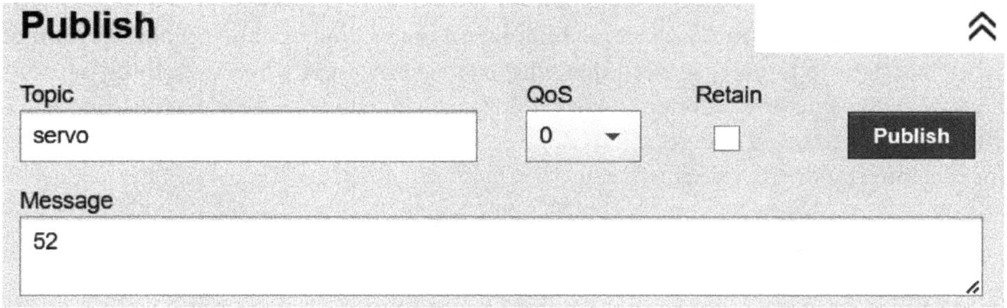

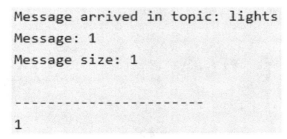

Figure 5.25 – Publishing MQTT messages on the servo topic

8. The message will be received in ESP32, and the servo motor will move to 52 degrees, as can be seen in *Figure 5.26*:

```
Message arrived in topic: servo
Message: 52
Message size: 2


----------------------
52
Moving servo to degree: 52
```

Figure 5.26 – Message arrived in ESP32 servo topic

9. Let's also send a message on the `lights` topic, and we will receive the following message on the LED topic and the LED will be turned on:

```
Message arrived in topic: lights
Message: 1
Message size: 1


----------------------
1
```

Figure 5.27 – Message arrived in ESP32 LED topic

Now, we will move on to the next section of this chapter, in which we will learn how to send alerts using webhooks in our IoT projects.

Adding real-time notifications using webhooks

In the ever-changing world of IoT, it's important for devices and faraway servers to talk effectively. Among the many ways they communicate, webhooks are useful. Webhooks help devices send quick alerts and instructions to faraway servers, like sending a text message when something happens. In this section, we'll dive into how webhooks work in IoT projects, showing how devices such as ESP32 can use them to send messages and get things done on faraway servers in real time. This helps devices stay connected and responsive in the IoT world.

What are webhooks and how do they work?

Webhooks are like virtual messengers in the world of technology. Imagine you have a friend who keeps an eye on your favorite website for you. Whenever something new happens on that site, your friend quickly sends you a message to let you know. In the digital realm, webhooks play a similar role. They allow different services and apps to communicate with each other in real time.

Here's how they work. Let's say you have an online store and want to know whenever a new order is placed. You set up a webhook that tells your store's system to send a message to another service whenever an order is made. When an order happens, the store quickly sends a message to that other service, almost like tapping them on the shoulder. This way, you get instant notifications without having to constantly check your store. Webhooks make it easy for different systems to talk to each other and share important information as soon as things happen.

Webhook example

In the following example, we will send a random number of webhooks whenever a button is pushed. We will make the following circuit:

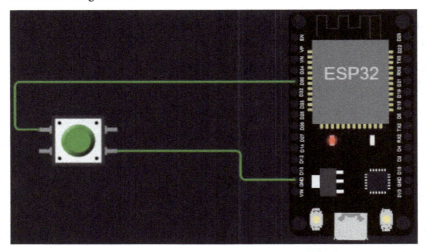

Figure 5.28 – ESP32 connected to push button

We have interfaced the push button to pin D35 using the internal pull-up configuration as we interfaced it in *Chapter 2*.

We will go to `https://webhook.site/` to get a free webhook:

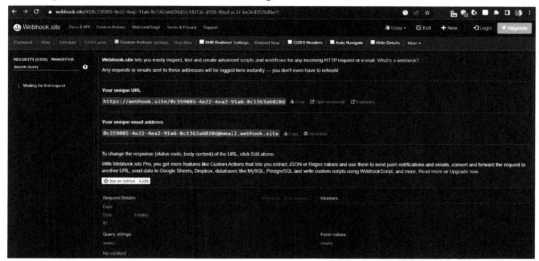

Figure 5.29 – webhook.site dashboard

We will copy our unique URL, as we will need this in our code. We will upload the following code to ESP32 using the Arduino IDE. The code is available at `https://github.com/PacktPublishing/Programming-ESP32-with-Arduino-IDE/tree/main/Chapter%205/ESP32_webhook`:

```
#include <WiFi.h>
#include <HTTPClient.h>
const char* ssid = "WiFi_SSID";
const char* password = "WiFi_Password";
const char* webhookURL = "Your_Unique_URL";
const int buttonPin = 35;
int buttonState = HIGH;
int lastButtonState = HIGH;
unsigned long lastDebounceTime = 0;
unsigned long debounceDelay = 50;

void setup() {
  Serial.begin(115200);
  pinMode(buttonPin, INPUT_PULLUP);
  digitalWrite(buttonPin, HIGH);
  WiFi.begin(ssid, password);
  while (WiFi.status() != WL_CONNECTED) {
```

```
      delay(1000);
    }
  }

void loop() {
  int reading = digitalRead(buttonPin);
  if (reading != lastButtonState) {
    lastDebounceTime = millis();
  }
  if ((millis() - lastDebounceTime) > debounceDelay) {
    if (reading != buttonState) {
      buttonState = reading;
      if (buttonState == LOW) {
        sendWebhookRequest(buttonState);
      }
    }
  }
  lastButtonState = reading;
}

void sendWebhookRequest(int switchStatus) {
  HTTPClient http;
  String url = String(webhookURL) + "?random=" + String(random(30));
  http.begin(url);
  int httpResponseCode = http.GET();
  if (httpResponseCode > 0) {
    Serial.print("Webhook request sent. Response code: ");
    Serial.println(httpResponseCode);
  } else {
    Serial.print("Error sending webhook request. HTTP response code:
");
    Serial.println(httpResponseCode);
  }
  http.end();
}
```

At the beginning of the code, the necessary libraries for Wi-Fi and HTTP communication are included. The Wi-Fi credentials, including the network's SSID and password, are set up. The webhookURL variable is used to hold the URL of the webhook endpoint, which is the address where the webhook request will be sent.

The button's pin number is defined as buttonPin, and initial values for various variables are set. The debounceDelay variable controls the time interval during which button debounce is considered.

In the setup() function, serial communication is initialized, and the pinMode variable is set for the button pin. The INPUT_PULLUP mode is used, which enables the internal pull-up resistor for the button. This ensures a stable reading when the button is not pressed.

ESP32 then tries to connect to the specified Wi-Fi network using the provided credentials. The code enters a loop until a successful Wi-Fi connection is established. During this time, the serial monitor outputs Connecting to WiFi... to provide feedback on the connection process. Once connected, the monitor displays Connected to WiFi.

Moving to the loop() function, the code continuously reads the current state of the button using the digitalRead() function. It also checks whether the button's state has changed since the last reading. If a change is detected, lastDebounceTime is updated with the current time in milliseconds.

Inside another conditional check, the code verifies whether enough time has passed to ensure the button has been debounced. If the button's state is found to be different from the last state and the debounce time has passed, buttonState is updated with the current button reading. If the button is pressed (low state), the code calls the sendWebhookRequest() function, which is responsible for initiating the webhook.

The sendWebhookRequest() function creates an HTTPClient instance and forms the URL for the webhook request, adding a random value to the URL parameters. The HTTP client then initiates a connection to the specified URL using the begin() function. A GET request is made to the webhook endpoint, and the HTTP response code is checked. If the response code is greater than 0, the serial monitor outputs Webhook request sent. Response code: followed by the actual response code. If there's an error, the monitor displays Error sending webhook request. HTTP response code: along with the response code. Finally, the HTTP client connection is closed using the end() function.

After uploading the code, when we push the button on pin D35, we will be able to see the alerts in the webhook.site user interface, as shown in the following figure:

Figure 5.30 – Webhook received at webhook.site

We can see the random numbers in the user interface. Webhooks are a useful addition to IoT projects, and we will make use of them in the following chapters for real applications.

In the next section, we will discuss a real-life analogy that could explain HTTP, MQTT, and webhooks altogether.

A real-life analogy of HTTP, MQTT, and webhooks

Imagine you're hosting a big party at your house. The party invitations are like HTTP requests. You send out invitations (requests) to your friends, telling them about the party details and asking them to reply. When your friends arrive at the party, they bring gifts (data) and hand them over to you, just like how a web server receives and processes HTTP requests.

Now, let's add webhooks to the mix. Think of webhooks as a special guest list you have. You've asked your friends to not only come to the party but also let you know when they're on their way so that you can be prepared. With webhooks, your friends send you messages whenever they're leaving their homes (events happening in their systems). This way, you can get ready to welcome them and ensure everything is in place when they arrive.

Lastly, imagine your party has a live band that plays music for everyone to enjoy. This band represents MQTT. Instead of you telling each guest when to dance, the band plays music that everyone can dance to. Similarly, MQTT is like a constant stream of music that devices listen to. If any device wants to dance (share information), it just needs to join the rhythm by subscribing to the band's music (subscribing to MQTT topics). This way, devices can communicate without needing to send individual messages, just like how everyone at the party can dance to the same music without needing personal instructions.

This analogy could be very useful for understanding these protocols; in the next section, we will compare all these protocols so that we can differentiate them better and select the best one according to our needs.

Comparing HTTP, webhooks, and MQTT

The following table compares the HTTP, webhooks, and MQTT protocols in terms of use case, communication style, protocol type, security, and scalability:

Aspect	HTTP	Webhooks	MQTT
Communication Style	Request-Response	Event-Driven	Pub-sub
Use Case	Data Retrieval, Information Exchange	Real-Time Notifications, Automation	Real-time data exchange, iot
Protocol Type	Stateless	Stateless	Stateful
Payload Type	Typically, JSON or XML	Custom Data	Custom Data
Security	Encrypted over SSL/TLS	Limited Security	Encrypted over TLS
Scalability	Suitable for Limited, Concurrent Requests	Can Handle Large Number of Requests	Highly Scalable

Connection	Request-Response	External Event	Persistent
Data Flow	One-way	One-way	Two-way
Error Handling	HTTP Status Codes	Manual Handling	MQTT Acknowledgments
Examples	Browser Requests, API Calls, Web Apps	Notifications from Third-Party Apps	IoT Device Communication

Table 5.1 – Comparison of HTTP, webhooks, and MQTT protocols

The preceding table gives us a good idea of all the protocols discussed in this chapter. While all these protocols are used in IoT development, they have different use cases and communication styles. The HTTP protocol works on a request-response model and is a web-browsing protocol. Webhooks are event-driven and are mostly used for notifications, and MQTT is based on a pub-sub model and is used for real-time data transfer.

Summary

In this chapter, we explored different data-based protocols for IoT applications. We first explored the HTTP protocol and learned how we could use HTTP with ESP32 to communicate with web servers and use ESP32 as a web server or HTTP client.

Continuing our exploration, we learned about the MQTT protocol, highlighting its real-time capabilities through the pub/sub model. By learning how to implement MQTT clients on ESP32, we acquired the ability to build dynamic and responsive IoT applications. Additionally, we harnessed the power of webhooks, using them to trigger actions based on events, thereby enhancing interactivity and connectivity with external services. This chapter equipped us with the expertise to choose the right protocol for specific project requirements.

In the next chapters, we'll use all the resources we have learned about in this chapter and previous chapters to work on some real-life practical projects using ESP32.

Part 3 – Practical Implementation

Now that you've grasped the fundamentals of ESP32, interfacing with sensors and displays, and explored data and network-oriented IoT protocols, it's time to apply this knowledge in practical, full-scale projects.

This part has the following chapters:

- *Chapter 6, Project 1 – Smart Plant Monitoring System Using ESP32, Messaging Services, and the Twitter API*
- *Chapter 7, Project 2 – Rent Out Your Parking Space*
- *Chapter 8, Project 3 – Logging, Monitoring, and Controlling Using ESP32*
- *Chapter 9, From Arduino IDE to Advanced IoT Development – Taking the Next Steps*

6

Project 1 – Smart Plant Monitoring System Using ESP32, Messaging Services, and the Twitter API

In this chapter, we will use all the knowledge we gained in the previous chapters and complete an innovative project where we'll integrate various sensors with a plant to create a smart and interconnected ecosystem.

Our project revolves around the concept of enhancing plant care and communication. We will dive into the details of interfacing sensors with an ESP32 microcontroller, enabling the plant to gather and process data about its environment. The data will be sent to the owner of the plant, which will set the foundation for informed decision-making.

What sets this project apart is its extensive use of messaging services and APIs to establish communication channels between the plant and the digital world. We will explore how the plant can send real-time updates via Gmail, WhatsApp, and Telegram, ensuring that you are always in the know of your plant's wellbeing, no matter where you are.

Furthermore, we'll harness the power of the Twitter API to enable our plant to communicate with the global community. The plant will autonomously tweet its updates, sharing its growth, health, and experiences with the world, thereby becoming a part of the vibrant online ecosystem.

In this chapter, we will cover the following topics:

- Interfacing sensors with ESP32

- Sending emails using SMTP

- Sending WhatsApp and Telegram messages using the Messaging Services API

- Writing tweets

Throughout this chapter, we will provide comprehensive step-by-step instructions, practical examples, and hands-on guidance to help you create a smart plant monitoring system. By the end of this journey, you will not only have a flourishing plant but also a deeper understanding of IoT, messaging services, and the integration of APIs, making you a proficient developer in the realm of IoT and smart systems.

Technical requirements

For this chapter, we will need the following hardware and software components:

- ESP32 dev kit

- Capacitive soil moisture sensor

- DHT22 temperature and humidity sensor

- Google account

- The CallMeBot API

- The Twitter API

- WhatsApp and Telegram accounts

All the code files used in this chapter will be available at `https://github.com/PacktPublishing/Programming-ESP32-with-Arduino-IDE/tree/main/Chapter6`

First, let's interface the sensors that will help us gather some useful data from our plant.

Interfacing sensors with ESP32

In our first topic, we'll dive into the foundational step of our project: connecting and interfacing two crucial sensors with the ESP32 microcontroller. These sensors – the moisture sensor and the DHT22 temperature and humidity sensor– play pivotal roles in providing essential data for our smart plant monitoring system. The moisture sensor allows us to monitor soil moisture levels, ensuring our plant receives the optimal amount of hydration, while the DHT22 sensor provides valuable insights into the surrounding environment, including humidity and temperature data. This initial phase sets the stage for our project's success by establishing the means to gather critical information about the plant's well-being and its immediate surroundings. We'll explore the wiring, configuration, and data retrieval from these sensors, laying a strong foundation for the interconnected ecosystem we aim to create for our smart plant.

In this section, we will learn how to connect these sensors with ESP32 and read the data from these sensors. Let's start by connecting them to ESP32.

Connecting the sensors

In the previous chapters, we interfaced the DHT22 sensor with ESP32, which helps us to read environmental data such as temperature and humidity. We will also be adding the moisture sensor. When choosing the moisture sensors, there were two options: *capacitive* and *resistive*. We chose to use capacitive moisture sensors, which operate on the principle of capacitance. This is the ability of two conductive materials separated by a non-conductive material (dielectric) to store electrical charge. In the context of a capacitive moisture sensor, the sensor's probes or electrodes act as the conductive plates, and the soil or medium being measured acts as the dielectric. When the sensor is inserted into the soil, the moisture content in the soil affects its dielectric properties. Dry soil has a low dielectric constant, while moist soil has a higher dielectric constant. As the moisture level changes, the capacitance between the sensor's electrodes also changes. The sensor measures this change in capacitance, which is then correlated to the soil's moisture content. By monitoring the capacitance variations, the sensor provides an accurate and real-time indication of soil moisture levels, making it a valuable tool for applications such as plant monitoring and irrigation control.

The following figure provides a visual guide, specifying the pins and their corresponding functions:

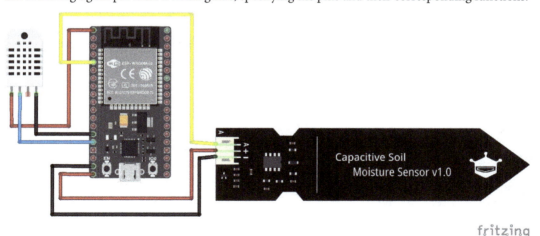

Figure 6.1 – ESP32 connection diagram with moisture and DHT22 sensors

Let's summarize the connection.

DHT22 has four pins; VCC is connected to 3.3V, though you could connect it to the Vin pin of ESP32. The SDA of DHT22 is connected to the D13 pin of ESP32, and the GND of DHT22 is connected to the GND of ESP32. There is one more pin in DHT22 labeled as NC that will not be connected to any pin. The DHT22 sensor uses the single-wire serial communication protocol in which only one data line is applied for data exchange and data control in the system (SDA).

The capacitive soil moisture sensor has three pins. VCC is connected to the Vin pin of ESP32, GND is connected to the GND of ESP32, and AOUT is the analog output pin that we connected to the D34 pin of ESP32.

After making the connection, you will have to place the soil moisture sensor inside the soil of the plant, as shown in the following figure:

Figure 6.2 – How to place the moisture sensor

After making the connections, we must write the code to read the environmental values of the plant.

Reading the sensor data

Let's open the Arduino IDE and upload the following code to the ESP32 microcontroller. This code will help us read the sensor data and print it on the serial monitor. The code can be found on GitHub at https://github.com/PacktPublishing/Programming-ESP32-with-Arduino-IDE/tree/main/Chapter%206/Read_sensors:

```
#include <DHT.h>
//Sensors interfacing & parameters
#define DHTPIN 13          // DHT22 data pin
#define DHTTYPE DHT22      // DHT22 sensor model
#define MoistureSensor 34  // Moisture pin
DHT dht(DHTPIN, DHTTYPE);
int moisturePin = MoistureSensor;
int moistureThresholds[] = {300, 700};  // Adjust these thresholds for
```

```
your setup
int tempThreshold = 30;
int humidityThreshold = 40;
...
...

...
String getMoistureStatus(int value) {
  if (value < moistureThresholds[0]) {
    return "Dry";
  } else if (value >= moistureThresholds[0] && value <=
moistureThresholds[1]) {
    return "Ok";
  } else {
    return "Wet";
  }
}
```

This program continuously reads sensor data and generates messages about the plant's condition, particularly its moisture status. Let's break down the code step by step:

- Library and sensor definitions:

  - The code includes the DHT library for the DHT22 sensor

  - It defines the DHT22 data pin as DHTPIN (pin 13) and specifies the sensor model as DHT22

  - It also defines the moisture sensor pin as MoistureSensor (pin 34)

  - The thresholds for moisture levels are set in moistureThresholds, the temperature threshold is set as tempThreshold, and the humidity threshold is set as humidityThreshold

- The setup() function:

  - The setup() function initializes the serial communication for debugging and starts the DHT22 sensor

- The loop() function:

  - In the loop() function, sensor readings are continuously taken at regular intervals

- Sensor readings:

  - The readTemperature and readHumidity functions read the temperature and humidity values from the DHT22 sensor

  - The readMoisture function reads the moisture value from the moisture sensor

- The `PlantMessages` function:

    - The `PlantMessages` function generates a message based on the sensor readings and thresholds

    - It also checks if the temperature is above the threshold and if the humidity is below the threshold, appending messages accordingly

    - Finally, it compiles all the messages into a summary message, including moisture status, values, and environmental conditions, and returns it

- The `getMoistureStatus` function:

    - The `getMoistureStatus` function determines the moisture status (*Dry*, *Ok*, or *Wet*) based on the moisture value and predefined thresholds

- Serial output:

    - The summary message generated in the `PlantMessages` function is printed to the Serial Monitor

- Delay:

    - The code includes a delay of 20 seconds (`delay(20000)`) to control the rate at which sensor readings and messages are generated

This code essentially monitors the plant's vital parameters, checks if the soil is dry, and provides messages regarding the plant's condition, helping users decide when to water the plant based on temperature, humidity, and soil moisture.

Now, we will upload the preceding code to ESP32 using the Arduino IDE and open the serial monitor. Depending on the plant's environment status, we will receive messages such as those as shown in the following figure:

```
Moisture Status is Dry. I need Water Now.
The weather is hot, which causes the soil to dry out more quickly. I will need
water more frequently.
Low Moisture Level, Water evaporates quickly. I will need water Frequently.
Summary of Data:
 Moisture Status : Dry
 Moisture Value : 0
 Temperature : 42.10
 Humidity : 18.00
Moisture Status is Dry. I need Water Now.
The weather is hot, which causes the soil to dry out more quickly. I will need
water more frequently.
Low Moisture Level, Water evaporates quickly. I will need water Frequently.
Summary of Data:
 Moisture Status : Dry
 Moisture Value : 0
 Temperature : 42.10
 Humidity : 18.00
```

Figure 6.3 – Sensor data on the serial monitor

This figure shows that the sensors have been interfaced successfully, and we can see the relevant messages on the serial monitor. In the next section, we will send these messages to the email address.

Sending emails using SMTP

Simple Mail Transfer Protocol (**SMTP**) is a fundamental communication protocol that's used for sending electronic mail (email) messages over the internet. It operates as a set of rules and conventions that enable email clients or servers to transmit messages to their intended recipients. SMTP governs the process of routing, relaying, and delivering emails, making it a core component of email communication worldwide. Its simplicity and efficiency make it a widely adopted protocol for ensuring the reliable exchange of electronic messages across diverse email platforms and services.

In this section, we'll dive into the integration of SMTP within our ESP32-powered smart plant monitoring system. Email communication proves to be an invaluable tool in keeping plant enthusiasts informed about the well-being of their green companions. By harnessing the power of SMTP, our system can send email notifications and updates directly to the user's inbox. Whether it's alerting you about dry soil conditions or extreme temperatures, or simply sharing routine plant health reports, SMTP enables seamless communication between your ESP32 device and your preferred email service.

To enable email sending through ESP32, we'll need to configure our Gmail account to grant access to the ESP32 application by setting up the necessary authentication credentials.

Setting up a Gmail account to send emails using ESP32

Follow these steps to configure our Gmail account for sending emails:

1. First, go to `https://myaccount.google.com/u/1/`.

2. Click on the **Security** tab.

3. Under **How you sign into Google**, click on **2-Step Verification**:

How you sign in to Google

Make sure you can always access your Google Account by keeping this information up to date

🛡 2-Step Verification	2-Step Verification is off	›
👥 Passkeys	Start using passkeys	›
⦂⦂⦂ Password	Last changed Aug 20, 2022	›

Figure 6.4 – Setting up 2-Step Verification in our Google account

4. Follow the required steps to enable 2-step verification. It will probably ask you to enter your phone number.

5. Once 2-step verification has been enabled, search for app password and select it from the search results:

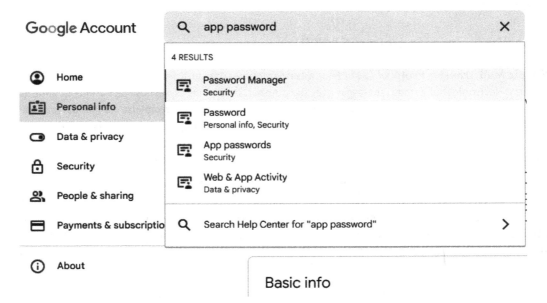

Figure 6.5 – Setting up an app password for ESP32

6.   In the **App passwords** area, select the other (custom name) and write the name of the device
     – for example, ESP32:

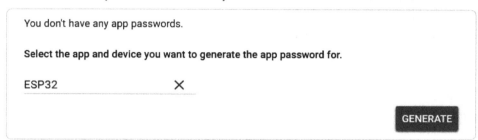

Figure 6.6 – Setting up app passwords

7.   Then, click on **GENERATE**; the password for your device will be generated, as shown here:

Generated app password

Your app password for your device

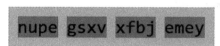

How to use it

Go to the settings for your Google Account in
the application or device you are trying to set
up. Replace your password with the 16-
character password shown above.
Just like your normal password, this app
password grants complete access to your
Google Account. You won't need to remember
it, so don't write it down or share it with
anyone.

DONE

Figure 6.7 – App password for ESP32

8.   Copy the app password for your device; we will use this in our code.

Now that we have configured the password for ESP32 to send emails, we will move on to the next step
and write the code for sending the messages.

Writing code for sending emails using ESP32

We will upload the following code to ESPP32 using the Arduino IDE. This code will help us send emails using our Gmail account. The code can be found on GitHub at `https://github.com/PacktPublishing/Programming-ESP32-with-Arduino-IDE/tree/main/Chapter%206/Send_Email`:

```
#include <DHT.h>
#include <WiFi.h>
#include <ESP_Mail_Client.h>

//Sensors interfacing & parameters

//WiFi Credentitals
#define WIFI_SSID "Your WIFI SSID"
#define WIFI_PASSWORD "WIFI PASSWORD"

//Email Credentials
…
…
…
  Serial.println(msg);
  sendEmail(msg);
  delay(10000);
}
//readTemperature function
//readHumidity() function
//readMoisture() function
//PlantMessages function
//getMoistureStatus function
```

Here's an explanation of the code:

- The following libraries are included:

  - DHT.h: This library is used to interface with the DHT22 temperature and humidity sensor

  - WiFi.h: This library provides the functions needed to connect ESP32 to a Wi-Fi network

  - ESP_Mail_Client.h: This library enables ESP32 to send emails using the SMTP protocol

- Sensor and parameter definitions:

  - The code defines some parameters related to sensors and Wi-Fi credentials. Use the sensor and parameters variables from the previous code (which we used in the *Reading the sensor data* section); we also defined `WIFI_SSID`, `WIFI_PASSWORD`, `SMTP_server`, `SMTP_Port`, `sender_email`, `sender_password`, `Recipient_email`, and `Recipient_name`. These parameters are used to configure the Wi-Fi connection and the email-sending process.

- Wi-Fi connection:

  - `connectWiFi()`: This function is responsible for connecting the ESP32 microcontroller to the Wi-Fi network specified by `WIFI_SSID` and `WIFI_PASSWORD`. It continuously attempts to connect to Wi-Fi and prints status messages until a successful connection is established.

- Sending emails:

  - `sendEmail(const String& messageText)`: This function is used to send an email. It sets up an SMTP session with the SMTP server, configures the email message (sender, recipient, subject, and content), and then sends the email. If the email is sent successfully, it prints a message. If there's an error, it prints the error reason.

- The `setup()` function:

  - `setup()`: In the `setup()` function, ESP32 initializes serial communication, connects to Wi-Fi using `connectWiFi()` and initializes the DHT sensor (temperature and humidity sensor) with `dht.begin()`.

- The `loop()` function:

  - `loop()`: The main `loop()` function continuously reads temperature, humidity, and soil moisture values, creates a message using the `PlantMessages` function, prints the message to the serial monitor, and sends the message as an email using the `sendEmail` function. It then waits for 10 seconds before repeating the process.

Important note

The code references functions such as `readTemperature()`, `readHumidity()`, `readMoisture()`, `PlantMessages`, and `getMoistureStatus`. You could place these functions from the previous code. Also, copy the sensor and parameters definition from the previous code.

This code provides a basic framework for monitoring environmental conditions and sending email notifications using an ESP32 microcontroller. To use it, you will need to customize credentials so that they match your specific setup.

After uploading the code, the following results will be sent to the email you provided:

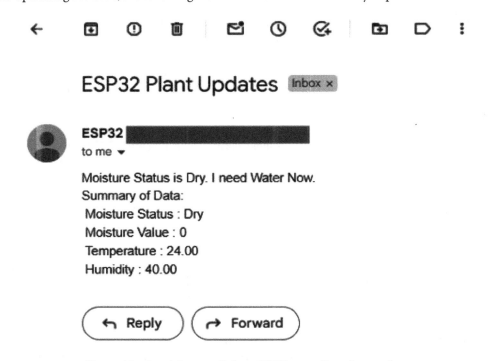

Figure 6.8 – Receiving emails from ESP32 regarding plant updates

In this section, we learned how to send an email using ESP32 using SMTP. In the next section, we will move forward and use the CallMeBot API to send WhatsApp and Telegram messages.

Using the CallMeBot API to send WhatsApp and Telegram messages

The CallMeBot API is a powerful tool that enables users to seamlessly send WhatsApp and Telegram messages programmatically. This versatile API simplifies the process of integrating messaging services into applications, making it accessible for a wide range of purposes. Whether it's sending automated notifications, alerts, or personalized messages, developers can harness the capabilities of CallMeBot to enhance user engagement and communication. By leveraging this API, businesses and individuals can create innovative solutions that connect with their target audience via WhatsApp and Telegram, enriching their digital interactions and streamlining communication channels. With the CallMeBot API, messaging integration has never been easier, providing a versatile platform for modern messaging needs.

In this section, we will add more functions to our project that will enable us to send WhatsApp and Telegram messages. We will start with the WhatsApp messages.

Setting up WhatsApp messages

To send WhatsApp messages using the CallMeBot API, follow these steps to set up the environment:

1. First, we will have to add +34 644 51 95 23 as a phone number to our phone contacts:

Figure 6.9 – Saving the CallMeBot API's WhatsApp number

2. Then, send a message stating `I allow CallMeBot to send me messages` to the new contact that we created using WhatsApp:

Figure 6.10 – Giving permission to CallMeBot

3. Wait until you receive a message stating `API Activated for your phone number. Your APIKEY is XXXXXX` from the bot:

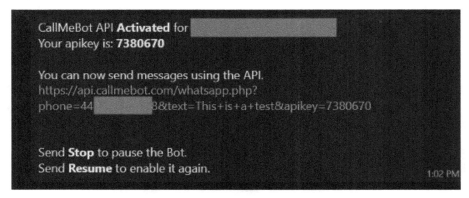

Figure 6.11 – Receiving the API key for WhatsApp from CallMeBot

4.   Now, paste the link provided into your browser:

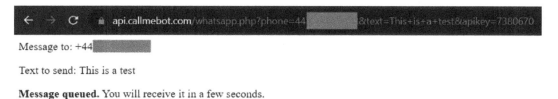

Message to: +44▮▮▮▮▮▮

Text to send: This is a test

Message queued. You will receive it in a few seconds.

Figure 6.12 – Testing the API using a browser

5.   You will receive a WhatsApp message:

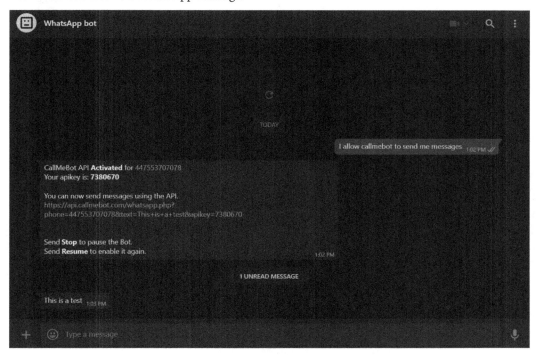

Figure 6.13 – Receiving a test message from the CallMeBot API on WhatsApp

As you can see, we have received a message on our WhatsApp account. In the following section, we will set up the environment for receiving Telegram messages, followed by the ESP32 code for both.

Setting up Telegram messages

Now, we will set up the CallMeBot API to send Telegram messages. Follow these steps:

1. Paste `https://api.CallMeBot.com/text.php?user=@myusername&text=This+is+a+test+from+CallMeBot` into your browser (replace the username with your own):

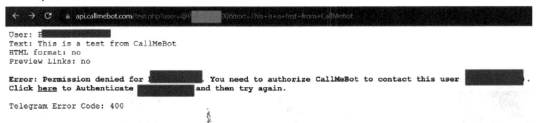

Figure 6.14 – Setting up the CallMeBot Telegram API

2. If you get a permission denied error, click **here** to authenticate; an authentication page will open:

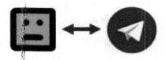

Telegram Authentication

Hello, Login using the button below to allow CallMeBot API to send you messages

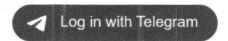

By signing up, you are indicating that you have read and agree to the Terms of Use and Privacy Policy.

Figure 6.15 – Telegram Authentication

3. Click on **Log in with Telegram**; you will receive a request via Telegram:

A, we received a request to log in on
api2.callmebot.com with your Telegram account.

To authorize this request, use the **'Confirm'** button
below.

Browser: Chrome 116 on Windows
IP: 2a02:2455:179f:5200:1ddc:31ab:0c5f:3117
(Ismaning, Germany)

If you didn't request this, use the 'Decline' button
or ignore this message.   1:55 pm

| Decline | Confirm |

Figure 6.16 – Authentication request on Telegram

4. Click **Confirm**. Now, if you paste the aforementioned URL again, you will see the following page:

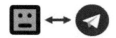

Telegram Authentication

You are currently logged in CallMeBot as A
(@Photon67000)

You can now send Text Messages to
@Photon67000 using the API URL below:
**http://api.callmebot.com/text.php?
user=Photon67000&text=This+is+a+test+from+CallMeBot**

Send a Test Message

By signing up, you are indicating that you have read and
agree to the Terms of Use and Privacy Policy.

Log out"

Figure 6.17 – Authentication successful – Send a Test Message

5.   Click on **Send a Test Message**; you will receive the following message in Telegram:

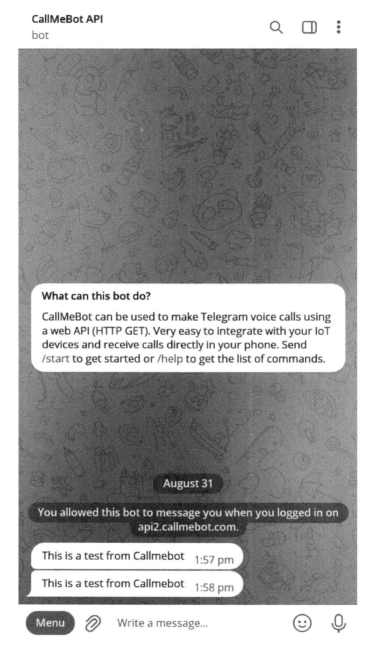

Figure 6.18 – Message received via Telegram

With that, we have received the test messages for both Telegram and WhatsApp by using a web browser. In the next section, we will update our previous code so that it will send messages on both platforms using ESP32.

The ESP32 code to send messages on WhatsApp and Telegram

In this section, we'll write some code to send Telegram and WhatsApp messages from the ESP32 microcontroller. We will upload the following code to ESP32. The code can be found on GitHub at https://github.com/PacktPublishing/Programming-ESP32-with-Arduino-IDE/tree/main/Chapter%206/Whatsapp_Telegram:

```
#include <DHT.h>
#include <WiFi.h>
#include <ESP_Mail_Client.h>
#include <HTTPClient.h>
#include <UrlEncode.h>
//Sensors interfacing & parameters
//WiFi Credentitals
...
...
...
  if (httpResponseCode == 200) {
    Serial.println("Telegram message sent successfully!");
  } else {
    Serial.print("Error sending Telegram message. HTTP code: ");
    Serial.println(httpResponseCode);
  }
  http.end();
}
```

Let's break down the code step by step:

- The sendWhatsAppMessage function is as follows:

  - This function sends a WhatsApp message using an external API

  - Input: Message content

  - It constructs an API URL, makes an HTTP request, and checks the response code

  - It prints success or error messages accordingly

- The `sendTelegramMessage` function is as follows:

  - It sends a Telegram message using an external API

  - Input: Message content

  - It constructs an API URL, makes an HTTP request, and checks the response code

  - It prints success or error messages accordingly

These functions enable automated messaging through WhatsApp and Telegram, utilizing external APIs. You need to replace placeholders with your authentication details and customize message content as needed for your application. Also, we will have to call these functions in the `loop()` function to allow them to send messages.

Now, we will upload the code to ESP32 and receive the messages via WhatsApp:

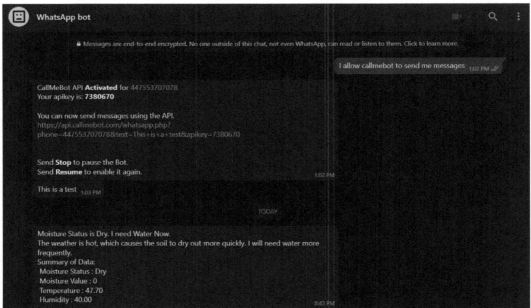

Figure 6.19 – Plant updates message on WhatsApp

Let's do the same for Telegram:

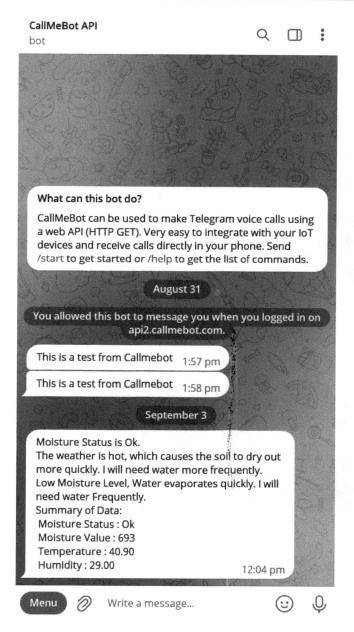

Figure 6.20 – Plant update message on Telegram

With that, we have learned how to send messages to Telegram and WhatsApp using ESP32. In the next section, we will use and set up the Twitter API to send tweet messages.

Publishing update tweets on Twitter

Using the Twitter API and ESP32, you can easily post tweets, providing a quick and efficient way to share updates and information on Twitter. In this section, we will set up the Twitter API so that we can publish the tweets from ESP32.

Setting up the Twitter API

Firstly, we will set up the Twitter API:

1. To publish the tweets on Twitter (now known as X), we will have to create an account. I have already created an account called `@plantNeedWater`:

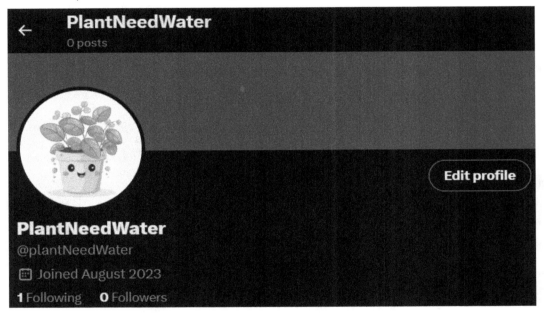

Figure 6.21 – Twitter @PlantNeedWater account

2. After making an account, sign up for a developer account at `https://developer.twitter.com/en`.

3. Select the **Free** account and click on **Get started**:

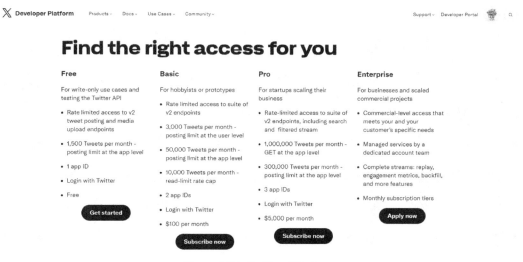

Figure 6.22 – Twitter API plans

4. Click on **Sign up for Free Account** and then accept the agreement and policy:

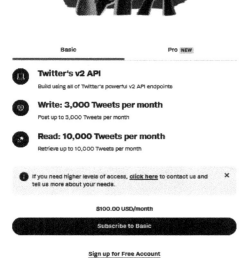

Figure 6.23 – Sign up for Free Account

5. Now, you will have to describe your use case of Twitter's data and API. You could explain the project you are doing and, depending on your case, explain it in 250 characters:

Developer agreement & policy

Describe all of your use cases of Twitter's data and API:

We need this information for data protection. Learn more

⚠ Required

☑ You understand that you may not resell anything you receive via the Twitter APIs

☑ You understand your Developer account may be terminated if you violate the Developer Agreement or any of the incorporated Developer Terms

☑ You accept the Terms & Conditions

By clicking on the box, and by otherwise accessing or using any Licensed Material, you indicate that you have read and agree to this Developer Agreement and the Twitter Developer Policy

Back   Submit

Figure 6.24 – Developer agreement & policy

6. A developer portal like this will open. Click on **Projects & Apps**:

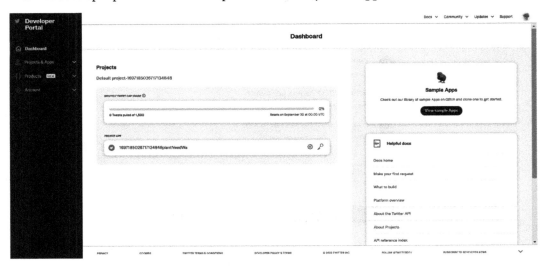

Figure 6.25 – Twitter developer portal

7.   Click on the application ID; it will open this portal. Then, click on **Set up** under **User authentication settings**, as shown in *Figure 6.26*.

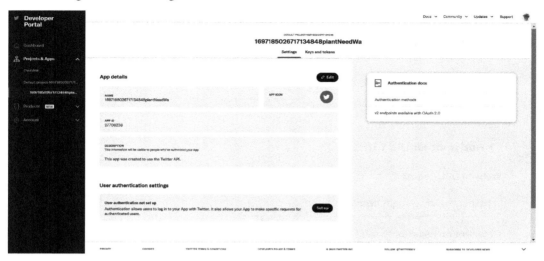

Figure 6.26 – Twitter project and apps

8.   Specify **Read and write** under **App permissions**:

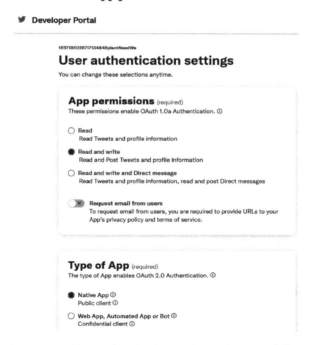

Figure 6.27 – User authentication settings – App permissions

9.   For **Website URL**, enter your website URL or `https://www.google.com`; write the same for **Callback URI / Redirect URL**. The other fields are optional. Then, click **Save**:

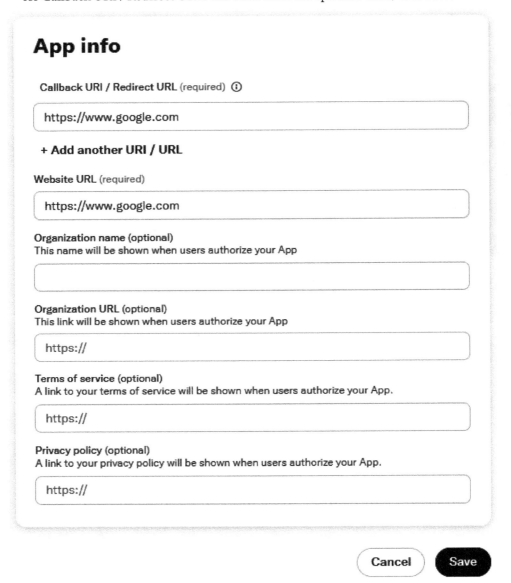

Figure 6.28 – User authentication settings – App info

10. Now, click on **Regenerate** under **Consumer Keys**; then, under **Authentication Tokens**, click **Generate**. This will generate access tokens and secret keys:

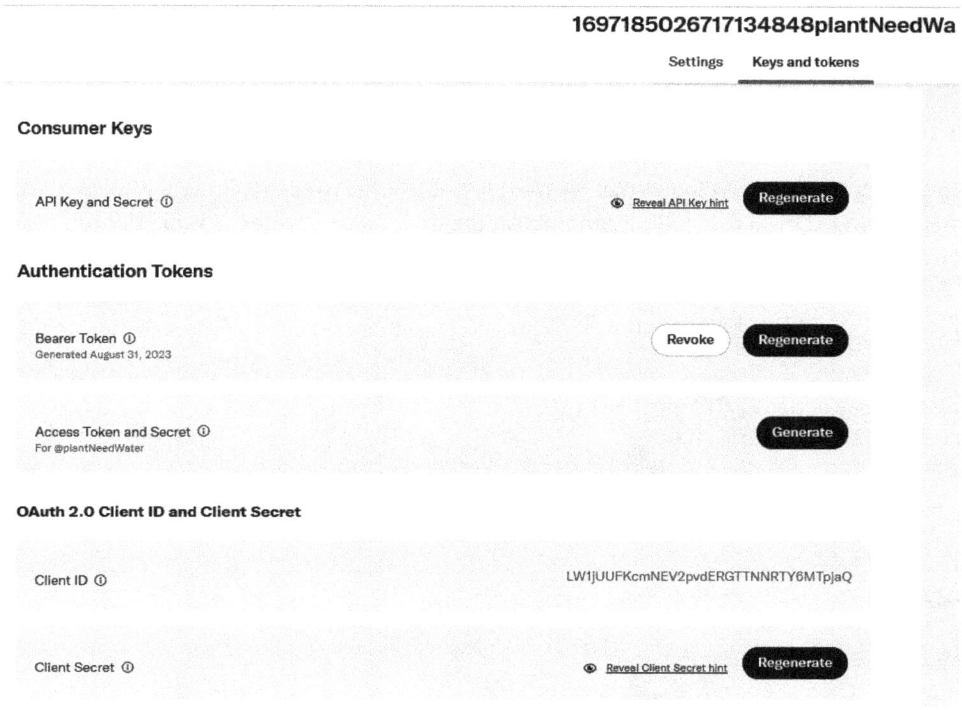

1697185026717134848plantNeedWa

Settings   **Keys and tokens**

Consumer Keys

API Key and Secret ⓘ   👁 Reveal API Key hint   Regenerate

Authentication Tokens

Bearer Token ⓘ
Generated August 31, 2023   Revoke   Regenerate

Access Token and Secret ⓘ
For @plantNeedWater   Generate

OAuth 2.0 Client ID and Client Secret

Client ID ⓘ   LW1jUUFKcmNEV2pvdERGTTNNRTY6MTpjaQ

Client Secret ⓘ   👁 Reveal Client Secret hint   Regenerate

Figure 6.29 – Generating leys

11. Copy the generated consumer keys and secrets and access tokens and secrets:

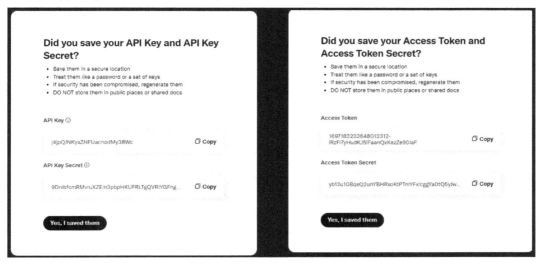

Figure 6.30 – Keys generated

Now that we have created the API keys, we will move on to the next part, in which we will write code for publishing the tweets.

Code for publishing the plant updates on X/Twitter

We have already set up the API keys that we need to publish the tweet. Now, we will write the code using the Arduino IDE so that ESP32 can publish the updates on Twitter as well. The code can be found on GitHub at https://github.com/PacktPublishing/Programming-ESP32-with-Arduino-IDE/tree/main/Chapter%206/twitter:

```
#include <DHT.h>
#include <WiFi.h>
#include <ESP_Mail_Client.h>
#include <HTTPClient.h>
#include <UrlEncode.h>
#include <WiFiClientSecure.h>
#include "time.h"
#include <TweESP32.h>
#include <TwitterServerCert.h>
#include <UrlEncode.h>
#include <ArduinoJson.h>
//Sensors interfacing & parameters
...

...

...

//send Tweet
void sendTweet(const char* tweetText) {
    twitter.timeConfig();
    client.setCACert(twitter_server_cert);
    bool success = twitter.sendTweet(const_cast<char*>(tweetText));
    if (success) {
        Serial.println("Tweet Sent");
    }
}
```

Let's break down the newly added sendTweet function:

- void sendTweet(const char* tweetText): This function is defined with the name sendTweet. It takes one parameter, const char* tweetText, which is a pointer to a constant character array. This parameter represents the text of the tweet that you want to send. The function does not return any value (void).

- `twitter.timeConfig();`: This line appears to be a call to a function or method named `timeConfig` of an object or library named `twitter`. It is related to configuring time settings, for authentication or timestamping purposes when interacting with the Twitter API.

- `client.setCACert(twitter_server_cert);`: This line sets the **Certificate Authority (CA)** certificate for a client object named `client`. In secure communication, especially when dealing with APIs over HTTPS, a CA certificate is used to verify the authenticity of the server's certificate. `twitter_server_cert` is likely a variable that holds the CA certificate required to establish a secure connection with the Twitter API server.

- `bool success = twitter.sendTweet(const_cast<char*>(tweetText));`: This line calls the `sendTweet` function of the `twitter` object or library, passing in `tweetText` as its argument. However, there's a type conversion happening here. The function returns a Boolean value (`bool`) indicating whether the tweet was sent successfully, and this value is stored in the `success` variable.

- `if (success) { Serial.println("Tweet Sent"); }`: This conditional statement checks the value of the `success` variable. If the value is `true`, it means that the tweet was sent successfully, and as a result, it prints `"Tweet Sent"` to the serial monitor as a confirmation message.

We must make sure that the credentials in the code are updated. Also, it is necessary to install the TweESP32 library. You can download that by downloading it as a ZIP file from `https://github.com/witnessmenow/TweESP32`. Then, you can go to the library manager in the Arduino IDE and click on **Add .zip library** to upload the library from the ZIP file. Make sure you install the other libraries in the code.

Important note

Change all the credentials for sending and receiving the messages, such as Telegram username, WhatsApp number, WhatsApp API key, sender email, sender email password, receiving email, recipient name, and Twitter API keys and secrets so that you can use them with your accounts.

After uploading the code, you will be able to see the tweet on your account:

Figure 6.31 – Plant updates tweet published

Not only the tweet, but the final code will also publish the messages on WhatsApp, Telegram, and email, as can be seen in *Figure 6.32*. The final code can be found on GitHub at `https://github.com/PacktPublishing/Programming-ESP32-with-Arduino-IDE/tree/main/Chapter%206/Final_code`:

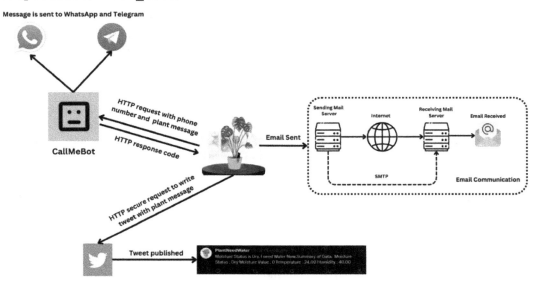

Figure 6.32 – Complete project overview

In essence, the project involves utilizing SMTP to dispatch emails through a Gmail account, as illustrated in the preceding figure. ESP32 interfaces with the CallMeBot API through HTTP requests, facilitating the transmission of messages to both WhatsApp and Telegram. Additionally, the project incorporates the configuration of a Twitter developer account, which furnishes secure credentials for composing tweets via requests.

Summary

In this chapter, we embarked on a comprehensive exploration of IoT applications, focusing on the vital task of environmental monitoring. We began by delving into the intricacies of reading moisture levels, as well as tracking temperature and humidity data. These critical measurements provide us with invaluable insights into our surroundings, enabling us to make informed decisions and take appropriate actions.

Building upon this foundation, we explored the power of email communication by employing SMTP. This allowed us to send messages and alerts directly to email recipients, providing a reliable means of information dissemination and communication.

Furthermore, we dived into the exciting realm of communication and automation. Leveraging the CallMeBot API, we honed our skills in sending specific messages through popular messaging platforms such as WhatsApp and Telegram.

In addition to real-time messaging, we dived into the world of social media and harnessed the Twitter API to publish tweets. This not only enabled us to share data and updates with a broader audience but also added an element of public engagement to our IoT projects.

Collectively, this chapter has equipped us with a diverse set of tools and skills for monitoring environmental conditions and orchestrating meaningful responses. Whether it's moisture levels, temperature, humidity, or instant messaging through WhatsApp, Telegram, email, or Twitter, we are now well prepared to design and implement IoT applications that are both informative and interactive.

In the next chapter, we will do another exciting IoT project using ESP32 in which we will learn how to integrate the payment option in our IoT projects.

7

Project 2 – Rent Out Your Parking Space

In this chapter, we will complete another exciting project that explores the intersection of technology, convenience, and practicality. Our mission is to create a prototype to rent out your parking space, with the help of an ESP32 microcontroller and the versatile PayPal API.

The concept of renting out your parking space might seem simple, but it's a brilliant example of how IoT and APIs can be harnessed to streamline everyday tasks and even generate income. This project not only serves as a prototype but also lays the foundation for a real-world application that can benefit both parking space owners and those in need of parking.

In this chapter, we will dive into the details of interfacing the ESP32 with the parking space, setting up a payment system using the PayPal API, and creating a seamless user experience for potential renters. We will explore the technical aspects of monitoring parking availability, accepting payments, and providing access control to the rented parking space.

However, the real beauty of this project lies in its potential for real-world application. As we conclude this chapter, we will discuss how this prototype can be extended to a fully functional service. Imagine a future where your vacant parking space generates income while helping others find convenient and secure parking. It's a win-win scenario that embodies the essence of IoT and the power of APIs in shaping our daily lives.

In this chapter, we will cover and perform the following applications:

- Interfacing sensors with ESP32
- Integrating the PayPal API
- Creating a user-friendly experience for potential renters
- Real-world implementation and project limitations
- Security concepts in IoT

Just like in the previous chapters, we will provide comprehensive step-by-step instructions, practical examples, and hands-on guidance to help you build your own parking space rental system. By the end of this chapter, you will not only have a working prototype but also the knowledge and skills to potentially launch a profitable parking space rental service. This chapter brings us one step closer to becoming proficient developers in the world of IoT and smart systems, making our daily lives smarter and more connected. Let's dive in and discuss the technical requirements for this project.

Technical requirements

For this project, we will need the following:

- An ESP32 Dev kit board
- A Servo motor
- An ultrasonic sensor
- A push button
- An RGB LED
- An SSD1306 OLED
- A PayPal account

Interfacing sensors with ESP32

In this section, we will dive into the hardware of our parking space rental project. Here, we will explore the integration of a diverse array of sensors and actuators with the ESP32 microcontroller, enabling us to enhance the functionality and user experience of our prototype.

Our project relies on the seamless coordination of various components to monitor parking space availability, handle secure payments through the PayPal API, and ensure a user-friendly experience. To achieve this, we will connect the ESP32 with essential components, including an ultrasonic sensor, an SSD1306 OLED I2C display, a Servo motor, an RGB LED, and a push button.

The ultrasonic sensor enables precise measurement of distances, a crucial aspect of monitoring parking spaces. The SSD1306 OLED I2C display provides visual feedback to users, displaying relevant information about parking availability and transactions. The Servo motor gives us the ability to control physical barriers, allowing for secure access to rented parking spaces. The RGB LED serves as a visual indicator, guiding users through the parking process. Finally, the push button offers a convenient way for users to interact with the system.

Throughout this section, we will explore how to connect and configure each of these sensors and actuators with the ESP32. We will provide you with detailed, step-by-step instructions and hands-on guidance, ensuring that you not only grasp the technicalities of interfacing these components with the ESP32 but also understand how they contribute to the overall functionality and efficiency of our parking space rental system.

Let's start with the connection diagram.

The connection diagram

In this system, the connection diagram is the roadmap to make all the components work together seamlessly. The SSD1306 display is linked to the I2C pins for data transmission, and it's powered through VCC and GND to maintain electrical stability. The button, serving as a user interface element, connects to pin D5 in a pull-up configuration, and the other pin is connected to GND. Our RGB LED, a common cathode type,is connected to pin D4 (red), D2 (green), and D15 (blue), providing a spectrum of visual cues. The Servo motor, facilitating controlled movement, relies on a power supply connected to GND and VCC, controlling what happens through pin D14. Lastly, the ultrasonic sensor, the distance-measuring workhorse, interfaces with the ESP32 by connecting its trigger to D13 and its echo to D12, allowing us to gauge distances with precision. This meticulously designed connection diagram is the backbone of our parking space rental system, ensuring each component collaborates harmoniously in delivering a user-friendly and efficient experience.

The following figure provides a visual guide, specifying the pins and their corresponding functions.

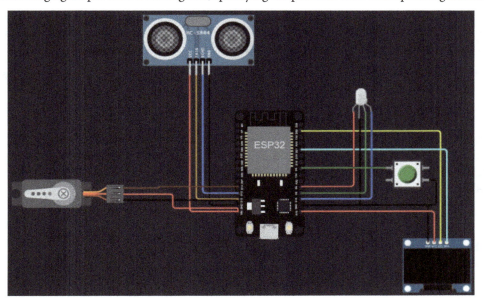

Figure 7.1 – The connection diagram

To summarize the connection, the SSD1306 OLED has four pins, and VCC is connected to the 3.3V; alternatively, you could connect it to the Vin pin of ESP32. SDA is connected to the D21 pin of ESP32 and SCL is connected to the D22 pin of ESP32, and we have connected the GND pin to the GND of ESP32 to make sure the GND is common. The OLED is employed for the user interface of the system.

The ultrasonic sensor, which is used here for the distance measurement, has four pins as well. The trigger pin of the ultrasonic sensor is connected to the D13 pin of ESP32, and the echo pin is connected to the D12 pin of ESP32. Furthermore, the VCC pin and GND pin are connected to the VCC and GND of ESP32, respectively, for the power. The ultrasonic sensor operates by emitting high-frequency sound waves, beyond the range of human hearing, measuring the time it takes for these waves to bounce off an object and return to the sensor. By calculating the "time of flight" and using the known speed of sound in the air, the sensor can precisely determine the distance to the object. This distance measurement is then provided as an output. The trigger pin is used to send the ultrasonic pulse, and the echo pin outputs the status of the received wave.

The push button is connected to the D5 pin of ESP32 and GND of ESP32; we are using the internal pull-up for the configuration of the button. The button will be used to open and close the Servo barrier.

A common cathode RGB LED is an LED with a shared cathode (negative) terminal for all three-color channels (red, green, and blue), allowing control of each color by applying a positive voltage independently. The common cathode RGB LED is used to indicate whether the parking space is available or occupied. It has four terminals and is connected to the GND of ESP32, while the D4, D2, and D15 pins of ESP32 are connected to the red, green, and blue of the LED, respectively.

The Servo motor is used in this project so we can open and close the barrier, since we are prototyping this project. The Servo motor has three terminals. VCC and GND are connected to the VCC and GND of ESP32, and the data pin is connected to D14 of ESP32.

After making the connections, we can write the code to read the distance using the ultrasonic sensor.

Reading the distance using the ultrasonic sensor

We will open the Arduino IDE and upload the following code to the ESP32 to read the distance, using the ultrasonic sensor. The code is available on GitHub (https://github.com/PacktPublishing/Programming-ESP32-with-Arduino-IDE/tree/main/chapter%207/Reading_distance):

```
const int trigPin = 13;
const int echoPin = 12;
const int redPin = 4;
const int greenPin = 2;
const int bluePin = 15;
int distanceRange = 50;
void setup() {
  Serial.begin(115200);
```

```
  pinMode(trigPin, OUTPUT);
  pinMode(echoPin, INPUT);
  pinMode(redPin, OUTPUT);
  pinMode(greenPin, OUTPUT);
  pinMode(bluePin, OUTPUT);
}
void loop() {
  int distance = getdistance();
  delay(1000);
}
int getdistance() {
  long duration;
  int distance;
  digitalWrite(trigPin, LOW);
  delayMicroseconds(2);
  digitalWrite(trigPin, HIGH);
  delayMicroseconds(10);
  digitalWrite(trigPin, LOW);
  duration = pulseIn(echoPin, HIGH);
  distance = (duration / 2) / 29.1;
  Serial.println("Distance: " + String(distance));
  if (distance > distanceRange) {
    digitalWrite(redPin, LOW);
    digitalWrite(greenPin, HIGH);
  } else {
    digitalWrite(greenPin, LOW);
    digitalWrite(redPin, HIGH);
  }
  return distance;
}
```

The code begins by defining some constants – trigPin and echoPin specify the pins for the ultrasonic sensor, and redPin, greenPin, and bluePin specify the pins for the RGB LED. distanceRange is set to 50, representing the threshold distance to change the LED color.

In the setup() function, the serial communication is initiated at a baud rate of 115200, and the specified pins are set to either output (to trigger the ultrasonic sensor and control the LED) or input (to read the echo from the ultrasonic sensor), as already discussed in the *The connection diagram* section.

The loop() function continuously runs the main logic. It starts by calling the getdistance() function to measure the distance using the ultrasonic sensor. Then, there's a one-second delay before the next measurement.

The `getdistance()` function triggers the ultrasonic sensor by sending a pulse from `trigPin`. It measures the time taken for the ultrasonic waves to bounce off an object and return to the sensor via `echoPin`. The distance is calculated using the speed of sound (29.1 ms for a meter) and the time of flight, which is equal to `duration`, and for our calculation, we have used `duration / 2` because the pulse will travel to the object and, after reflection, will travel back to the sensor. The distance is printed to the serial monitor in cm.

Depending on the measured distance, the code changes the LED color. If the distance is greater than `distanceRange`, it turns the LED green (indicating that the object is far). If the distance is less than or equal to `distanceRange`, it turns the LED red (indicating that the object is within the specified range).

The distance value is then returned from the `getdistance()` function.

You will see the following distance results on the serial monitor:

```
Distance: 46
Distance: 46
Distance: 46
Distance: 46
Distance: 46
Distance: 46
Distance: 106
Distance: 106
Distance: 106
```

Figure 7.2 – The distance in cm on the serial monitor

Make sure to change the `distanceRange` value according to your requirements. In the next section, we will interface the Servo motor and push button.

Reading the push button and controlling the Servo motor

Next, we will upload the following code to the ESP32, using the Arduino IDE, to read the push button and open or close the barrier. The code is available on GitHub (https://github. com/PacktPublishing/Programming-ESP32-with-Arduino-IDE/tree/main/ chapter%207/Reading_Pushbutton_controlling_servo):

```
#include <ESP32Servo.h>
#define BUTTON 5
Servo myservo;  // Create a Servo object
const int servoPin = 14;
bool barrier = false;
```

```
void setup() {
  Serial.begin(115200);
  pinMode(BUTTON, INPUT_PULLUP);
  myservo.attach(servoPin); // Attaches the servo on the specified pin
}
void loop() {
  if (!barrier) {
    if (!digitalRead(BUTTON)) {
      openServo();
      barrier = true;
      delay(1000);
    }
  }
  if (barrier) {
    if (!digitalRead(BUTTON)) {
      closeServo();
      barrier = false;
    }
  }
}

void openServo() {
  Serial.println("Servo open");
  myservo.write(0);
}
void closeServo() {
  delay(1000);
  Serial.println("Servo closed");
  myservo.write(180);
}
```

Let's look at the code:

- `#include <ESP32Servo.h>`: This line includes the `Servo` library, which is used for controlling the Servo motor. Make sure to install this library using the Arduino Library Manager.

- `#define BUTTON 5`: This defines a BUTTON constant with the value 5, representing the GPIO pin where the button is connected.

- `Servo myservo;`: This line creates a `Servo` object called `myservo`, which will be used to control the servo motor.

- `const int servoPin = 14;`: This defines another constant, `servoPin`, which specifies the GPIO pin where the servo motor is connected.

- `bool barrier = false;`: This Boolean variable `barrier` is used to keep track of the state of the barrier (Servo). When the barrier is `false`, the barrier is considered closed, and when it's `true`, the barrier is open.

- `void setup()`: The `setup()` function is used for initialization tasks. It does the following:

  - Initializes serial communication at a baud rate of `115200`.

  - Sets the `BUTTON` pin as an input with a pull-up resistor. This means that the button will read `LOW` when pressed and `HIGH` when released.

  - Attaches the `myservo` object to the GPIO pin specified in `servoPin`.

- `void loop()`: The `loop()` function is where the main program logic is executed repeatedly. It does the following:

  - Checks the state of the barrier

  - If the barrier is not currently open and the button is pressed (i.e., the `!barrier` and `!digitalRead(BUTTON)` conditions are met), it calls the `openServo()` function, which opens the barrier, sets the barrier to `true`, and adds a delay of one second

  - If the barrier is open (the barrier is `true`) and the button is pressed, it calls the `closeServo()` function, which closes the barrier and sets the barrier to `false`

  The following truth table shows the status of the barrier and the button.

Barrier	Button	Status
0	0	Button is pushed to open the barrier.
1	0	Button is pushed to close the barrier.
0	1	Barrier is open. Waiting for the button press.
1	1	Barrier is closed. Waiting for the button press.

Table 7. 1 – The truth table for the status of the barrier and the button

- `void openServo()`: This function is responsible for opening the Servo barrier. It sets the angle of the Servo motor to 0 degrees, representing the open position. It also prints `"Servo open"` to the serial monitor.

- `void closeServo()`: This function is used to close the Servo barrier. It sets the angle of the Servo motor to 180 degrees, representing the closed position. It adds a delay of one second to give the barrier time to close and then prints `"Servo closed"` to the serial monitor.

In the next section, we will display a **Quick Response (QR)** code on the SSD1306 OLED, which will open a PayPal payment link when scanned.

Showing a QR code on the OLED

QR codes function as two-dimensional barcodes that encode information in a matrix of black squares arranged on a white background. Each QR code can store various types of data, such as text, URLs, or contact information. The code's pattern serves as a visual representation of data that can be quickly and accurately scanned by a QR code reader, typically found in smartphones. The information is then decoded, enabling users to access the embedded content, link to websites, or perform other actions without manual input.

Next, we will upload the following code, using the Arduino IDE, to the ESP32, showing the PayPal payment link as a QR code on the SSD1306 OLED. The code is available on GitHub (`https://github.com/PacktPublishing/Programming-ESP32-with-Arduino-IDE/tree/main/chapter%207/QRCode_OLED`):

```
#include <Wire.h>
#include <Adafruit_GFX.h>
#include <Adafruit_SSD1306.h>
#include "qrcode.h"

#define SCREEN_WIDTH 128
#define SCREEN_HEIGHT 64
#define OLED_RESET -1

Adafruit_SSD1306 display(SCREEN_WIDTH, SCREEN_HEIGHT, &Wire, OLED_
RESET);
QRCode qrcode;
String paypalLink = "https://paypal.me/username"; //insert your paypal
link from here

void setup()
{
  Serial.begin(115200);
  if (!display.begin(SSD1306_SWITCHCAPVCC, 0x3C)) {
    Serial.println(F("SSD1306 allocation failed"));
    for (;;);
  }
  showScantoPay();
}

void loop()
{
}

void showScantoPay(void) {
```

```
display.clearDisplay();
display.setTextSize(2); // Change the font size to 2
display.setTextColor(WHITE);
uint8_t qrcodeData[qrcode_getBufferSize(3)];
qrcode_initText(&qrcode, qrcodeData, 3, 0, paypalLink.c_str() );
int scale = 2; // Change this for different sizes
for (uint8_t y = 0; y < qrcode.size; y++)
{
  for (uint8_t x = 0; x < qrcode.size; x++)
  {
    if (qrcode_getModule(&qrcode, x, y))
    {
      display.fillRect(x * scale, y * scale, scale, scale, WHITE);
    }
  }
}
display.setCursor(65, 5); // Adjust the position as needed
display.println("Scan");
display.setCursor(65, 25); // Adjust the position as needed
display.println("to");
display.setCursor(65, 45); // Adjust the position as needed
display.println("Open.");

display.display();
}
```

Let's review the code:

- The libraries include:

  - `Wire.h`: This library is used for I2C communication

  - `Adafruit_GFX.h` and `Adafruit_SSD1306.h`: These libraries are used to control and display graphics on the SSD1306 OLED display

  - `"qrcode.h"`: This is a custom library for generating QR codes

  Make sure to install these libraries using the Arduino Library Manager.

- The constants:

  - `SCREEN_WIDTH` and `SCREEN_HEIGHT`: These constants define the width and height of the OLED display in pixels.

  - `OLED_RESET`: This constant specifies the reset pin for the OLED display. In this code, it's set to `-1`, which means it's not used.

- Object initialization:

  - `Adafruit_SSD1306 display(SCREEN_WIDTH, SCREEN_HEIGHT, &Wire, OLED_RESET)`: An instance of the `Adafruit_SSD1306` class is created. This object is used to control the OLED display.

- Global variables:

  - `QRCode qrcode`: An instance of the `QRCode` structure is created. This is used to generate the QR code.

  - `String paypalLink`: This variable holds the URL or text that will be encoded into the QR code. Make sure to add your username at the end of the PayPal link.

- The `setup()` function:

  - Serial communication is started at a baud rate of `115200`.

  - The OLED display is initialized using `display.begin(SSD1306_SWITCHCAPVCC, 0x3C)`. If the initialization fails, it prints an error message and enters an infinite loop.

  - The `showScantoPay()` function is called to display the QR code and message on the OLED screen.

- The `loop()` function:

  - The `loop()` function is empty, as there are no continuous tasks to perform in this code

- The `showScantoPay()` function:

  I.   This function displays the QR code and message on the OLED display.

  II.   It clears the display using `display.clearDisplay()`.

  III. The QR code is generated using the `qrcode_initText()` function from the custom QRCode library. The QR code is created based on the `paypalLink` string.

  IV.   The QR code is then displayed on the OLED screen by drawing white rectangles for the QR code modules, using `display.fillRect()`.

  V.   A text message, `"Scan to open the barrier"`, is added to the display, using `display.setCursor()` and `display.println()`.

  VI.   Finally, the content is displayed on the OLED using `display.display()`.

The output of the code is shown in the following figure:

Figure 7.3 – The QR code on the SSD1306 OLED

In the next section, we will set up Webhooks to receive a PayPal notification whenever someone makes a payment.

Integrating the PayPal API

In this section, we will set up the Webhooks that will enable us to receive a notification related to the payment in the ESP32. To set up the Webhooks, we will complete the following steps:

1. Firstly, we will go to `https://www.webhook.site` and get a unique URL, as highlighted in the following figure:

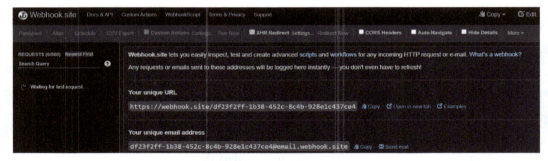

Figure 7.4 – A unique URL on Webhook.site

2. Then, to test our Webhook, we will use the PayPal **Instant Payment Notification** (**IPN**) simulator. It will help us to simulate the payment notification for testing. To access the IPN simulator, go to `https://developer.paypal.com/dashboard/ipnsimulator` using your web browser.

3. Paste the unique URL into the IPL URL handler, and select **Web Accept** as the transaction type.

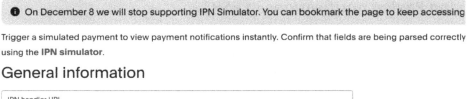

Figure 7.5 – The PayPal IPN simulator

4. For testing, leave all other values to default, and then go to the bottom of the page and click on **Send IPN**.

Figure 7.6 – Sending an IPN using the IPN simulator

5. You will receive the data at `https://www.webhook.site`, as shown in the following figure:

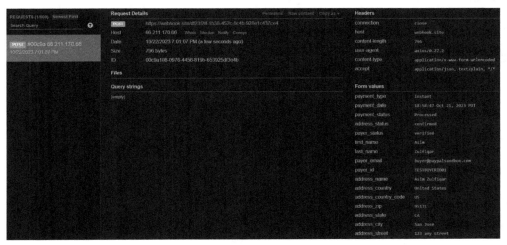

Figure 7.7 – The IPN received at Webhook.site

Now, we have set up the Webhook, and we have successfully received the data at `Webhook.site` but we will need to receive this data in ESP32 to decide whether the payment has been made or not.

Receiving PayPal notifications in ESP32

The notifications received from PayPal are in the **JavaScript Object Notation (JSON)** format. JSON is a lightweight data-interchange format that is easy for humans to read and write, and also straightforward for machines to parse and generate. It is primarily used to transmit data between a server and a web application as an alternative to XML. JSON employs a simple and clear structure, representing data as key-value pairs within objects, which can be nested to create complex structures. Arrays, which are ordered lists of values, also play a crucial role in JSON. The format supports various data types, including strings, numbers, Booleans, objects, arrays, and null values. Its simplicity, universality, and human-readable nature make JSON widely adopted in web development and data exchange scenarios.

To receive the PayPal notification in ESP32, we will upload the following code in the ESP32 using the Arduino IDE. The code is available on GitHub (`https://github.com/PacktPublishing/Programming-ESP32-with-Arduino-IDE/tree/main/chapter%207/Reading_webhook_paypal`):

```
#include <WiFi.h>
#include <HTTPClient.h>
#include <ArduinoJson.h>
#include <NTPClient.h>
#include <WiFiUdp.h>
#include <time.h>

WiFiUDP ntpUDP;
NTPClient timeClient(ntpUDP, "pool.ntp.org");
...
...
...
bool parseTimestamp(String timestampStr, struct tm &createdTime) {
  if (strptime(timestampStr.c_str(), "%Y-%m-%d %H:%M:%S",
&createdTime)) {
    return true;
  } else {
    Serial.println("Failed to parse timestamp.");
    return false;
  }
}
```

Let's review the code:

- We have included the following libraries:

  - `#include <WiFi.h>`: This includes the Wi-Fi library to enable wireless network communication

  - `#include <HTTPClient.h>`: This imports the `HTTPClient` library to make HTTP requests

  - `#include <ArduinoJson.h>`: This includes the `ArduinoJson` library to parse JSON data

  - `#include <NTPClient.h>`: This imports the `NTPClient` library for time synchronization using the **Network Time Protocol (NTP)**

  - `#include <WiFiUdp.h>`: This includes the `WiFiUdp` library for UDP communication

  - `#include <time.h>`: This imports the `time` library for time-related functions

- Global variables and constants:

  - `WiFiUDP ntpUDP`: This defines a UDP object for NTP time synchronization

  - `NTPClient timeClient(ntpUDP, "pool.ntp.org")`: This initializes the NTP client with the UDP object and NTP server address

  - `ssid` and `password`: Variables that store the Wi-Fi network SSID and password

  - `apiKey`: A variable that stores an API key used for authentication

  - `url`: The URL of the web service where payment data is retrieved

  - `LastModifiedHeader`: Stores the "Last-Modified" header received from the server

  Make sure to change `apiKey`, `url`, `ssid`, and `password`.

- The `setup()` function:

  - Initializes serial communication with a baud rate of `115200`

  - Connects to the specified Wi-Fi network (`ssid` and `password`)

  - Uses a `while` loop to wait until the ESP32 successfully connects to the Wi-Fi network

  - Prints a message to the serial monitor when the connection is established

- The `loop()` function:

    - Repeatedly calls the `checkPayment()` function at a regular interval of 6 seconds (6,000 milliseconds)

- The `checkPayment()` function:

    - Responsible for checking and processing payment data.

    - Declares a string variable, `amountPaid`, to store the payment amount.

    - Sets the `timeLimitMinutes` to 2, which is the time limit for processing payment data. Data older than two minutes will be considered old.

    - Updates the time using NTP and gets the current epoch time.

    - Checks whether the ESP32 is connected to the Wi-Fi network.

    - Creates an `HTTPClient` object called `http` to make an HTTP GET request to the specified URL.

    - Adds headers to the HTTP request, including `"accept,"` `"api-key,"` and "If-Modified-Since" if `lastModifiedHeader` is not empty.

    - Executes the HTTP GET request and stores the HTTP response code in `httpCode`.

    - If the request is successful (`HTTP_CODE_OK`), it parses the JSON response using the `parseJsonData()` function.

    - If the response indicates that there is no new data (`HTTP_CODE_NOT_MODIFIED`), it prints a message.

    - If there is an HTTP error, it prints the error code.

    - If the request fails to connect, it prints a failure message.

    - The function ends by closing the HTTP connection and returning the payment amount as an integer.

- The `parseJsonData()` function:

    - This parses the JSON response received from the server to extract payment data

    - The function takes the JSON payload, a reference to `amountPaid`, the current time, and the time limit as parameters

    - It uses the `ArduinoJson` library to deserialize the JSON data

- It parses `timestamp`, calculates the time difference, and checks whether the data is within the time limit

- If the data is within the time limit, it extracts and prints the payer's name, email, and amount paid

- If the data is too old, it prints a message and returns `false`

- The `parseTimestamp()` function:

  - This parses a `timestamp` string and populates the `createdTime` structure

  - The function returns `true` if parsing is successful and `false` otherwise

After uploading the code, send an IPN notification using the IPN simulator, and you will see a similar output in the serial monitor. Test it a few times by changing the payer's name, email, and `mc_gross` (i.e., `Amount paid`):

```
Connecting to WiFi...
Connected to WiFi
Name: Asim Zulfiqar
Email: buyer@paypalsandbox.com
Amount Paid: 12.34
```

Figure 7.8 – An IPN notification in the ESP32 serial monitor

Now that we have completed and understood the important parts of this project, we will combine everything to complete it.

Creating a user-friendly experience for potential renters

By now, you will have noticed that the code contained in each of the preceding sections was just a small part of this project. In this section, we will combine everything to create a user-friendly experience for potential renters. The following is the flow chart for this project:

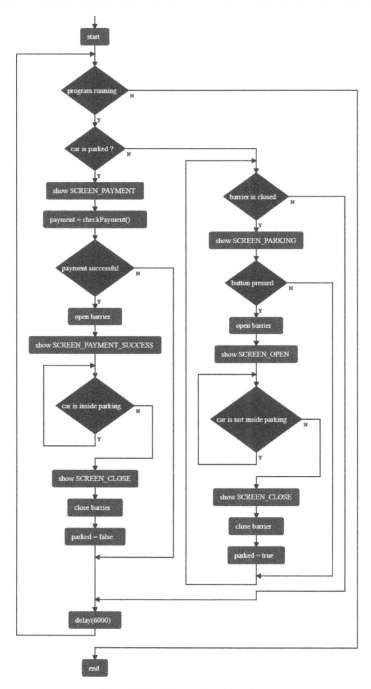

Figure 7.9 – The project flow chart

The preceding flow chart shows the flow of the commands and instructions for various scenarios – that is, when the payment has not been made and the car is not parked or parked, and when the payment has been made and the car is parked or not. The flow chart will help us understand and create a logic to write the final code of the project. The final code has all the functionalities that we have previously discussed in this chapter. It will wait for the button press, read the sensor data, wait for the payment, and show the parking status on the OLED. The code is available on GitHub (`https://github.com/PacktPublishing/Programming-ESP32-with-Arduino-IDE/tree/main/chapter%207/Rent_out_Parking_Complete`):

```
#include <Wire.h>
#include <Adafruit_GFX.h>
#include <Adafruit_SSD1306.h>
#include "qrcode.h"
#include <WiFi.h>
#include <HTTPClient.h>
#include <ArduinoJson.h>
#include <NTPClient.h>
#include <WiFiUdp.h>
#include <time.h>
#include <ESP32Servo.h>

enum ScreenStatus
...

...

...

    case SCREEN_OTHER:
      display.setTextSize(1);
      display.println("Some other screen");
      break;
    }
    display.display();
  }
}
```

The libraries that are included in this code were discussed in the previous section. An enum named `ScreenStatus` is defined to represent different screen states of the parking system. We have used two flag variables, `parked` and `barrier`, to track the parking status:

- The main `loop` function operates in two main states – when the car is not parked and when the car is parked. The flow chart in *Figure 7.9* illustrates the flow of the main `loop` function:

  - While the car is not parked:

    - Continuously checks for the barrier to be lifted (using a button press)

    - If the button is pressed, it opens the barrier, updates the screen, and sets the barrier flag to `true`

  - While the car is parked:

    - Displays the payment screen, checks for the payment status using `checkPayment()`, and waits for successful payment

    - When payment is successful, it opens the barrier, updates the screen, and waits for the car to leave before resetting the parking state

- The `updateDisplay()` function is responsible for updating the OLED display to show different screens or information based on the current `currentScreen` state.

- Screen detection:

  - The function begins by checking whether `currentScreen` is different from `lastScreen`. This check ensures that the display is only updated when the screen state changes.

- QR code generation (`SCREEN_PAYMENT`):

  - When `currentScreen` is set to `SCREEN_PAYMENT`, the code generates a QR code with the PayPal payment link (`paypalLink`) and displays it on the OLED screen. This allows users to scan the QR code for payment.

- Displaying content:

  - For each screen state, specific content is printed on the OLED screen. This content includes instructions, messages, and, in the case of `SCREEN_PAYMENT`, the QR code.

- Displaying an update:

  - After configuring the display for the current screen state, the `display.display()` function is called to update the OLED display with the new content

After uploading the code, you will see the following state – the barrier is closed, and the OLED shows SCREEN_PARKING.

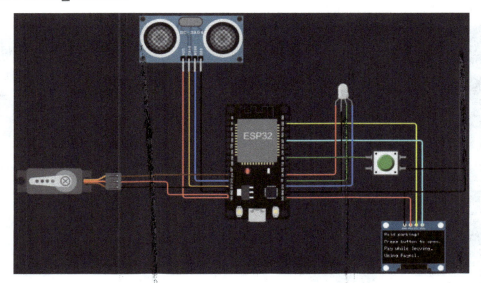

Figure 7.10 – The initial stage of the project

When you push the button, the barrier will open, and the OLED will show SCREEN_OPEN, as shown in the following figure:

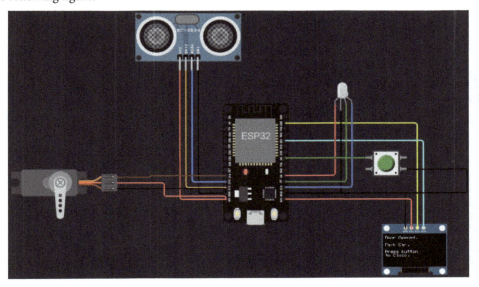

Figure 7.11 – The OLED and Servo status when the button is pressed and the barrier is closed

Now, as the OLED suggests that the barrier has opened, you can park your car now. When the user parks the car and then you press the button again, we will see the QR code on the OLED and that the barrier is closed, as shown in the following figure:

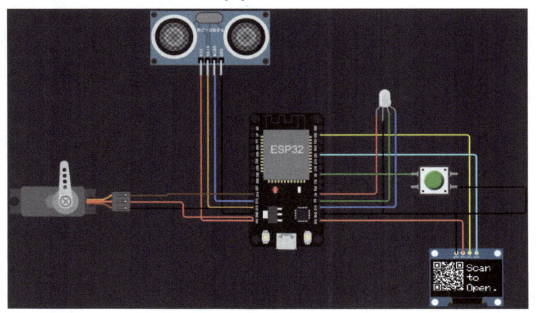

Figure 7.12 – The Servo and OLED status when the barrier is closed,
and the QR code for the payment is shown on the OLED

Now, when the user returns, they will not be able to access the door with the button press. They will have to scan the QR code; when scanned, the PayPal user interface will open. They will have to pay $1, and once the payment is successful, we will get a notification in ESP32 using the Webhook, get the following response on the OLED, and the barrier will open:

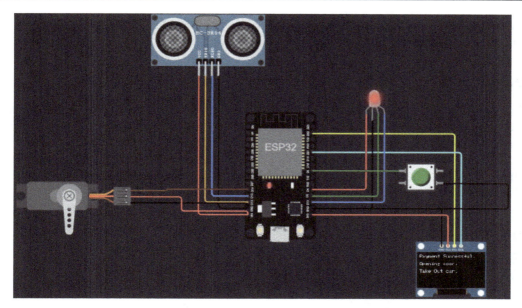

Figure 7.13 – The OLED and Servo status when the payment is successful

Now, the OLED suggests the user removes the car from the parking space, and it will keep the barrier open unless the distance is greater than `distanceRange`. When the distance read by the ultrasonic sensor is greater than `distanceRange`, ESP32 will assume that the car has been removed, and it will go back to the initial screen and the barrier will close.

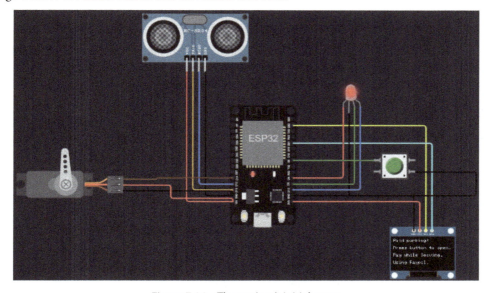

Figure 7.14 – The project's initial stage

Once the project is in its initial stage, the door can be accessed using the push button. Next, we will discuss future enhancements and real-world implementation.

Real-world implementation and project limitations

The project we have developed is a prototype that employs a Servo motor to simulate the function of a barrier gate. In actual operational scenarios, it's important to note that the SG90 Servo motor used in this prototype is insufficient to serve as an effective barrier gate. In practical applications, a dedicated parking barrier system is required, which, depending on its configuration, can be integrated with the ESP32. An example of a more robust setup might involve using a relay board to control the barrier, as shown in *Figure 7.15*.

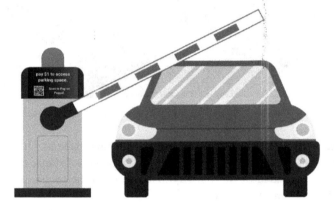

Figure 7.15 – A practical implementation of the project

Additionally, for real-world scenarios, access to a parking space should only be granted after a successful payment. In our prototyping, we used the PayPal IPN simulator to test payment functionality. To get notifications when someone pays you on PayPal, we will complete the following steps:

1. Log in to your PayPal account and go to **Settings**.
2. Go to the **Seller Tools** tab, and then click on the **Instant payment notifications** option.

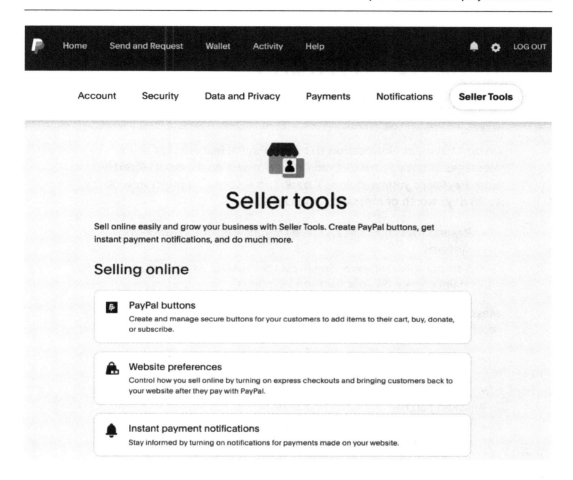

Figure 7.16 – PayPal | Seller Tools

3. Click on **Choose IPN Settings**.

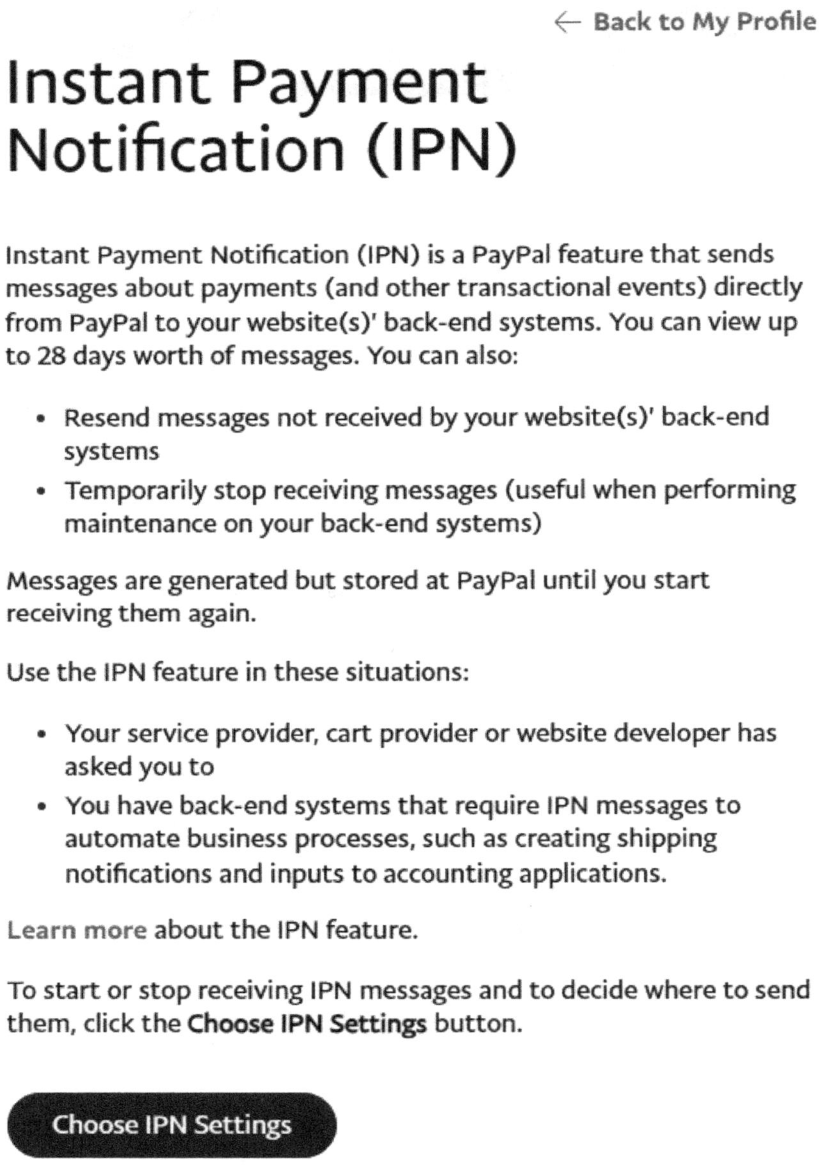

← **Back to My Profile**

Instant Payment Notification (IPN)

Instant Payment Notification (IPN) is a PayPal feature that sends messages about payments (and other transactional events) directly from PayPal to your website(s)' back-end systems. You can view up to 28 days worth of messages. You can also:

- Resend messages not received by your website(s)' back-end systems
- Temporarily stop receiving messages (useful when performing maintenance on your back-end systems)

Messages are generated but stored at PayPal until you start receiving them again.

Use the IPN feature in these situations:

- Your service provider, cart provider or website developer has asked you to
- You have back-end systems that require IPN messages to automate business processes, such as creating shipping notifications and inputs to accounting applications.

Learn more about the IPN feature.

To start or stop receiving IPN messages and to decide where to send them, click the **Choose IPN Settings** button.

Choose IPN Settings

Figure 7.17 – PayPal IPN settings

4. Paste your Webhook unique URL into the notification URL and enable the notifications.

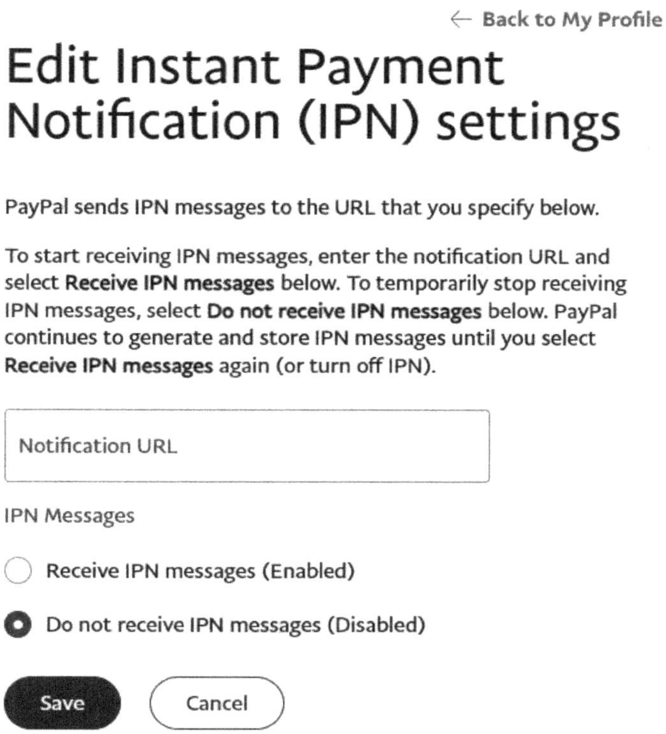

← **Back to My Profile**

Edit Instant Payment Notification (IPN) settings

PayPal sends IPN messages to the URL that you specify below.

To start receiving IPN messages, enter the notification URL and select **Receive IPN messages** below. To temporarily stop receiving IPN messages, select **Do not receive IPN messages** below. PayPal continues to generate and store IPN messages until you select **Receive IPN messages** again (or turn off IPN).

Notification URL

IPN Messages

○ Receive IPN messages (Enabled)

● Do not receive IPN messages (Disabled)

Save   (Cancel)

Figure 7.18 – Setting up IPNs

Now, whenever a payment is made to your account, you will receive an IPN and will be able to control the barrier accordingly. Next, we will discuss the limitations of the current setup.

Current project limitations

The project we have completed showcases a parking space prototype with certain limitations:

- **Limited payment security**: The prototype lacks a secure payment processing mechanism, and payment data is exposed through a public webhook service, posing significant security risks

- **User authentication**: User authentication and authorization are not implemented in the prototype, leaving the system open to unauthorized access and usage

- **Data privacy concerns**: The system does not address data privacy concerns or regulatory requirements to handle sensitive user and payment data

However, this project will enable you to understand the concept of integrating payment options into your projects at a basic level. In the next section, we will briefly discuss security concepts in IoT, just to give you a very basic idea of security in IoT.

Security concepts in IoT

In the field of the **Internet of Things (IoT)**, ensuring robust security is paramount to safeguarding connected devices and the data they generate. Several key security concepts are integral to fortifying IoT ecosystems. Some of them are defined here:

- **Authentication**: Authentication is a critical security concept in IoT, verifying the identity of devices and users seeking access to a network. This process involves confirming the legitimacy of entities through various mechanisms such as passwords, biometrics, or digital certificates. By implementing strong authentication protocols, IoT systems can stop unauthorized access and mitigate the risk of compromised devices compromising the entire network.

- **Encryption**: Encryption plays a pivotal role in securing data transmitted between IoT devices and networks. Employing encryption algorithms ensures that the information exchanged remains confidential and tamper-resistant. Both symmetric and asymmetric encryption methods are applicable in IoT contexts, allowing for the protection of sensitive data from interception and unauthorized access.

- **Public or Private Key Infrastructure (PKI)**: PKI forms the backbone of secure communication in IoT. PKI utilizes pairs of public and private keys to facilitate secure data exchange. In the IoT context, these keys enable encrypted communication and authentication. The public key is openly shared, while the private key remains confidential, ensuring the integrity and confidentiality of the transmitted data.

By integrating these security concepts, IoT ecosystems can establish a robust defense against unauthorized access, data breaches, and other potential threats, thereby fostering a secure and trustworthy interconnected environment.

Summary

In this chapter, we embarked on a practical project focused on enabling the rental of parking spaces, through the integration of Webhooks and PayPal IPN. To bring this project to life, we used various components, including ultrasonic sensors, Servo motors, and OLED displays in the prototyping phase. These components allowed us to create a system that facilitates the access and payment process for parking spaces.

Looking ahead to the next chapter, we will delve into the development of a data logger, expanding our exploration of IoT applications into a different realm. This project promises to further extend our understanding and practical skills in the realm of IoT.

8

Project 3 – Logging, Monitoring, and Controlling using ESP32

In this chapter, we will start another exciting journey to explore the capabilities of the ESP32 microcontroller in the realm of home automation and monitoring. The mission of this chapter is to demonstrate how ESP32 can be harnessed to enhance the convenience, security, and efficiency of your daily life.

Our focus will be on logging, monitoring, and controlling various aspects of your home using the versatile ESP32 platform. We'll deploy sensors in key areas such as the kitchen, bathroom, bedroom, and living room to collect valuable data. This data will be efficiently stored in an InfluxDB database, providing a robust foundation for analysis and monitoring.

The heart of our monitoring system lies in Grafana, a powerful tool that allows us to visualize and gain insights from the data collected. We'll delve into the technical aspects of setting up Grafana, creating informative dashboards, and setting alert mechanisms for a proactive approach to home management.

But that's not all! We'll take home automation a step further by integrating a servo motor to simulate control of the main door. This dynamic feature will be orchestrated through the **Message Queuing Telemetry Transport** (**MQTT**) protocol, enabling you to remotely manage access to your home with ease and security.

In this chapter, we will cover the following main topics:

- Interfacing sensors with ESP32 for monitoring temperature, light, and motion in various areas of the house
- Setting up InfluxDB Cloud and logging the data
- Creating a user-friendly dashboard in Grafana
- Controlling the main entrance gate using the MQTT protocol

Just as in our previous chapters, we'll provide comprehensive step-by-step instructions, practical examples, and hands-on guidance to assist you in building your own home monitoring and control system. By the end of this chapter, you'll not only have a fully functional home monitoring system, but you'll also possess the knowledge and skills to extend it to meet your unique needs and preferences.

Technical requirements

For this project, we will need the following:

- An ESP32 board
- Servo motor
- PIR motion sensor
- Light-detecting resistor module
- DHT22 temperature and humidity sensor
- InfluxDB Cloud account (free account)
- Grafana cloud account (free account)
- HiveMQ public MQTT broker

All the code files used in this chapter will be available at `https://github.com/PacktPublishing/Programming-ESP32-with-Arduino-IDE/tree/main/chapter%208`

Interfacing sensors and actuators with ESP32

In this section, we'll dive into the hardware components of our home monitoring and control project. Here, we will explore the seamless integration of a wide range of sensors and actuators with the ESP32 microcontroller, allowing us to transform our ordinary home into a smart and efficiently managed living space.

Our project hinges on the precise coordination of various elements to log data and monitor different rooms in our home, offering us valuable insights and control. To achieve this, we will connect the ESP32 microcontroller to a set of essential components, including DHT22 sensors, motion sensors, **Light Dependent Resistor** (**LDR**) modules, and an additional servo motor for the living room.

Each room in our home as depicted in *Figure 8.1*, will be equipped with a set of sensors. The DHT11 sensors will provide temperature and humidity data, the motion sensors will detect human presence, and the LDR modules will measure light levels. These sensors work in tandem to collect data from each room, giving us a comprehensive understanding of the environment.

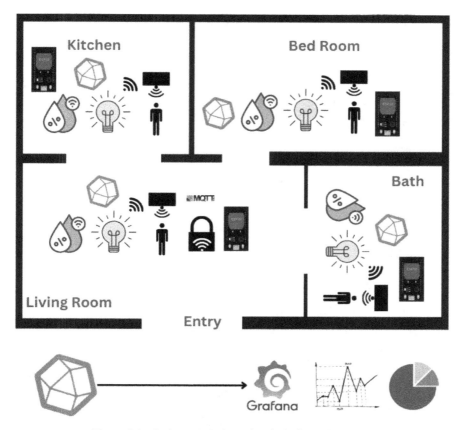

Figure 8.1 – Project scenario and technical requirements

In the living room, we'll take home automation to the next level by incorporating a servo motor. This motor will be controlled using the MQTT protocol, allowing us to simulate a door lock. With this added functionality, you can remotely control access to your living room, enhancing both convenience and security.

Throughout this section, we will guide you through the process of connecting and configuring each of these sensors and actuators with the ESP32 microcontroller.

Let's start our journey by examining the connection diagram and bringing our smart home vision to life.

Connection diagram

For each of the rooms, except the living room, we have a consistent setup of sensors to log and monitor the environment. Each room features a DHT sensor for temperature and humidity, an LDR module for light levels, and a motion sensor for detecting human presence.

The connections for these sensors are as follows and can be seen in *Figure 8.2*:

- DHT sensor:
  - VCC: Connected to a 3.3V or 5V power source
  - GND: Connected to the ground (0V)
  - Data (D12): Connected to pin D12 on the ESP32 microcontroller

- LDR module:
  - VCC: Connected to a 3.3V or 5V power source
  - GND: Connected to the ground (0V)
  - Data (D13): Connected to pin D13 on the ESP32 microcontroller

- Motion sensor:
  - VCC: Connected to a 3.3V or 5V power source
  - GND: Connected to the ground (0V)
  - Data (D14): Connected to pin D14 on the ESP32 microcontroller:

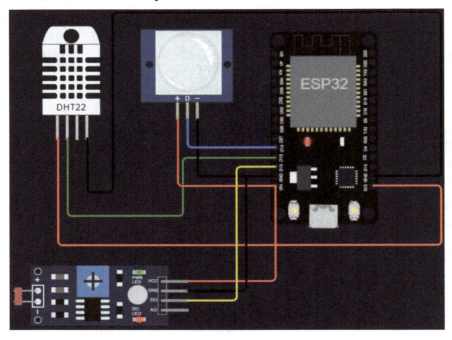

Figure 8.2 – Connection diagram for the kitchen, bathroom, and bedroom on the ESP32 microcontroller

For the living room, we introduce an extra component, the servo motor, which is utilized to simulate a door lock. It will be triggered when we receive an MQTT message, as shown in *Figure 8.3*:

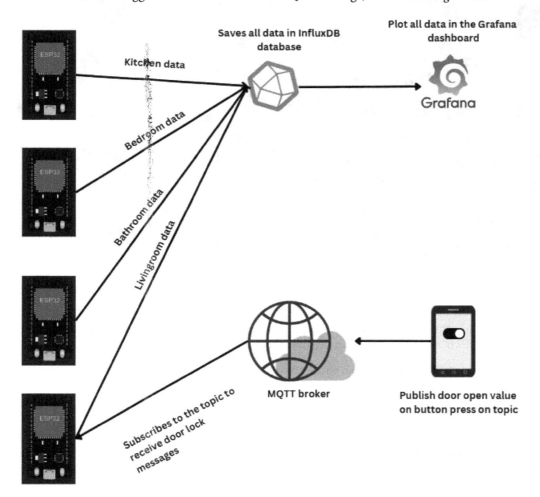

Figure 8.3 – Project data flow

The connections for this motor are as follows and can be seen in *Figure 8.4*:

- Servo motor (living room):

  - Data (D15): Connected to pin D15 on the ESP32

  - VCC: Connected to a 3.3V or 5V power source

- GND: Connected to the ground (0V):

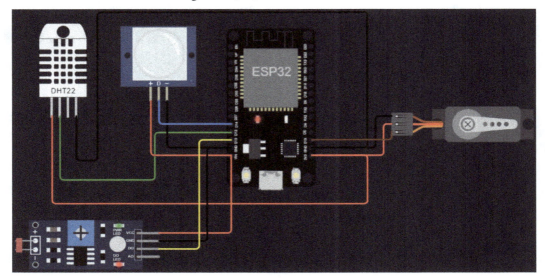

Figure 8.4 – Connection diagram for the living room

This connection diagram ensures that each component in every room works together seamlessly to log data and provide real-time monitoring, enabling efficient data collection and control while maintaining electrical stability and user-friendly functionality.

After making the connections, we can write the code to read the sensor data.

Reading the sensor data

We will open the Arduino IDE and upload the following code to the ESP32 microcontroller so that it can read the sensor data using the DHT22, motion sensor, and LDR. The code is available on GitHub at https://github.com/PacktPublishing/Programming-ESP32-with-Arduino-IDE/tree/main/chapter%208/read_sensors:

```
#include <Adafruit_Sensor.h>
#include <DHT_U.h>
…
…
…
void setup()
{
  Serial.begin(115200);
  setupSensors();
}
```

```
void loop()
{
  readSensors();
  delay(1000);
}
```

Let's review the code:

- The code starts by defining the pins for the sensors: DHTPIN for the DHT22 sensor, LDR for the light-dependent resistor, and motionsensor for the motion sensor.

- The setupSensors() function is responsible for initializing the sensors. It begins by initializing the DHT sensor and getting sensor information. It also sets pinMode for the LDR and motion sensor as inputs.

- The readSensors() function reads data from the sensors. It retrieves temperature and humidity data from the DHT sensor, motion sensor state, and light level from the LDR. Then, it prints the data to the Serial Monitor.

- In the setup() function, serial communication is initiated at a baud rate of 115200, and the setupSensors() function is called to initialize the sensors.

- The loop() function continuously reads sensor data using readSensors() and then adds a delay of 1 second before the next reading.

You will see the following results on the serial monitor:

```
Temperature : 26.20
Humidity : 25.00
Motion : 1
Light : 0
Temperature : 26.20
```

Figure 8.5 – The sensor's data printed on the serial monitor

Next, we will send the data to the InfluxDB database. For that, we will set up an InfluxDB Cloud account.

Setting up InfluxDB Cloud and logging the data

InfluxDB is a high-performance, open source time series database designed for efficiently storing and querying timestamped data. It is particularly well suited for applications that collect and analyze data that changes over time, such as sensor readings, application metrics, and system monitoring data.

Time series data is a type of data where each data point is associated with a specific timestamp. It is used to record changes or measurements over time, making it ideal for tracking trends, patterns, and historical data. In time series data, time is a critical dimension, and the data points are typically sorted in chronological order.

For example, let's consider a DHT sensor that measures temperature and humidity. The sensor records readings at regular intervals and stores them with timestamps. Here's a simplified representation of time series data from a DHT sensor:

Timestamp	Temperature (°C)	Humidity (%)
2023-11-01 10:00:00	25.2	45.3
2023-11-01 10:05:00	25.4	45.2
2023-11-01 10:10:00	25.25	45.6
2023-11-01 10:15:00	25.3	45.2

Table 8.1 – The DHT sensor as time series data

In this example, the DHT sensor records temperature and humidity measurements at 5-minute intervals, and each data point is associated with a specific timestamp. This chronological arrangement of data points allows you to analyze how temperature and humidity change over time, making it a classic example of time series data. InfluxDB is an ideal database for efficiently storing and querying such data.

Cloud database setup

First, we will set up the InfluxDB Cloud database to log the data in the database. To do this, we will follow these steps:

1. First, go to https://www.influxdata.com/products/influxdb-cloud/.

2. Click on **Log In** and then select **Log in to InfluxDB Cloud 2.0**, as shown in *Figure 8.6*:

Figure 8.6 – Log in to InfluxDB Cloud 2.0

3. Complete the login procedure using your Google account, Microsoft account, or email address, as shown in *Figure 8.7*:

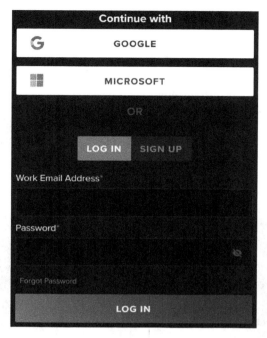

Figure 8.7 – InfluxDB login screen

4. If you will be logging in for the first time, it will ask you some questions about your role and organization.

5. Once you've logged in, you will see the Resource Center, as shown in the following figure:

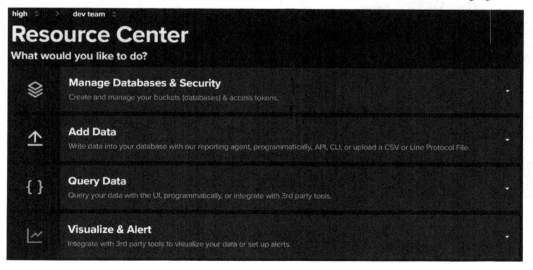

Figure 8.8 – InfluxDB Resource Center

6. First, we'll create a bucket.

> **What's a bucket?**
>
> A *bucket* is a fundamental concept that's used to organize and store time series data. Buckets act as containers for data and determine how data is retained and queried. Each bucket has its own data retention policy, which defines how long data is kept and what happens to older data when new data arrives. This allows you to efficiently manage historical data within InfluxDB. Buckets also help in partitioning data and access control, making it easier to organize and secure time series data.

To create a bucket, click on **Manage Databases & Security**. Then, under **Database Manager**, click **GO TO BUCKETS**, as shown in *Figure 8.9*:

Figure 8.9 – InfluxDB – Manage Databases & Security

7. There, you will see all your buckets. Let's create a new bucket. To do so, click + **CREATE BUCKET**, as shown in *Figure 8.10*:

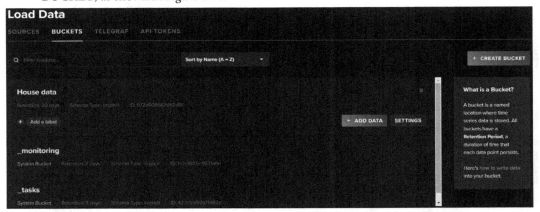

Figure 8.10 – How to create a bucket in InfluxDB

8. Name the bucket Home data and click on **CREATE**, as shown in *Figure 8.11*:

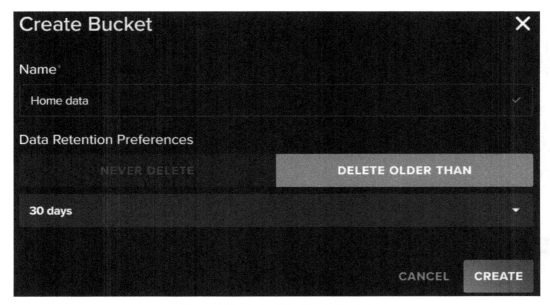

Figure 8.11 – InfluxDB – Create Bucket

9. Once the bucket has been created, you will see the bucket in the list and some information under that, such as bucket ID. We will copy and save this bucket ID and the bucket's name, which is **Home data**. In this case, we will need this ID while logging data:

Figure 8.12 – InfluxDB bucket name and ID

10. Furthermore, we will need the cluster URL and organization ID. To get that, click on the organization's name on top, as shown in *Figure 8.13* (in my case, it is **dev team**). Then, click **Settings**:

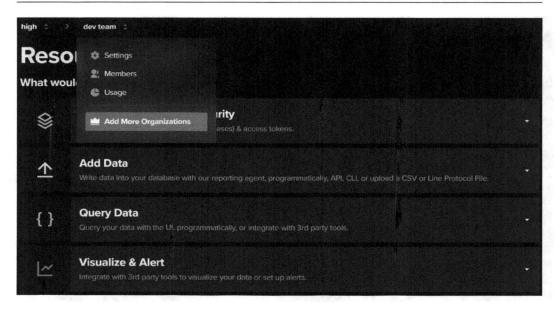

Figure 8.13 – InfluxDB organization settings

11. A settings page will open, as shown in the following figure. Copy and save the **Organization ID** and **Cluster URL (Host Name)** values:

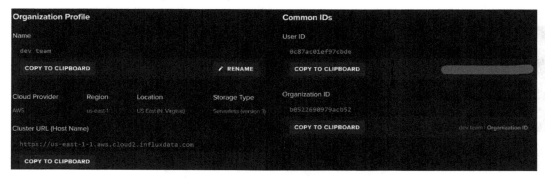

Figure 8.14 – InfluxDB – Organization ID and Cluster URL (Host Name)

12. Lastly, we will need an API token. To get that token, click on **GO TO TOKENS**, as shown in *Step 6* and *Figure 8.9*. You will see the list of created tokens if you created some previously; otherwise, click on **GENERATE API TOKEN** and select **All Access API Token**, as shown in *Figure 8.15*:

Figure 8.15 – GENERATE API TOKEN in InfluxDB

13. Give your token a name and click **SAVE**:

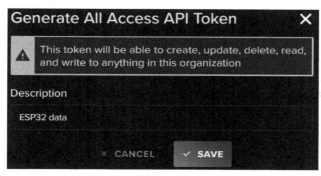

Figure 8.16 – Generate All Access API Token

14. Now, you need to copy and save the token as you will not be able to access it again. You will be notified of this, as shown in *Figure 8.17*:

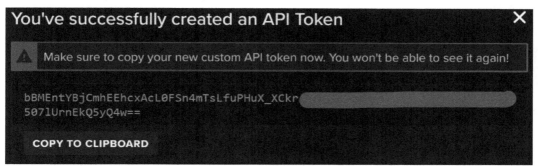

Figure 8.17 – Copying the InfluxDB API token

With that, we have set up InfluxDB Cloud to log the data from ESP32 and gathered the required data, which includes the bucket name, bucket ID, organization ID, cluster URL, and API token. We will use all these credentials in our code to log data in the ESP32 microcontroller.

Logging data to InfluxDB

To log the data, we will need the credentials that we gathered in the previous section and make sure we change them with our credentials. Then, we will upload the following code using the Arduino IDE to ESP32 so that we can log the sensor data to the bucket in InfluxDB. The code can be found on GitHub at https://github.com/PacktPublishing/Programming-ESP32-with-Arduino-IDE/tree/main/chapter%208/kitchen_data:

```
#include <Adafruit_Sensor.h>
#include <DHT_U.h>
#include <WiFiMulti.h>
#include <InfluxDbClient.h>
#include <InfluxDbCloud.h>

// InfluxDB configuration
const char* INFLUXDB_URL = "ClusterURL"; // cluster URL
const char* INFLUXDB_TOKEN = "API Token" //api token
const char* INFLUXDB_ORG = "org ID"; //organization ID
const char* INFLUXDB_BUCKET = "Home data"; //bucket name
...
...
...
void setup() {
  Serial.begin(115200);
  setupWifi();
  setupSensors();
}

void loop() {
  readSensors();
  writeToInfluxDB();
  delay(1000);
}
```

Let's take a closer look at the code:

- Include the necessary libraries:

  - The code includes several libraries, including Adafruit_Sensor, DHT_U for the DHT sensor, WiFiMulti for managing Wi-Fi connections, InfluxDbClient for interfacing with InfluxDB, and InfluxDbCloud for InfluxDB cloud-specific functionality. Make sure you install them using the Arduino Library Manager.

- Wi-Fi and InfluxDB configuration:

  - This sets up Wi-Fi configuration, including `SSID` and `password`.

  - The InfluxDB configuration includes the InfluxDB URL, API token, organization ID, and the bucket name where data will be stored. Make sure you change them with your credentials.

- Pin definitions:

  - This defines the pins for various sensors and the DHT sensor type (DHT22)

- DHT sensor setup:

  - This initializes the DHT sensor, sets its type, and retrieves sensor information for temperature and humidity

- Time zone configuration:

  - This sets the time zone information (`TZ_INFO`) for time synchronization

- InfluxDB client configuration:

  - This configures the InfluxDB client instance with the provided InfluxDB URL, organization, bucket, and API token

  - This initializes a data point (`dbdata`) named `House_data` to store sensor readings

- The `setupWifi()` function:

  - It sets up Wi-Fi in *Station* mode.

  - It attempts to connect to the specified Wi-Fi network using the `wifiMulti` object and prints a message while waiting for a successful connection.

- The `setupSensors()` function:

  - It initializes the DHT sensor and retrieves sensor information

  - It configures the LDR and motion sensor pins as inputs

  - It synchronizes the time with NTP servers for accurate time tracking

  - It checks the connection to InfluxDB and sets tags for the data point

- The `readSensors()` function:

  - It clears the fields of the `dbdata` data point to prepare for new data.

  - It reads temperature and humidity data from the DHT sensor and adds it to the data point

  - It reads the motion sensor state, light level from the LDR, and Wi-Fi signal strength (RSSI) and adds them to the data point

- The `writeToInfluxDB()` function:

  - It prints the data point in line protocol format to the serial monitor.

  - It attempts to write the data point to the InfluxDB database using the InfluxDB client. If the write fails, it prints an error message.

- The `setup()` function:

  - It initializes serial communication at a baud rate of `115200`

  - It calls the `setupWifi()` and `setupSensors()` functions to configure Wi-Fi and sensors

- The `loop()` function:

  - In the main loop, it repeatedly reads sensor data using the `readSensors()` function

  - It then sends the data to the InfluxDB database using the `writeToInfluxDB()` function

  - There is a 1-second delay between each data transmission to avoid overwhelming the database with rapid updates

Once the code has been uploaded, you will see the following results on the serial monitor:

```
Connecting to Wi-Fi
Syncing time......
Synchronized time: Fri Nov  3 09:53:27 2023

Connected to InfluxDB: https://us-east-1-1.aws.cloud2.influxdata.com
Writing: House_data,device=kitchen,SSID
temperature=26.20,humidity=25.00,rssi=-94i,motion_sensor=0i,light=0i
Waiting 1 second
```

Figure 8.18 – Data written to the InfluxDB serial monitor

Now, when you click on the home data bucket that was indicated in *step 9* and *Figure 8.11*, you will see the following UI:

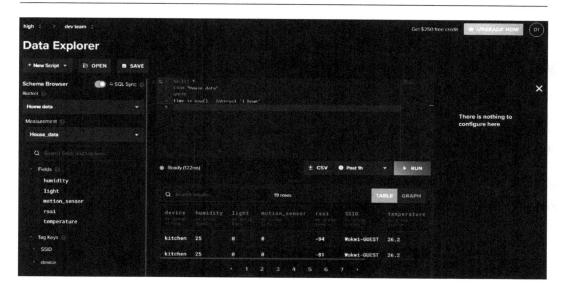

Figure 8.19 – InfluxDB data explorer

In the preceding figure, we set **Bucket** to **Home data** and **Measurement** to **House_data**. A query will be created automatically that will show us the logged data in the form of a table or graph.

In the preceding example, we logged the data of the kitchen. Upload the same code to the other ESP32 microcontrollers in the living room, bathroom, and bedroom. Make sure you change the device name concerning the room. You can change it by modifying the #define DEVICE "kitchen" parameter. The code for the other rooms is available on GitHub at https://github.com/PacktPublishing/Programming-ESP32-with-Arduino-IDE/tree/main/chapter%208.

Once all the devices have been added, you will be able to see all these devices in the InfluxDB **TABLE** area, as shown in *Figure 8.20*:

device	humidity	light	motion_sensor	rssi	SSID	temperature	time
bathroom	25	0	0	-91	Wokwi-GUEST	26.2	2023-11-03T11:14:55.666Z
bathroom	25	0	0	-83	Wokwi-GUEST	26.2	2023-11-03T11:15:18.873Z
bedroom	25	0	0	-70	Wokwi-GUEST	26.2	2023-11-03T11:15:12.736Z
kitchen	25	0	0	-91	Wokwi-GUEST	26.2	2023-11-03T11:15:27.365Z
livingroom	25	0	0	-75	Wokwi-GUEST	26.2	2023-11-03T11:15:06.184Z
livingroom	25	0	0	-85	Wokwi-GUEST	26.2	2023-11-03T11:15:42.332Z

Figure 8.20 – Data in the form of a table in InfluxDB

Next, we will set up the Grafana cloud to visualize this data.

Monitoring and visualization using the Grafana cloud

Grafana is an open source platform for data visualization and monitoring. It allows users to create interactive and customizable dashboards that display real-time or historical data from various sources, including databases, time series databases such as InfluxDB, and more. Grafana is widely used for monitoring system performance, IoT devices, application metrics, and other data sources, making it a valuable tool for gaining insights from complex datasets through visually appealing and customizable graphs, charts, and panels.

First, we will set up the Grafana cloud:

1.   Go to https://grafana.com/auth/sign-in. Sign in if you already have an account or register if you are using Grafana for the first time.

2.   Once you've logged in, you will have to click on **Add Stack**, as shown in the following figure:

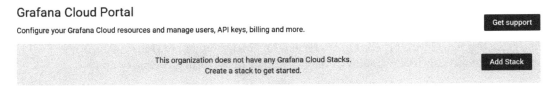

Figure 8.21 – Grafana Cloud Portal

3.   Give your instance a name and click on **Add Stack**, as shown in the following figure.

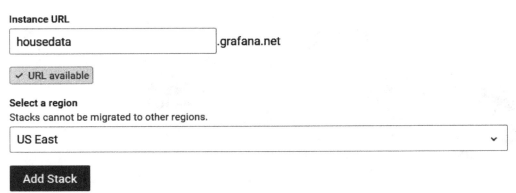

Figure 8.22 – Add a Grafana Cloud Stack

4. It will take some time to launch. Once launched, click on **Launch** under **Grafana**, as shown in *Figure 8.23*. You can explore other options as well, such as **Prometheus**, which is used for monitoring data:

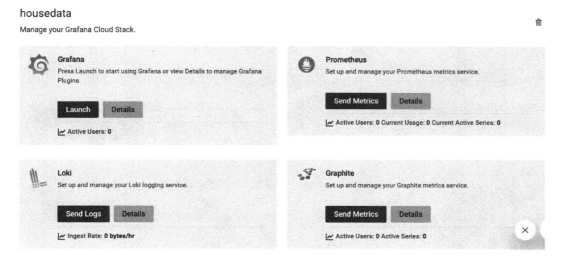

Figure 8.23 – Launching the Grafana stack

5. Once Grafana has launched, it will ask you to add a new connection, as shown in the following figure. Search for `FlightSQL` and select it:

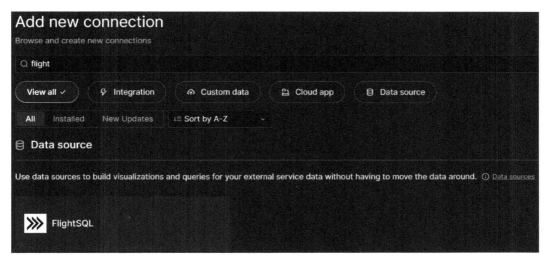

Figure 8.24 – Adding a new connection in Grafana

6. Click on **Install via grafana.com**, as shown in the following figure:

Figure 8.25 – Installing FlightSQL in Grafana

7.   Another window will open. Click **Install plugin**:

Figure 8.26 – Installing and managing the FlightSQL plugin

8.   Once installed, click **Manage instance**, then **Get plugin**, as shown in the following figure:

Figure 8.27 – Get plugin

9.   Once the plugin has been installed, go back to Grafana's main page and navigate to the **Add new connection** page, as shown in *step 5* and *Figure 8.24*. Here, click **Add new data source**:

Figure 8.28 – FlightSQL plugin added to Grafana

10. The **Settings** page will open, as shown in the following figure:

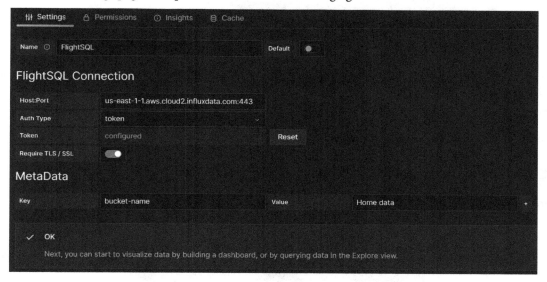

Figure 8.29 – FlightSQL plugin – the Settings page

11. We will have to add the following data:

   - **Host:Port**: Add the cluster URL without `https://` at the start; at the end, add `:443` to the cluster URL

   - **Auth Type**: Select **Token** here

   - **Token**: Paste the API token ID of InfluxDB

   - **Require TLS / SSL**: Enable this

   - In **MetaData**, we will set **Key** to `bucket-name` and **Value** to `Home data`

12. After adding this data, click **Save**; you will see a status of **OK**, as shown in *Figure 8.29*. Now, click on **building a dashboard**, as shown in *Figure 8.29*. At this point, we are ready to build our dashboard, as can be seen in *Figure 8.30*:

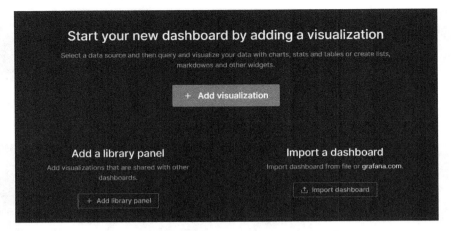

Figure 8.30 – Adding a new visualization in Grafana

In the next section, we will add visualizations and build the dashboard.

Creating a dashboard and visualizing the data

In this section, we will visualize the temperature, humidity, motion sensor, and LDR data:

1.   Click + **Add visualization**, as shown in *Figure 8.30*. We'll be asked for the data source, as shown in *Figure 8.31*:

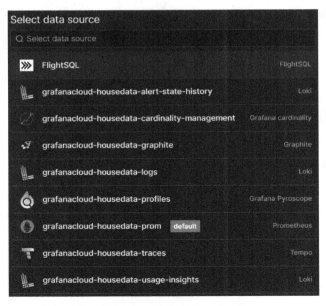

Figure 8.31 – Selecting FlightSQL as the data source

2.   Select **FlightSQL**; the following user interface will appear:

Figure 8.32 – Newly created empty panel

3.   In the **Query** section, click **Edit SQL**, as shown in *Figure 8.33*:

Figure 8.33 – The Query section in the Grafana panel

Add the following query:

```
select time,temperature as Kitchen from "House_data" WHERE
"device"='kitchen'
```

4. Once this query has been added, you will see the data in the dashboard:

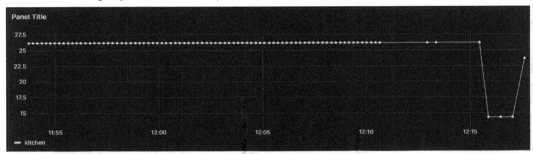

Figure 8.34 – Kitchen data graph in panel

5. Now, we will add more queries for the living room, bedroom, and bathroom. To do that, in the **Query** section, click on + **Add query**, as shown in *Figure 8.33*, and add the following queries one by one:

```
select time,temperature as bedroom from "House_data" WHERE
"device"='bedroom'

select time,temperature as livingroom from "House_data" WHERE
"device"='livingroom'

select time,temperature as bathroom from "House_data" WHERE
"device"='bathroom'
```

Now, you will see all four graphs in the visualization, as shown in *Figure 8.35*. In the right-hand area, change the panel's title and unit to Celsius:

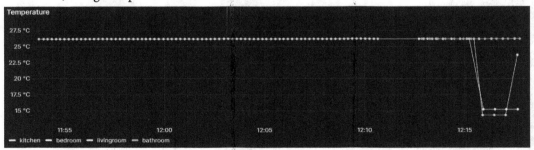

Figure 8.35 – Every room's temperature data in Grafana

6. Save the panel. Similarly, we will create a panel for humidity data using the following queries:

```
select time,humidity as Kitchen from "House_data" WHERE
"device"='kitchen'

select time,humidity as bedroom from "House_data" WHERE
"device"='bedroom'

select time,humidity as livingroom from "House_data" WHERE
"device"='livingroom'

select time,humidity as bathroom from "House_data" WHERE
"device"='bathroom'
```

7. After adding the queries, change the panel's title and unit to percentage; you will see the following panel:

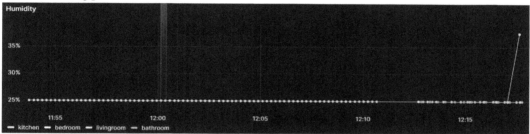

Figure 8.36 – Every room's humidity data in Grafana

8. Save the panel. Similarly, you can add the motion sensor and LDR data. The query for the kitchen motion sensor is as follows:

```
select time,motion_sensor as kitchen from "House_data" WHERE
"device"='kitchen'
```

For LDR, the query is as follows:

```
select time,light as kitchen from "House_data" WHERE
"device"='kitchen'
```

9. For the other devices, just change the device's name. Once you've done this, you will see the following dashboard:

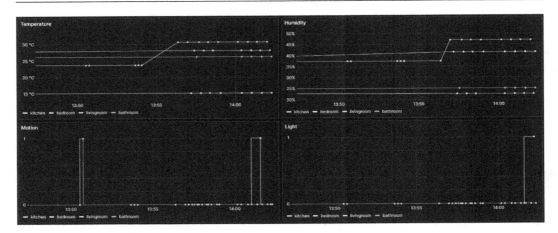

Figure 8.37 – Temperature, humidity, motion, and temperature data added to the dashboard

Furthermore, you can set up alerts in Grafana by going to the **Alerts** option. The user interface is very straightforward, and you will just have to follow the provided steps to create alerts. These alerts can be sent to your email address.

In the next section, we will focus on controlling the main entrance gate.

Controlling the main entrance gate using the MQTT protocol

In this section, we will learn how we can control the appliances in IoT projects using the MQTT protocol. We will use the HiveMQ public MQTT broker, whose credentials are available at https://www.hivemq.com/mqtt/public-mqtt-broker/.

For the living room ESP32 microcontroller, we will upload the following code so that we can send the data to InfluxDB as well as receive the MQTT message to control the door lock. The connection diagram for the living room is provided in *Figure 8.4*. The code is available on GitHub at https://github.com/PacktPublishing/Programming-ESP32-with-Arduino-IDE/blob/main/chapter%208/livingroom/livingroom.ino:

```
#include <Adafruit_Sensor.h>
#include <DHT_U.h>
#include <WiFiMulti.h>
#include <InfluxDbClient.h> //https://github.com/tobiasschuerg/
InfluxDB-Client-for-Arduino.git
#include <InfluxDbCloud.h>
#include <PubSubClient.h>
#include <ESP32Servo.h>
// WiFi configuration
```

```
WiFiMulti wifiMulti;
#define DEVICE "livingroom"  //change device name
...
...
...
// Servo setup
Servo doorLock;
int servoPosition = 90; // Initial position
// MQTT settings
const char *mqttServer = "broker.hivemq.com";
const char *clientID = "client_ID";
const char *topic = "/door/lock";
WiFiClient espClient;
PubSubClient mqttclient(espClient);
...
...
...
void callback(char *topic, byte *payload, unsigned int length)
{
  if (strcmp(topic, "/door/lock") == 0)
  {
    if (payload[0] == '1')
    {
      // Open the door lock
      doorLock.write(0); // Adjust the servo position for the open
state
      Serial.println("door opened");
      delay(500);       // Keep it open for 5 seconds
      // Close the door lock
      doorLock.write(servoPosition); // Return to the initial position
    }
  }
}
void setup()
{
  Serial.begin(115200);
  setupWifi();
  setupSensors();
  mqttsetup();
  xTaskCreatePinnedToCore(mqttTask, "MQTT Task", 8192, NULL, 1, NULL,
0);
}
```

The preceding code is like the previous code, except that we added the MQTT functionalities using **Free Real-Time Operating System (FreeRTOS)**. This is an open source and highly configurable operating system that's designed for embedded systems and microcontrollers. It provides a small, efficient, and real-time kernel that supports multitasking, task prioritization, synchronization, and interrupt handling. FreeRTOS is commonly used in resource-constrained devices and applications that require real-time responsiveness and reliability. We are using FreeRTOS for multitasking – that is, running two loops at once. The first loop is for MQTT and the other loop is to send the data to InfluxDB. The details of RTOS will be discussed in the next chapter. Let's take a look at the new functions that were added to the previous code:

- MQTT communication:

  - This sets up an MQTT client to connect to the MQTT broker (in this case, `broker.hivemq.com`) with a specified client ID and topic (`"/door/lock"`). The callback function handles incoming MQTT messages. If a message with a payload of `1` is received, it opens a simulated door lock using the servo motor.

- Reconnect to MQTT:

  - The `reconnect()` function is responsible for re-establishing the MQTT connection in case it gets disconnected. It subscribes to the specified MQTT topic after reconnecting.

- MQTT task:

  - The code creates a separate FreeRTOS task called `mqttTask` that manages the MQTT communication. This is an example of running MQTT in a separate task to avoid blocking the main loop.

  - The `xTaskCreatePinnedToCore` function is used in the context of FreeRTOS to create a new task (a thread-like execution unit) that runs in a separate thread of execution on a specific core of the microcontroller. Here's an explanation of its parameters:

    - `mqttTask`: This is the task function that you want to create and run in a separate thread. In your code, `mqttTask` is the name of the function that handles MQTT-related logic.

    - `MQTT Task`: This is a human-readable name or description for the task. It's used mainly for debugging and identifying the task in your code. It does not affect the task's behavior.

    - `8192`: This parameter specifies the stack size for the task in words. The stack is a memory region where the task's local variables and execution context are stored. The size you specify is typically in words, and `8192` words will occupy 8,192 * 4 bytes (32,768 bytes or 32 KB) of memory for the stack.

    - `NULL`: This is a pointer to any parameters you want to pass to the task function. If your task function requires any parameters, you can pass them here as a pointer.

- 1: This parameter specifies the priority of the task. Tasks with higher priority values will run before tasks with lower priority values. The range of priorities typically depends on the specific FreeRTOS port and configuration but is usually 0 (highest priority) to the maximum value supported.

- NULL: This is a pointer to a variable that receives the task's handle. You can use this handle to manipulate and control the task later, such as suspending or deleting it.

- 0: This parameter specifies the core on which the task should be pinned. In your code, it's set to 0, indicating that the task should run on core 0. If you have multiple cores available, you can set this to 1 to run the task on core 1.

- Setup:

  - In the setup() function, serial communication is initialized, Wi-Fi is configured, the sensors and InfluxDB are set up, and the MQTT client is initialized. Additionally, mqttTask is created to run the MQTT communication in a separate task.

- Loop:

  - The loop() function reads sensor data and writes it to InfluxDB. The MQTT communication is handled in mqttTask.

After uploading the code, we can test the servo motor using a smartphone app. To test this, follow these steps:

1. Install the IoT MQTT panel application from the Play Store or App Store:

Figure 8.38 – IoT MQTT Panel on Android

2. Click on **SETUP A CONNECTION**, as shown in *Figure 8.39*:

You do not have any connection to communicate with MQTT broker. If you are using this application for the first time, we highly recomend to go through FAQ and User Guide from main menu.

SETUP A CONNECTION

Figure 8.39 – SETUP A CONNECTION

3. Fill in the credentials with your MQTT broker details, as shown in *Figure 8.40*:

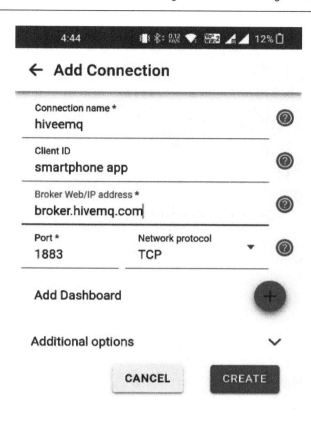

Figure 8.40 – Add Connection

4. Click on **Add Dashboard**; you will see the following screen. Give the dashboard a name and then click **Save**:

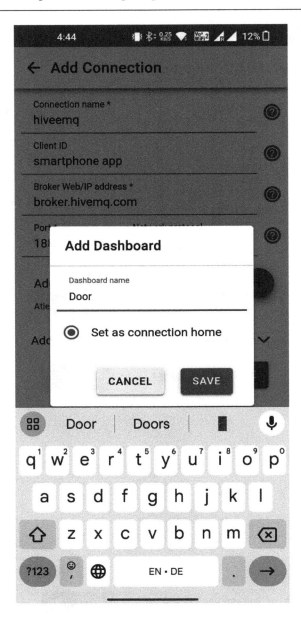

Figure 8.41 – Add Dashboard

5. After that, save the connection.

6. You will see the connection in the list; click on the connection you have created.

7. You will see the following screen. Click **ADD PANEL**:

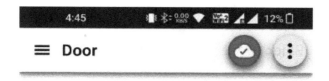

Current dashboard does not have any panel

ADD PANEL

Figure 8.42 – ADD PANEL

8.   Select **Button**:

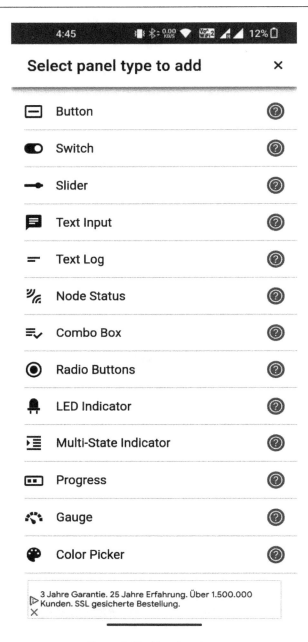

Figure 8.43 – Panel options

9. Fill in the data and click **Create**. We will provide **Topic** and **Payload** details. When this button is pressed, the payload will be sent:

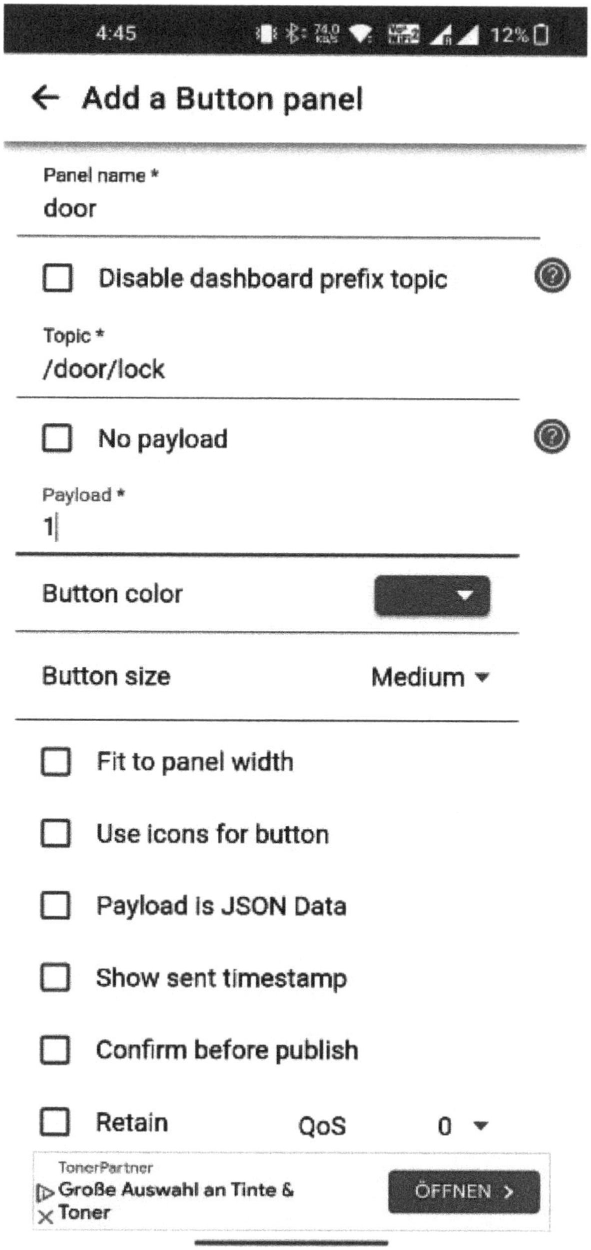

Figure 8.44 – Add a Button panel

10. A button will appear, as shown in *Figure 8.45*. Click on the button to send an MQTT message:

Figure 8.45 – A DOOR button to open the door

11. When you send an MQTT message, that will also appear on the serial monitor and the servo motor will move, as shown in *Figure 8.46*:

```
Connecting to Wi-Fi
Syncing time.
Synchronized time: Fri Nov  3 14:21:39 2023

Connected to InfluxDB: https://us-east-1-1.aws.cloud2.influxdata.com
Writing: House_data,device=livingroom,SSID=Wokwi-GUEST temperature=26.20,humidity=25.00,rssi=-83i,motion_sensor=0i,light=0i
Received message on topic: /door/lock
Message payload: 1
door opened
```

Figure 8.46 – The ESP32 serial monitor when the door is opened

With that, we have come to the end of this chapter, where we used an InfluxDB Cloud database to store data and Grafana to visualize it.

Summary

In this chapter, we delved into the world of data logging and visualization for IoT applications. Our focus shifted toward utilizing InfluxDB Cloud for data logging, harnessing the power of Grafana to create insightful data visualizations, and implementing MQTT with the HiveMQ public broker to remotely control a door lock. This chapter extended our practical IoT skills, enabling us to log, analyze, and visualize data while also providing the means for remote device control.

In this chapter, our focus revolved around leveraging cloud-based solutions for data storage and visualization, specifically utilizing InfluxDB Cloud and the Grafana cloud. These platforms, built on the robust infrastructure of **Amazon Web Services** (**AWS**), offer comprehensive application development services. However, alternative deployment options are also available to provide flexibility to users.

One viable option is to harness AWS directly, utilizing services such as AWS EC2, which functions as a virtual machine on the cloud. This approach allows users to independently install Grafana and InfluxDB, providing a tailored and controlled environment. Importantly, the installation process in this scenario is cost-free. However, there will be a cost for the AWS services.

Alternatively, for those seeking a more localized setup, deploying Grafana and InfluxDB on a Raspberry Pi or even a personal computer is a viable choice. This local deployment not only offers greater control over the configuration but also eliminates cloud-related costs. Users can explore these options based on their specific needs and preferences.

In the upcoming chapter, we will bring our journey in this book to a conclusion. We will also explore the next steps we can take to further enhance our understanding of IoT and unlock additional capabilities of the ESP32 platform.

9

From Arduino IDE to Advanced IoT Development – Taking the Next Steps

As we approach the final chapter of this informative and practical journey, it is valuable to revisit the extensive ground we've covered while exploring IoT through the lens of the ESP32 microcontroller with the Arduino IDE. In the preceding sections, we have dived into the foundational aspects of interfacing with ESP32 using the Arduino IDE, exploring communication protocols to facilitate seamless interaction, and understanding IoT data and network protocols. Now armed with this foundational knowledge, we are ready for advanced development, prepared to reveal the next tier of opportunities.

In this concluding chapter, we will enhance our proficiency by exploring advanced development strategies. We will investigate the capabilities of **Espressif IoT Development Framework (ESP-IDF)**, draw comparisons with Arduino IDE development, and unlock the potential of FreeRTOS and ESP32 by understanding their features.

The exploration extends to PlatformIO, a versatile development platform that unfolds new possibilities for efficient and flexible programming. We will discuss the tip of some more advanced cloud solutions, providing a comprehensive view of the extensive possibilities awaiting in the IoT domain.

As we conclude this journey, the final chapter will present a comprehensive embedded IoT and software roadmap. This roadmap will synthesize the knowledge you've acquired, furnishing a strategic guide for your ongoing exploration into the field of IoT development. The aim is not only to conclude this book but to prepare you for a future characterized by innovation and mastery in the dynamic field of IoT.

In this chapter, we will address the following topics:

- Power of ESP-IDF: A comparison with the ESP32 Arduino core
- Understanding RTOS use cases and features
- PlatformIO — an alternative to the Arduino IDE

- Enterprise clouds
- A complete IoT embedded and software roadmap

Let's dive into the concluding chapter and unlock the doors to advanced development with ESP32, shaping a pathway to limitless possibilities.

Power of ESP-IDF

In the first chapter of this book, I highlighted that when it comes to ESP32 development, there are two paths one can take: the **ESP32 Arduino core** and **ESP-IDF**. These are essentially two different toolkits or approaches you can take to work with the ESP32 microcontroller, each offering its own set of features and advantages.

The ESP Arduino core, being beginner-friendly, has been used in this book using the Arduino IDE, but to unlock the full potential of ESP32, ESP-IDF is recommended, which provides more features and a low-level approach for ESP32 development. In this section, we will explore the power of ESP-IDF and will compare it with the ESP32 Arduino core, which will give you a starting point to get started with ESP-IDF.

What is ESP-IDF?

ESP-IDF is an official development framework for ESP32 microcontrollers and supplies a collection of libraries, tools, and APIs tailored for the development of applications using ESP32 microcontrollers. It provides a variety of features typically required for IoT applications and is structured to deliver a versatile and comprehensive platform.

A key benefit of the ESP-IDF framework is its complete support for both standard C and standard C++ programming languages, enabling the creation of efficient and high-performance code. Furthermore, the major advantage of ESP-IDF over the Arduino framework is that it receives updates earlier than the Arduino framework because of its native support.

Moreover, ESP-IDF offers a range of functionalities for constructing IoT applications, including the following:

- Advanced Bluetooth and Wi-Fi connectivity support
- An extensive set of drivers for diverse sensors, peripherals, and communication protocols
- Backing for **over-the-air** or **OTA** updates (the capability of remotely updating and upgrading software or firmware on a device without requiring physical access) and secure boot
- Integration with FreeRTOS, a real-time operating system for microcontrollers. (FreeRTOS is discussed in the next section)

For additional information on ESP-IDF, refer to the following resources:

- ESP-IDF programming guide: `https://docs.espressif.com/projects/esp-idf/en/latest/esp32/`
- ESP-IDF GitHub: `https://github.com/espressif/esp-idf`
- *Developing IoT Projects with ESP32*: `https://www.packtpub.com/product/developing-iot-projects-with-esp32-second-edition`
- *Internet of Things Projects with ESP32*: `https://www.packtpub.com/product/internet-of-things-projects-with-esp32/`

ESP-IDF versus the Arduino ESP32 core

The Arduino ESP32 core used in this book offers a low barrier to entry and is beginner-friendly, whereas ESP-IDF, being the official development framework, provides more features and a low-level approach. There are a few additional differences, as follows:

- ESP-IDF has full support for C and C++ programming languages, while the Arduino platform also supports these languages but not in the full implementation of them. Therefore, the full advantage of C and C++ features can be leveraged using ESP-IDF.
- Another difference is in OTA updates. Both platforms support OTA firmware updates, but with the Arduino ESP32 core, the process is less optimized compared to ESP-IDF; that is, ESP-IDF offers a more integrated and efficient experience.
- ESP-IDF, as the official development framework, has consistent support for the latest versions of ESP32 microcontrollers and their features. Any new release of ESP32 ensures full compatibility and support within the ESP-IDF framework.

To elaborate more, ESP-IDF has several features that are either not present in the Arduino ESP32 core or have limited support, such as the following:

- FreeRTOS support
- Efficient memory management and debugging tools
- Support for multi-core CPUs
- Frequent updates and faster adoption of new ESP versions

The following table illustrates the advantages and disadvantages of both development frameworks:

ESP-IDF	Arduino ESP32 core
✓ Native FreeRTOS support	— Limited RTOS support
✓ Task-based applications	— `setup()` and `loop()` functions
✓ Multi-core by default	— Single core by default
✓ Support for new ESP32 releases	— Limited support for new ESP32 releases
— Less beginner-friendly	✓ Beginner-friendly
— Smaller community	✓ Large community

Table 9.1 – ESP-IDF and Arduino ESP32 core comparison – advantages, and disadvantages

The ESP Arduino core, utilizing the Arduino IDE, is beginner-friendly and boasts a large community. It is straightforward to initiate using the Arduino IDE. It employs the C++ programming language, though not in its complete implementation; nevertheless, it aids in transitioning to ESP-IDF for advanced development.

In this section, FreeRTOS has been frequently referenced; in the next section, we will dive into its definition and features.

Understanding RTOS use cases and features

An **RTOS** is specialized software that manages tasks with precise timing requirements, ensuring timely execution in embedded systems and applications. It is designed for applications where a predictable response time is critical, such as in robotics and **industrial control systems (ICS)**.

To understand an RTOS, we will take an example of the approach that we have taken in this book of the "super loop architecture," in which the main program consists of a continuous loop (a "super loop" or `loop()` function) that executes sequentially. This loop repeatedly performs tasks, checks conditions, and responds to events, as can be seen in *Figure 9.1*:

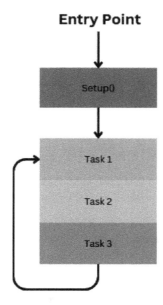

Figure 9.1 – Super loop architecture

In contrast, an RTOS allows for the concurrent execution of multiple tasks. In the case of a multi-core processor, true multitasking is achievable, as can be seen in *Figure 9.2*, while on a single-core processor, multitasking is emulated by dividing CPU time among tasks based on priority. Tasks with higher priority receive more CPU time and are executed more frequently:

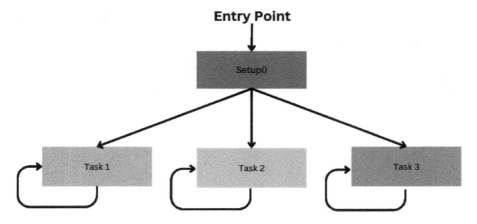

Figure 9.2 – Task execution in an RTOS

Now that we understand what an RTOS is, we will discuss FreeRTOS in the next section, which is a version of RTOS integrated into ESP-IDF.

FreeRTOS

FreeRTOS is an open source RTOS kernel that is integrated into ESP-IDF as a component. ESP-IDF FreeRTOS is derived from vanilla FreeRTOS but incorporates substantial modifications to both API and kernel behavior to facilitate dual-core **symmetric multiprocessing** (**SMP**) support. SMP is a computational design in which a single operating system governs and coordinates the activities of two or more identical CPUs (cores) that are interconnected and share access to a central main memory.

FreeRTOS example using the Arduino IDE

We can use FreeRTOS using the Arduino IDE as well, but the support is very limited. However, to show how task creation and execution work in FreeRTOS, we will perform the following example in the Arduino IDE.

We will take two LEDs and connect them to the D12 and D13 pins, and the cathode of both LEDs should be connected to the current limiting resistor and then to the GND pin, as shown in the following diagram:

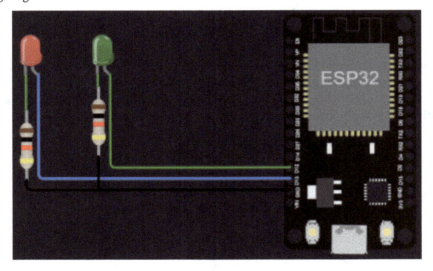

Figure 9.3 – LED blinking using RTOS: connection diagram

For each of these LEDs, we will create a task, and each task will contain its own loop for LED blinking. Here are the steps:

1. Firstly, we will import the necessary libraries:

    ```
    include <Arduino.h>
    #include <freertos/FreeRTOS.h>
    #include <freertos/task.h>
    ```

2. Then, we will define the pin numbers of the LEDs:

```
const int led1Pin = 13;  // Pin number for the first LED
const int led2Pin = 12;  // Pin number for the second LED
```

3. We will create a task function for the first LED, as follows:

```
void led1Task(void *parameter) {
    pinMode(led1Pin, OUTPUT);
    while (1) {
        digitalWrite(led1Pin, HIGH);
        vTaskDelay(500 / portTICK_PERIOD_MS);
        digitalWrite(led1Pin, LOW);
        vTaskDelay(500 / portTICK_PERIOD_MS);
    }
}
```

This task is responsible for toggling the first LED on and off at a 500 ms interval. The vTaskDelay function is a part of FreeRTOS and is used to introduce a delay in a FreeRTOS task. It takes a parameter representing the time to delay by in ticks, and portTICK_PERIOD_MS is a constant that represents the number of ticks per ms.

4. Similarly, we will create a task for the second LED and toggle the LED after every 1 second, as follows:

```
void led2Task(void *parameter) {
    pinMode(led2Pin, OUTPUT);
    while (1) {
        digitalWrite(led2Pin, HIGH);
        vTaskDelay(1000 / portTICK_PERIOD_MS);
        digitalWrite(led2Pin, LOW);
        vTaskDelay(1000 / portTICK_PERIOD_MS);
    }
}
```

5. Finally, we will define tasks in the setup() function, as follows:

```
void setup() {
    xTaskCreate(led1Task, "LED1 Task", 4096, NULL, 1, NULL);
    xTaskCreate(led2Task, "LED2 Task", 4096, NULL, 1, NULL);
}
```

In the setup() function, we create instances of both LED tasks using xTaskCreate. Each task is assigned a name, stack size (4096 bytes), and priority (1). The NULL parameters are used for task parameters and task handles, which are not needed in this example.

6. Since we are not using the super loop architecture, the `loop()` function will remain empty:

```
void loop() {
    // Empty loop as tasks handles the work in the background
}
```

The preceding example demonstrates the use of FreeRTOS tasks to concurrently control two LEDs with different blinking patterns. The tasks run independently in the background, allowing for simultaneous execution of LED blinking routines. Now, when you upload the code, you will see the LEDs blinking at different frequencies.

In conclusion, this example serves as an introduction to the capabilities of FreeRTOS within the Arduino IDE, providing a glimpse of its task management features. However, it's essential to recognize that FreeRTOS offers a vast set of functionalities that can be further explored within ESP-IDF for ESP32. The true depth of FreeRTOS implementation and integration with ESP32 is revealed in ESP-IDF, offering a comprehensive platform for advanced development. For a deeper exploration, refer to the FreeRTOS documentation within ESP-IDF at `https://docs.espressif.com/projects/esp-idf/en/latest/esp32/api-reference/system/freertos.html`.

PlatformIO – an alternative to the Arduino IDE

PlatformIO is an open source development ecosystem that simplifies embedded systems development, including the ESP32 microcontroller, and is an alternative to the Arduino IDE, which developers often use. Unlike the Arduino IDE, which is more beginner-friendly and limited in features, PlatformIO provides a more robust and versatile environment for embedded systems development.

It supports a wide range of microcontrollers, including ESP32, and offers advanced features such as project configuration management, a powerful build system, and integrated testing. This alternative is particularly popular among experienced developers seeking a more flexible and efficient development workflow for their ESP32 projects.

One key benefit of using PlatformIO is that developers can seamlessly develop ESP32 applications using either the Arduino core or ESP-IDF within the same IDE, offering them the flexibility to choose the framework that best suits their project requirements.

Using PlatformIO to upload code to ESP32

In this section, we will delve into the process of utilizing PlatformIO to harness the capabilities of the ESP32 Arduino core. Also, this section includes a guide that can help you upload all the code of this book using PlatformIO. We will follow the next steps:

1. Firstly, make sure you have installed VS Code. VS Code is a powerful yet simple code editor. The installation process is simple: just download the installation file for your OS and then install it by running the executable. The installation file can be downloaded from `https://code.visualstudio.com/`.

2. Once VS Code is installed, go to the VS Code extension pack, then find and install PlatformIO IDE extensions. Complete instructions with visuals can be found at `https://docs.platformio.org/en/latest/integration/ide/vscode.html#installation`.

3. After installing the extension, you can click on the platform extension and select **Create New Project**, as shown in the following figure:

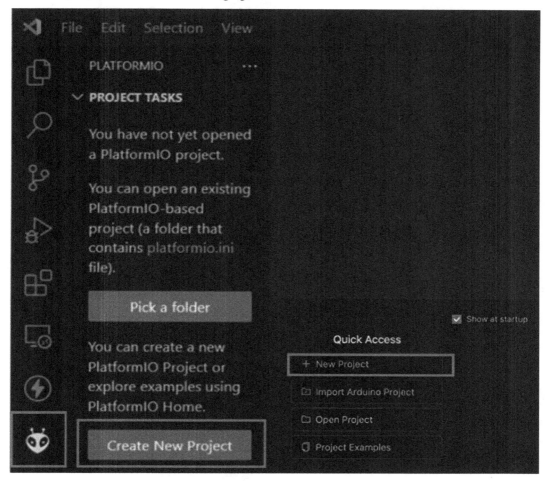

Figure 9.4 – Creating a new project in the PlatformIO IDE

4. A project wizard will open. Give the project a name, select your ESP32 board from the list, and select a framework. We are selecting **Arduino**, but here, you have the option to select **ESP-IDF** as well. Click on **Finish**:

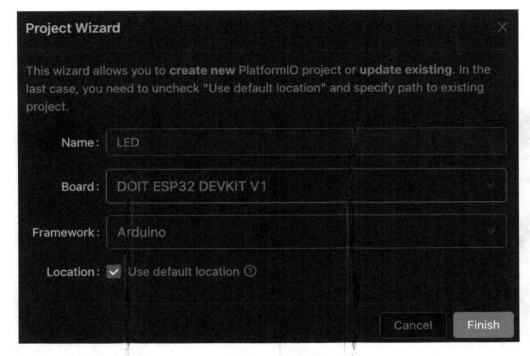

Figure 9.5 – Project wizard

5.   It will take some time to set up the project. Once the project is ready, you will see the following file structure. The `platformio.ini` file serves as a pivotal configuration file where developers define project settings, target platforms, build options, and library dependencies, providing a centralized and easily shareable blueprint for their embedded systems projects:

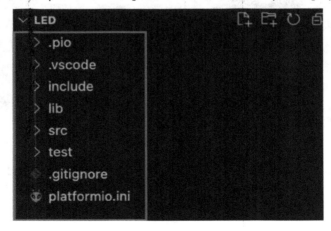

Figure 9.6 – PlatformIO project file structure

6. The `platformio.ini` file generated for this simple `hello world` project has the following content:

```
[env:esp32dev]
platform = espressif32
board = esp32dev
framework = arduino
monitor_speed = 115200
lib_deps =
    Arduino
    ; Add any additional libraries here if needed.
```

7. Then, we will paste the `hello world` code that we wrote in *Chapter 1* into the `main.cpp` file in the `src` folder, as can be seen in the following figure:

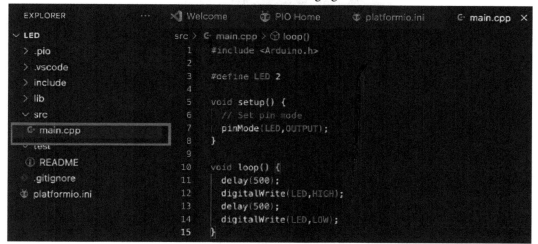

Figure 9.7 – PlatformIO main.cpp file

8. Then, to build and upload the code, we will go back to the PlatformIO home page, and from its menu, we will click on **Build**, which will build the code and report errors if there are any in the terminal, as can be seen in the following figure:

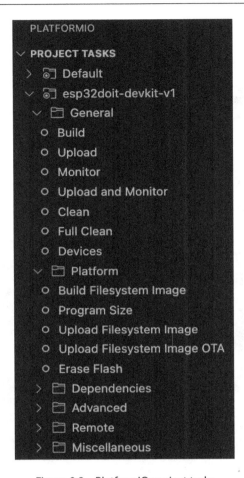

Figure 9.8 – PlatformIO project tasks

9. When the build is complete, you will see the following output in the terminal:

Figure 9.9 – PlatformIO build complete

10. Once the build is complete, select **Upload** to upload the code to ESP32. The LED will start blinking, and you will see the following output on the serial monitor:

Figure 9.10 – PlatformIO upload completion

11. Similarly, clicking on **Monitor** will open a serial monitor, and you will be able to see the serial prints.

> **Important note**
>
> You can follow the same steps to upload all the code of this book using PlatformIO. You will only have to add dependencies to the `platformio.ini` file and replace the `main.cpp` file with the code provided in this book.

The PlatformIO IDE is simple to use; most of the features available on the platform are comparable to the Arduino IDE, plus it contains some additional features. I hope this small section has provided you with a good starting point to explore PlatformIO. You can upload and build the examples and projects of this chapter using PlatformIO. The documentation of PlatformIO is comprehensive and can be found at `https://docs.platformio.org/en/latest/what-is-platformio.html`.

Enterprise clouds

This book is tailored for beginners, providing a foundation for IoT fundamentals. Throughout our journey, we've explored various data and network-based protocols, along with incorporating third-party services and databases such as the HiveMQ **Messaging Queuing Telemetry Transport** (**MQTT**) broker, InfluxDB Cloud, and Grafana Cloud. These services operate on what we call "enterprise clouds" — large and robust cloud systems commonly employed by businesses. As we conclude, it's valuable to introduce the concept of enterprise clouds, showcasing their significance in the tech landscape.

In this section, we'll narrow our focus to **Amazon Web Services** (**AWS**) and Azure IoT and delve into their IoT services. This sneak peek will offer insights into the workings of these substantial cloud services and how they can be beneficial for ESP32 and IoT projects.

AWS IoT services

AWS provides a comprehensive set of IoT-related services to enable the development, deployment, and management of IoT applications. Some key AWS IoT services include the following:

- **AWS IoT Core**: AWS IoT Core is the central service that enables communication between IoT devices and the cloud. ESP32 devices can connect to AWS IoT Core using MQTT or HTTP to send and receive messages. This allows you to leverage AWS IoT Core for device management, communication, and security.

- **AWS IoT Device Management**: This service helps in onboarding, organizing, and managing IoT devices at scale and can be used to manage fleets of ESP32 devices, enabling tasks such as OTA updates and device monitoring.

- **AWS IoT Greengrass**: ESP32 devices can run AWS IoT Greengrass core software, extending AWS IoT services to the edge. This is beneficial for local processing and reducing latency.

- **AWS IoT Analytics**: IoT Analytics is a fully managed service that helps process, enrich, store, and analyze IoT data. ESP32-generated data can be processed and analyzed in AWS IoT Analytics, providing insights into device telemetry.

- **AWS IoT Events**: This service allows you to detect and respond to events from IoT sensors and applications. It enables the creation of complex event-processing logic to trigger actions based on predefined patterns.

- **AWS IoT Things Graph**: IoT Things Graph simplifies the integration of different devices and services by providing a visual representation of IoT workflows. It allows developers to model and deploy IoT applications quickly.

These AWS IoT services collectively provide a robust platform for building scalable, secure, and efficient IoT applications across various industries.

Azure IoT services

As with AWS, Microsoft Azure offers a comprehensive suite of IoT services to support the development and deployment of IoT solutions. Some key Azure IoT services include the following:

- **Azure IoT Hub**: ESP32 devices can connect to Azure IoT Hub for bidirectional communication. Azure IoT Hub provides features such as device provisioning, messaging, and device twin management.

- **Azure IoT Central**: Azure IoT Central is a fully managed solution that simplifies the development and deployment of scalable and secure IoT applications. It can simplify the development of ESP32-based IoT applications with pre-built templates and scalable SaaS solutions.

- **Azure IoT Edge**: Azure IoT Edge extends cloud intelligence to edge devices, allowing them to run containerized workloads locally. This facilitates real-time analytics and reduces latency by processing data closer to the source.

- **Azure Stream Analytics**: Azure Stream Analytics is a real-time analytics service that processes streaming data from devices and sensors. It can be used to derive insights, detect anomalies, and trigger actions based on real-time data.

- **Azure Time Series Insights**: This service provides a fully managed, scalable, and real-time data analytics platform for IoT applications. It helps analyze and visualize time-series data generated by IoT devices.

These Azure IoT services collectively offer a robust and scalable platform for building, deploying, and managing IoT applications, catering to a wide range of industries and use cases.

To boost your IoT skills, it's crucial to learn more about these IoT services and clouds. While this section mentions the basic idea here, exploring the official documentation of AWS and Azure is a great next step. The docs provide detailed insights, clear guidelines, and a variety of features that can really help you get better at using these platforms for your IoT projects.

A complete IoT embedded and software roadmap

In *Chapter 1*, we discussed the IoT four-layer architecture, including the sensing, networking, data processing, and application layers. The first three chapters explained the sensing layer of IoT, in which we learned about the communication protocols used by sensors and how to interface different sensors with ESP32. *Chapter 4* explained network protocols such as Wi-Fi, **Bluetooth Low Energy** (**BLE**), and cellular communication, and in *Chapter 5*, we learned about data protocols such as HTTP, MQTT, and Webhooks. Furthermore, we completed three projects that explained how data is processed, manipulated, and presented in the form of visualization. This cumulative approach lays a robust foundation for IoT development.

Moving forward from our foundational discussions, this section unveils a complete IoT roadmap, carefully crafted by considering various job requirements in these fields. The roadmap is neatly split into two categories: *IoT embedded developer* and *IoT application developer*. Think of these categories as friendly guides, outlining clear paths for those who want to dive deep into the inner workings of embedded systems or for those who fancy crafting applications in the ever-exciting field of IoT.

Roadmap for IoT embedded development

An IoT embedded developer is primarily focused on foundational aspects of IoT, dealing with hardware and low-level software for devices, and requiring expertise in embedded programming languages and microcontroller architectures. The roadmap is divided into the programming languages, concepts, and tools required:

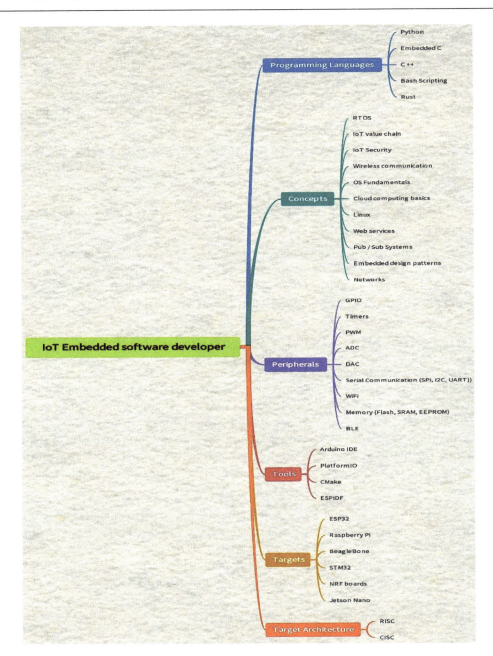

Figure 9.11 – IoT embedded software developer roadmap

Figure 9.11 depicts an IoT embedded software developer roadmap, and its contents are explained in the following sections.

Programming languages

Knowing different computer languages is super important when you're getting into embedded systems. Make sure you're good with embedded C and C++ because they're like the ABCs of this journey. Python is another important language to learn, bringing extra flexibility to your skills. While it's not a must, learning the basics of Bash scripting can be useful, and playing around with Rust can add a special touch to what you know. Just remember — C++ and embedded C are like the starting point: the basics you really need to begin your embedded adventure.

Concepts

Understanding specific concepts is key to feeling comfortable in the world of IoT. You must get the hang of RTOS, the IoT value chain, wireless communication, OS fundamentals, Linux, **publish/subscribe (pub/sub)** systems, embedded design patterns, and networks. These are like the must-haves in your toolkit for developing IoT solutions without feeling lost. While it's nice to know a bit about IoT security, cloud computing basics, and web services, focusing on the must-haves will give you a solid foundation and make your journey in IoT development much smoother.

Tools

Equipping yourself with the right tools is crucial for navigating the field of embedded systems. The Arduino IDE serves as a beginner-friendly platform, allowing you to write, compile, and upload code to your devices effortlessly. PlatformIO expands your toolkit, offering a versatile ecosystem for IoT development and streamlining the process of managing libraries and projects. CMake steps in as a powerful tool assisting in the building, testing, and packaging of software projects. ESP-IDF, tailored for ESP32 development, provides a comprehensive set of libraries and tools, enhancing your ability to work seamlessly with ESP32 microcontrollers. These tools collectively empower you to efficiently develop and deploy your embedded projects, ensuring a smooth and productive journey in the field of embedded systems.

Targets and peripherals for embedded development

Understanding target architectures is fundamental, with **reduced instruction set computing (RISC)** and **complex instruction set computing (CISC)** standing out as key concepts. The distinction between these architectures becomes particularly crucial during the development of embedded IoT solutions.

To put theory into practice, consider experimenting with various targets and development boards such as STM32 (Blue/Black Pill), ESP32/NodeMCU, Raspberry Pi, BeagleBone, and Jetson Nano, each offering unique capabilities.

To make meaningful progress with these targets, a grasp of target peripherals is essential. Dive into the details of microcontroller peripherals, ranging from **general-purpose input/output (GPIO)** and timers to **pulse-width modulation (PWM)**, **analog-to-digital converters (ADCs)**, and **digital-to-analog converters (DACs)**. Understand the details of serial communication protocols such as **Serial Peripheral Interface (SPI)** and **Inter-Integrated Circuit (I2C)**, and **universal asynchronous receivers-transmitters (UARTs)**, and familiarize yourself with key functionalities including Wi-Fi, memory (flash,

static random-access memory (SRAM), electrically erasable programmable read-only memory (EEPROM)), and BLE. This understanding empowers you to harness the full potential of your chosen targets and peripherals, paving the way for effective and efficient embedded development endeavors.

Roadmap for IoT applications development

An IoT application developer works on higher layers of the IoT stack, creating software applications that collect, process, and visualize data from IoT devices. This role demands proficiency in higher-level programming languages and cloud platforms and emphasizes software development and user-friendly application creation. The following diagram shows the roadmap and tech skills required to be an IoT application developer:

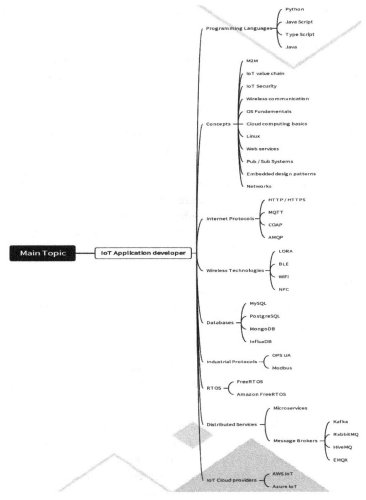

Figure 9.12 – IoT application developer roadmap

Embarking on the journey of becoming an IoT application developer requires versatility and a broad range of knowledge. While you don't need to be an expert in everything, having a grasp of several areas is beneficial. As an IoT application developer, you'll need to familiarize yourself with frontend and backend development, and it's nice to have some familiarity with cross-platform mobile development.

Programming languages

Consider the TypeScript, JavaScript, Python, and Java programming languages as essential tools in your toolkit. Feel free to choose from various frameworks based on your comfort level or prior experience.

Frameworks

When diving into frontend development for IoT applications, you have a range of frameworks to choose from. React, known for its component-based structure, Angular, offering a comprehensive frontend development environment, Vue, known for its simplicity and flexibility, and Svelte, recognized for its lightweight and efficient approach, are all excellent options to consider.

For the backend development aspect of IoT applications, several frameworks cater to different preferences and needs. ExpressJS, with its minimalist and flexible design, NestJS, offering a scalable and modular structure, FastAPI, known for its speed and ease of use, Flask, a lightweight and versatile Python framework, Django, a high-level Python web framework, Spring Boot, a Java-based framework designed for simplicity, and Go, renowned for its efficiency and performance, provide a diverse set of tools to support your backend development endeavors.

Concepts

Dive into the details of the IoT value chain, comprehending the journey from data acquisition to meaningful insights. Prioritize IoT security, understanding the measures needed to safeguard your applications and devices. Explore the details of wireless communication, OS fundamentals, and cloud computing basics, each contributing to the seamless functioning of your IoT applications. Familiarize yourself with Linux, a key operating system in this domain, and grasp the essentials of web services, pub/sub systems, system integration, networks, and **machine-to-machine** (**M2M**) communication. Embrace design patterns to enhance the efficiency and structure of your applications. In the realm of RTOSs, focus on understanding event loops, a crucial aspect that empowers you to work seamlessly with these systems. These foundational concepts collectively form the backbone of your knowledge, enabling you to navigate and excel in the dynamic field of IoT application development.

IoT protocols

Understanding fundamental internet protocols is important in the field of IoT application development. HTTP and its secure counterpart, HTTPS, serve as the cornerstone for web communication, enabling seamless data transfer between clients and servers. MQTT, a lightweight messaging protocol, facilitates efficient communication in IoT networks, allowing devices to publish and subscribe to data. **Constrained Application Protocol** (**CoAP**) is tailored for resource-constrained devices, ensuring efficient communication in constrained environments. Additionally, the **Advanced Message Queuing Protocol (AMQP)** plays a crucial role in enabling effective message-oriented communication between devices and systems in IoT applications. These protocols collectively provide a robust foundation for establishing reliable and secure communication channels within IoT ecosystems.

Message brokers

In the domain of IoT application development, message brokers play a vital role in facilitating communication between various components. Explore Kafka, recognized for its distributed and fault-tolerant design, RabbitMQ, a flexible and highly available message broker, HiveMQ, designed specifically for MQTT communication, EMQX, an open source MQTT broker, and **enterprise service bus (ESB)** examples such as WSO2, which facilitates the integration of diverse applications.

Databases

A well-rounded knowledge of databases is crucial for effective IoT application development. Familiarize yourself with relational databases such as MySQL and PostgreSQL, each offering robust data management capabilities. Dive into the realm of NoSQL databases with MongoDB, known for its flexible and scalable document-oriented structure, and Cassandra, a highly distributed and fault-tolerant database. Understand the role of Redis Cache in providing fast and efficient in-memory data storage. Lastly, explore InfluxDB, a time-series database tailored for handling timestamped data. Additionally, be versed in keystore databases, essential for the secure storage and management of cryptographic keys. This diverse range of databases equips you with the flexibility to handle different data structures and use cases within your IoT applications.

IoT platforms

Navigating the landscape of IoT platforms, also known as **application enablement platforms (AEPs)**, is crucial for streamlined development. Explore platforms such as ThingsBoard, offering an open source solution for device management and data visualization, The Things Industries, specializing in **Long Range Wide Area Network (LoRaWAN)** network management, Mainflux, an open source AEP for **industrial IoT (IIOT)**, and ThingWorx, renowned for its comprehensive IoT application development capabilities.

IoT cloud providers

In the realm of IoT, cloud services play a pivotal role in providing scalable and efficient solutions. There are two categories of AEPs, one being AEPs, and the other known as hyperscalers. Familiarizing yourself with these platforms and cloud providers equips you with the tools to harness the power of the cloud for your IoT applications.

This roadmap serves as a valuable guide to help you make informed decisions about what to learn next in the dynamic field of IoT development. It outlines key programming languages, concepts, tools, and targets, offering a structured path for both IoT embedded developers and IoT application developers. However, it's important to note that this roadmap represents a starting point, not the end of your learning journey. The field of IoT is continually evolving, and there's always more to explore and discover. As you progress through these foundational elements, you'll gain a solid footing to dive deeper into specific areas of interest, adapt to emerging technologies, and continuously expand your skill set. This roadmap lays the groundwork for your IoT endeavors, providing a foundation upon which you can build and shape your expertise in the ever-evolving landscape of IoT development.

Summary

In this concluding chapter, we have dived into a comprehensive comparison between the ESP32 Arduino core and ESP-IDF, gaining insights into their respective strengths and applications. Our journey led us to become acquainted with RTOSs and the versatility of PlatformIO as an IDE. Additionally, we broadened our horizons by learning about enterprise cloud services such as AWS and Azure and understanding their offerings in the IoT landscape. As we wrapped up, we introduced a final roadmap, a strategic guide to help you navigate the expansive world of IoT development, providing avenues for continuous learning and exploration beyond the domain of this book.

Furthermore, I would like to congratulate you on reaching and completing this final chapter. You've unlocked the potential to shape the future of interconnected technology, and as you reflect on your journey, remember that knowledge is a continuous adventure, and this accomplishment is just one milestone on your path to personal and professional growth.

May your newfound knowledge of IoT pave the way for innovative contributions in this dynamic field. Well done!

Index

Packtpub.com

Subscribe to our online digital library for full access to over 7,000 books and videos, as well as industry leading tools to help you plan your personal development and advance your career. For more information, please visit our website.

Why subscribe?

- Spend less time learning and more time coding with practical eBooks and Videos from over 4,000 industry professionals

- Improve your learning with Skill Plans built especially for you

- Get a free eBook or video every month

- Fully searchable for easy access to vital information

- Copy and paste, print, and bookmark content

Did you know that Packt offers eBook versions of every book published, with PDF and ePub files available? You can upgrade to the eBook version at packtpub.com and as a print book customer, you are entitled to a discount on the eBook copy. Get in touch with us at customercare@packtpub.com for more details.

At www.packtpub.com, you can also read a collection of free technical articles, sign up for a range of free newsletters, and receive exclusive discounts and offers on Packt books and eBooks.

Other Books You May Enjoy

If you enjoyed this book, you may be interested in these other books by Packt:

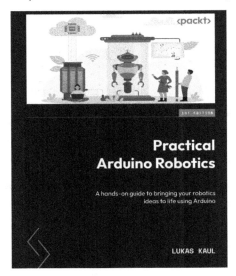

Practical Arduino Robotics

Lukas Kaul

ISBN: 978-1-80461-317-7

- Understand and use the various interfaces of an Arduino board
- Write the code to communicate with your sensors and motors
- Implement and tune methods for sensor signal processing
- Understand and implement state machines that control your robot
- Implement feedback control to create impressive robot capabilities
- Integrate hardware and software components into a reliable robotic system
- Tune, debug, and improve Arduino-based robots systematically

Arduino Data Communications

Robert Thas John

ISBN: 978-1-83763-261-9

- Explore data storage formats for both local and remote storage solutions
- Build projects that leverage the variety of communication standards
- Set up a database to host data transmitted from various projects
- Use MQTT and RESTful APIs to send data from devices to remote systems
- Prepare for multiple devices using high availability measures
- Use LoRa by implementing a gateway and a client
- Transmit temperature and humidity data over RS-485 and HC-12

Packt is searching for authors like you

If you're interested in becoming an author for Packt, please visit `authors.packtpub.com` and apply today. We have worked with thousands of developers and tech professionals, just like you, to help them share their insight with the global tech community. You can make a general application, apply for a specific hot topic that we are recruiting an author for, or submit your own idea.

Share Your Thoughts

Now you've finished *Hands-on ESP32 with Arduino IDE*, we'd love to hear your thoughts! Scan the QR code below to go straight to the Amazon review page for this book and share your feedback or leave a review on the site that you purchased it from.

`https://packt.link/r/1837638039`

Your review is important to us and the tech community and will help us make sure we're delivering excellent quality content.

Download a free PDF copy of this book

Thanks for purchasing this book!

Do you like to read on the go but are unable to carry your print books everywhere?

Is your eBook purchase not compatible with the device of your choice?

Don't worry, now with every Packt book you get a DRM-free PDF version of that book at no cost.

Read anywhere, any place, on any device. Search, copy, and paste code from your favorite technical books directly into your application.

The perks don't stop there, you can get exclusive access to discounts, newsletters, and great free content in your inbox daily

Follow these simple steps to get the benefits:

- Scan the QR code or visit the link below

https://packt.link/free-ebook/9781837638031

- Submit your proof of purchase
- That's it! We'll send your free PDF and other benefits to your email directly

www.ingramcontent.com/pod-product-compliance
Lightning Source LLC
Chambersburg PA
CBHW080629060326
40690CB00021B/4866